SELLING U.S. OUT

★ ★ ★

J.R. MARTIN

BEAVER'S POND
PRESS

ISBN 13: 978-1-59298-496-1

Library of Congress Catalog Number: 2012908589

Printed in the United States of America

Second Printing: 2013

16 15 14 13   5 4 3 2

Author photograph by Liz Allen Photography
Cover design by Lori Campbell
Interior design by James Monroe Design, LLC.

BEAVER'S
POND
PRESS

Beaver's Pond Press, Inc.
7108 Ohms Lane
Edina, MN 55439–2129
(952) 829-8818
www.BeaversPondPress.com

To order, visit www.BeaversPondBooks.com
or call (800) 901-3480. Reseller discounts available.

To Jill, our children, and grandchildren
as well as all who have served and sacrificed for
"The Glorious Cause of America."

Contents

Acknowledgements. . . . . *vii*

CHAPTER ONE
Selling U.S. Out—How and Why? 1

CHAPTER TWO
The Glorious Cause of America 7

CHAPTER THREE
Selling Our Freedom I 13

CHAPTER FOUR
Selling Our Freedom II 29

CHAPTER FIVE
Selling Our Freedom III. 49

CHAPTER SIX
The Free Trade Myth 83

CHAPTER SEVEN
The Decline of U.S. Manufacturing 119

CHAPTER EIGHT
Corporate Greed & Corruption—Selling Out America 149

CHAPTER NINE
Political Scandal and Corruption 205

CHAPTER TEN
America's Best Days Lie Ahead 267

CHAPTER ELEVEN
The Path Forward 281

Closing Thoughts 341

Addendum 343

Bibliography 359

About the Author 375

Acknowledgements

This book was a labor of love that began in 2009 and would not have been completed without the support of my lovely wife, Jill. She is my Abigail Adams! I am deeply grateful to her and to our son, Blake, for the patience and understanding given to me while I worked on "the book." Special thanks also to my daughter Crystal and my son-in-law Kurt for the feedback and support they provided to me. Blake has asked me to mention and thank another member of our family, Simon, our 100lb Black Lab, who faithfully slept by my desk as I wrote.

Much appreciation goes out to my mentor, John Riddle, who coached and guided me through this process. John is the author of numerous books and also founded and sponsors the national "I Love To Write Day" (ilovetowriteday.org) which is now celebrated in over 25,000 schools across America. I thank the wonderful people at Beaver's Pond Press (beaverspondpress.com), especially Dara Beevas and Tom Kerber for their guidance and support, Lily Coyle for her professional project management, Wendy Weckwerth for her outstanding editorial support, James Monroe for the beautiful book design, and the other staff members who assisted with the completion and distribution of *Selling U.S. Out.*

I am very grateful to Lori Campbell for her creative, inspiring, and quite possibly, award-winning cover design that fully captures and illustrates the essence of this book. I appreciate the feedback that she and her family, as well as many of their friends, provided on this book and cover design. Thanks also to Liz Allen, owner of Liz Allen Photography (lizallenphotography.com), for the professional photos used on the book cover and web site. I wish to thank my dear Texas friend, Tom Haynes, who provided me with invaluable feedback and support while I was writing this book. We lived in Texas for many years and consider it our second home.

Special thanks go out to James Rautman, Trent Hilborn, and Mark Mazur of A2f Pictures LLC (a2fpictures.com) for producing a world-class video to promote the ideas in *Selling U.S. Out*. I thank my friend and colleague Mike Danielson, President and CEO of M.R. Danielson Advertising (mrdan.com) for the wonderful website, and for the promotional assistance provided by him and his staff.

I want to thank the late Randy Pausch for writing *The Last Lecture* which I read in early 2011 while recovering from major surgery. Randy's book is truly a gift that inspired me to finish writing *Selling U.S. Out* and to dedicate the remainder of my life to making a positive difference in the world. Thank you Randy!

Finally, I wish to thank my family in Pittsburgh, whom I love and appreciate, as well as our many friends across the country who provided me with their invaluable feedback and support.

CHAPTER ONE

Selling U.S. Out—How and Why?

The things that will destroy America are prosperity at any price, peace at any price, safety first instead of duty first and love of soft living and the get-rich-quick theory of life.

—THEODORE ROOSEVELT

I have been involved in international business for most of the past twenty-five years. My business travels have taken me to Asia, Europe, South America, Mexico, Canada, and the Middle East. Prior to my career in business, I served for nine years in the U.S. Navy. A few years ago I did some work for a foreign-owned company that had factories in communist China. A former colleague referred them to me, and they said they wanted my assistance establishing a U.S. operation.

After engaging with this company, I was surprised to discover that they were already doing tens of millions of dollars of business in the U.S.— unincorporated and tax-free. Concerned about what I learned and its broader implications, I consulted with a highly respected corporate tax attorney. After I explained how this company was set up and operating in the U.S., he advised me that what they were doing may or may not be legal—it was in a "gray area." It seemed they were exploiting loopholes in the U.S.-China tax treaty signed by the Reagan administration in 1986. This being the case, I contacted my U.S. Congressman and Senator to advise them of this situation so that they could close these loopholes. I was extremely disappointed by the disinterest shown by both my U.S. congressman and senator about what I considered a very serious issue. If this relatively small foreign-owned company had figured out how to game the U.S. tax system, then surely other much larger companies were doing the same thing.

Around the same time that I was working through this issue, my lovely daughter Crystal, who also reminds me of Abigail Adams, and now has a family of her own, gave me David McCullough's books *1776* and *John Adams* as gifts. I have a passion for American history and read both with great enthusiasm and interest. Mr. McCullough is a brilliant author, who I deeply admire and respect. His books along with what I learned from my encounter with the foreign-owned company gaming the U.S. tax system, inspired me to research and write *Selling U.S. Out*. I was deeply moved while reading about the courage, sacrifice, and patriotism of the first Americans. What would they think about our nation's current state of affairs? Would they question our patriotism? Our commitment to liberty and independence? Our commitment to "The Glorious Cause of America"? How would they view our massive foreign debt—especially to nations (such as communist China) that do not grant their citizens basic human rights? How would our Founding Fathers view our current trade and economic policies? How would they view our nation's membership in the World Trade Organization (WTO)? How would they view the North American Free Trade Agreement (NAFTA) and other similar agreements? Would they view us as willing to sell our freedom and independence for material gain? What would Washington and Adams think about the corrupt and destructive power of the two major political parties in America? How would they judge today's capitalism? Would they equate capitalism with American patriotism? I have attempted to address these and other questions throughout this book.

As Roosevelt warned, America is being destroyed; our liberty and our children's futures are literally being sold out by those who seek prosperity at any price, love soft living, and embrace a get-rich-quick theory of life. However, it is within our collective power to reverse course and begin rebuilding our country. I discuss specific ideas and actions each of us can take to help rebuild America throughout the book and summarize them in the final chapter. Time is of the essence. We must rise above partisan politics and quickly come together as pragmatic, patriotic Americans working for the common good. Alexis de Tocqueville, a French historian and author of *Democracy in America*, wrote that, "The greatness of America lies not in being more enlightened than any other nation, but rather in her ability to repair her faults." It is time for us to unite in the common cause of rebuilding America by putting America and Americans first again! I believe we must start by cleaning up and opening up our political process. My sincere hope is that this book will inspire those who read it to take positive action.

Selling U.S. Out is not about some grand conspiracy. It is about how the toxic combination of ignorance, negligence, political ideology, corruption, and greed drove bad trade and economic policies that culminated in the economic collapse of 2008. The collapse was not just a financial crisis, it was an overall failure of the U.S. economic and financial systems. While the trillions of dollars the U.S. government borrowed and injected into the system averted a total system meltdown, the borrowed money did not address the underlying issues that caused the system to fail. If we do not address the underlying issues, it is only a matter of time before the system fails again with catastrophic consequences for the U.S. economy and our overall way of life.

As Paul Craig Roberts, former Assistant Secretary of the Treasury, explains in an article published in February 2009 *(Roberts, counterpunch. org)*, the seeds for our economic system failure were sown after World War II. While we preached "free markets" and "free trade," Japan, Germany, and other countries scoffed at us while maintaining tightly controlled access to their markets and employing industrial policy to rebuild their economies. Once rebuilt, they aggressively attacked open U.S. markets, destroying U.S. industries. By the late 1970s the U.S. had either given away or lost major industries to Japan, Germany, and other countries. Those we hadn't lost or given away, such as the automotive industry, were in steep decline. The de-industrialization and resulting economic decline of America was in full swing. As a result of Cold War politics and a naive assumption that our economy was large enough to absorb these losses, we did nothing to fix our trade policies and ignored the need to implement our own industrial policy or economic strategy to help guide the total strategic effort of our nation. These are the root causes and the beginnings of what grew into the 2008 economic and financial system failure. I discuss these ideas further in chapters three through seven and in chapter eleven.

Ongoing economic decline in the U.S. led to the election of Ronald Reagan in 1980. Instead of changing U.S. trade policy and creating a national economic strategy or industrial policy, the Reagan administration focused on deregulation and the expansion of trade (i.e., outsourcing and offshoring) with communist China. They granted them most-favored-nation (MFN) trade status, which greatly reduced tariffs on Chinese imports. This cleared the way for American investors and corporations to begin abandoning their home market to start pouring money into communist China instead, providing them with technology and knowledge of American markets. Thus began our record trade deficits and U.S. job losses through outsourcing and offshoring to China. The Reagan administration also began running record budget deficits that marked the beginning of our $15.5 trillion national debt. They began reversing the financial system regulatory reforms put into place after the Great Depression by passing a series of new laws to "deregulate" the savings and loan industry. This enabled fraud and other forms of corruption that led to massive bank failures and emergency government intervention in 1986. The total cost of the government "bailout" was $125 billion or five percent of our $2.1 trillion national debt in 1986. Instead of fixing U.S. trade policy (the system's primary problem), the Reagan administration introduced three new problems into the mix: financial system deregulation, "free trade" (outsourcing and offshoring) with communist China, and trillions of dollars in debt. On the surface, this appeared to "fix" the U.S. financial and economic system. However, all it really did was temporarily mask the symptoms of the original problem. It's kind of like taking a drug to mask the symptoms of a life-threatening disease. You feel good for the moment, but if the disease isn't cured, it becomes fatal.

Subsequent administrations, including the Clinton administration, continued to follow the pattern established by the Reagan administration—deregulation, expanded free trade (outsourcing and offshoring), and increased national debt. The de-industrialization and economic decline of America continued. In 1999 Clinton signed the Gramm-Leach-Bliley Act into law, which repealed the financial system and regulatory reforms enacted during the Great Depression with the passage of the Glass-Steagall Act in 1933. This massive deregulation paved the way for a reenactment of the same reckless behaviors that caused the stock market crash of 1929. Thanks to the passage of Gramm-Leach-Bliley, it was October 1929 all over again in September 2008! George W. Bush further expanded trade with China, creating more record trade deficits. His trade and economic policies added approximately $6 trillion to the national debt. Chapters six through nine expands on these observations.

Even after the economic and financial meltdown of 2008, the U.S. government hasn't acknowledged or addressed the root cause of our economic and financial system failure—flawed trade policy coupled with no national economic strategy or industrial policy. I discuss current U.S. trade policy in chapter six and ideas for a new U.S. trade policy coupled with a national economic strategy in chapter eleven.

The Obama administration continues to expand free trade and add trillions more to our national debt. The message from our government seems to be: *Don't worry, be happy. Things aren't as bad as they seem and are gradually getting better. And we have the statistics to prove it. Please continue to consume more and take on more debt to keep America strong! There is no need to concern yourself with our trade policy or national debt. All is well!*

Also, don't worry about paying taxes, serving in the military, or doing any of the other bothersome things we used to require of all U.S. citizens. While we like to talk a lot about the need to make sacrifices, we won't bother you unless you volunteer. By the way, here's a flag pin you can wear to display your patriotism. Oh, and if you are a veteran—thank you for your service. Sorry, we almost forgot to mention that. It's all good. Just look at our statistics.

Speaking of statistics, has anyone else noticed how the U.S. economic statistics seem to be improving as the election draws near? Funny thing, I noticed the same phenomenon when Bush ran for reelection in 2004. Then we had the economic collapse in 2008. But I'm sure this is just a coincidence.

Now let's begin our journey together, starting with a short review of early American history as it pertains to U.S. economic and trade policies. This lays an important foundation for the rest of this book, so please travel with me back to 1776.

CHAPTER TWO

The Glorious Cause of America

Our Nation's Miraculous Birth

It is nothing short of a miracle that this country we call the United States of America exists at all and that it has endured for more than 200 years! While most of us take this country and the freedoms we enjoy for granted, the birth of our great nation was brought about and has been sustained by tremendous personal sacrifice, honor, courage, perseverance, unselfish service, and a dedication to what the first Americans called "The Glorious Cause." Their early dedication is affirmed in our Declaration of Independence to which the signers pledged their lives, fortunes, and sacred honor. Indeed, many of those brave souls and those who supported or fought in the American Revolution did sacrifice their lives and fortunes to bring about the birth of this great nation that Ronald Reagan called the last hope of man on earth.

The Glorious Cause

To some, President Reagan's claim that the United States of America is the last hope of man on earth might seem arrogant and self-serving. However, I believe that Reagan was referring to what our forefathers called The Glorious Cause, which is not defined by ethnicity or geography but by a universal truth that is articulated in our Declaration of Independence with the words,

We hold these truths to be self-evident, that all men are created equal, that they are endowed by their Creator with certain unalienable Rights, that among these are Life, Liberty and the pursuit of Happiness.—That to secure these rights, Governments are instituted among Men, deriving their just powers from the consent of the governed . . . .

The universality of this truth is demonstrated by those who came to our shores during the Revolution and since to pledge their lives and fortunes for this glorious cause. One such person was a brilliant young French nobleman, Gilbert du Motier, the Marquis de Lafayette. As told in David McCullough's book *1776*, Lafayette heard about the American Revolution at a dinner party in Germany and because of his innate love of liberty, he chose to offer his life and his fortune to the glorious cause, believing that "the welfare of America is closely bound up with the welfare of mankind." So *at his own expense*, and at the risk of being imprisoned, he secretly outfitted a vessel and sailed to South Carolina—arriving in June 1777, more than two years after the Battles of Lexington and Concord. He then proceeded to Philadelphia, offered his services to Congress *without pay*, and was made a major general. Lafayette served under George Washington from 1777 to 1783. He served valiantly and was instrumental in helping America achieve independence. After the war Lafayette returned to his native France. His honorable, selfless service and the service of so many others during and since the American Revolution are active testaments to the glorious cause. Their sacrifices stand in stark contrast to the rampant corruption and greed tolerated in America today.

Our Founding Principles

As discussed in *The Rise & Decline of Constitutional Government in America* by Thomas G. West and Douglas A. Jeffrey, the Declaration of Independence lays out the principles on which our nation and constitutional form of government is founded. These principles are . . .

Equality

Equality is the first of the founding principles as stated in the Declaration of Independence: "We hold these truths to be self-evident, that all men are created equal . . . ." This same principle appears in the opening of the Massachusetts Constitution of 1780, which was written mostly by John Adams and served as the model for the United States Constitution. It states, "All men are born free and equal, and have certain natural, essential, and unalienable rights; among which may be reckoned the right of enjoying and defending their lives and liberties; that of acquiring, possessing, and protecting property; in fine, that of seeking and obtaining their safety and happiness."

Natural Rights

This is the second principle declared in the Declaration of Independence stating that human beings are "endowed by their Creator with certain unalienable Rights that among these are Life, Liberty, and the pursuit of Happiness." Out of this principle of the natural rights of liberty and property comes the Bill of Rights, the first ten amendments to the Constitution, which were officially adopted in 1791.

Consent

This principle is expressed in the Declaration by these words: "That to secure these rights, Governments are instituted among Men, deriving their just powers from the consent of the governed." This principle is further expressed in the preamble to the U.S. Constitution with the words "We the people," and in the closing of Lincoln's Gettysburg Address with " . . . and that government of the people, by the people, for the people, shall not perish from the earth."

Revolution

This principle is expressed in the Declaration as follows: "whenever any Form of Government becomes destructive of these ends, it is the Right of the People to alter or to abolish it, and to institute new Government, laying its foundation on such principles and organizing its powers in such form, as to them shall seem most likely to effect their Safety and Happiness." This right of revolution follows logically from the other principles. Since government exists to protect natural rights, and government derives its just powers from consent, the people have the right to get rid of it and set up a new government if the current one fails in its duties to the people. However, the Declaration also cautions that "Prudence, indeed, will dictate that Governments long established should not be changed for light and transient causes." As we have seen throughout history and are witnessing around the world today, revolution can be a dangerous thing. There is no guarantee that a worse form of government, such as a dictatorship, will not emerge. Our founders were counseling us that a nation should only embark on the dangerous path of revolution after serious consideration and when the outcome is likely to secure liberty and a general improvement in the lives of the people.

The Founding Fathers were men of integrity and great wisdom who understood the nature of man. The system of government they designed comprehends and protects us against human nature, which is why the Constitution has endured for more than 200 years. The principles upon which our government was founded are as relevant today as they were in 1789. These same principles are the vital foundation of our future.

Capitalism and Patriotism

In today's America there is a tendency to equate capitalism with patriotism and the liberty that was secured as a result of the American Revolution. In fact, since the founding of our country, there has been a conflict between capitalism and patriotism; the former is concerned only with securing wealth and the latter is concerned with securing liberty and freedom. In 1776, the vast majority of colonial "capitalists" opposed American independence and separation from England. They preferred to maintain the status quo to avoid a disruption in trade relations with England and the financial losses that would result. They were perfectly content to sacrifice freedom for financial security. In fact, the New York Chamber of Commerce opposed the Revolutionary War and many of its members assisted the British *(McCullough, 1776)*. They valued their business interests above all else. On the other hand, the patriots who signed the Declaration and those who battled for independence committed their Lives, Fortunes, and sacred Honor to secure the freedoms we take for granted. I wonder how those first patriots and the Founding Fathers would feel about the trillions of dollars we now owe to communist China, Japan, and the Middle East. Do you think they might question our commitment to the Glorious Cause of America? Would they view us, like the capitalists and loyalists of their era, as willing to sacrifice our freedoms for financial gain?

Our ancestors took a cautious and pragmatic approach to capitalism because they understood that its power could either help build or destroy American democracy. Throughout the nineteenth century and into the early twentieth, Americans struggled with trying to create a stable financial system that supported instead of threatened our democracy. It was an evolutionary process that culminated in the banking and financial system reforms passed after the collapse of Wall Street in 1929 and the Great Depression. Prior to enactment of these banking and financial system reforms, bank failures and economic depressions were common occurrences in America. In fact, before the Great Depression of the 1930s, the U.S. had four depressions and twenty-nine recessions, which in most cases were caused by financial "panics" and bank failures *(Wikipedia)*. The combination of the financial system reforms enacted after the Great Depression, along with other financial system reforms implemented in the late nineteenth and early twentieth centuries, created "American" capitalism. Unlike other forms of capitalism, American capitalism of this era was a stable system with checks and balances created to ensure that our financial systems served the country's common good and helped build—not destroy—the American economy and democracy. This system served us very well until the 1980s, when our political leaders began to dismantle it in favor of unregulated "global" capitalism. The dismantling of American capitalism in favor of the unregulated global model unleashed the same destructive forces that created financial instability in America throughout the nineteenth and early twentieth centuries. Worse yet, it turned the financial systems we created to build our nation into engines of American economic and national destruction. The global unregulated capitalist system exploits workers and resources world-wide without regard for the common good—it doesn't care about America or Americans, just about return on investment. Is it any wonder, then, that today's capitalists are selling out America in favor of communist China? Neither global capitalism nor communism values human rights, freedom, or liberty. One is dedicated to the pursuit of wealth and the other to the accumulation of political power—a perfect match made in hell!

Trade and Commerce

From the beginning, international trade has played an important role in our nation's economy. However, until the 1970s, the United States was primarily an exporting nation with trade surpluses. Throughout most of our history, we utilized tariffs to control imports and protect key industries. Tariffs were our government's primary source of revenue until the early 1900s. It was the Republican Party that promoted and supported this policy, as it was articulated by Congressman William McKinley in 1888:

> Free foreign trade gives our money, our manufactures, and our markets to other nations to the injury of our labor, our trades people, and our farmers. Protection keeps money, markets, and manufactures at home for the benefit of our own people.

McKinley would be stunned to see his Republican Party today promoting the so-called free-trade agreements that are driving record trade deficits and destroying our national economy.

CHAPTER THREE

Selling Our Freedom I

There are two ways to conquer and enslave a nation.
One is by the sword. The other is by debt.

—JOHN ADAMS

National Debt and Trade Imbalance

Our national debt is skyrocketing! As of the writing of this book, our national debt was $15.5 TRILLION and rising *(DeficitsDoMatter.org)*! This amount is rapidly increasing as our government continues to borrow more and more money. Furthermore, if you add to this debt the government's future obligations for increases in Social Security, Medicare, and Medicaid, our total national debt is a staggering $61 TRILLION! These are incomprehensible numbers for most of us, so allow me to try and put them into perspective. If you break $15.5 trillion down to every man, woman, and child now living in the U.S., each of us currently owns $49,000 of the total national debt! Then, if you factor in the money our government is obligated to pay for increases in Social Security, Medicare, and Medicaid, then each of is now in debt to the tune of more than $195,000! That means each child born in the U.S. today begins life with this debt. We are literally mortgaging our children's futures to finance our current standard of living. This skyrocketing debt is unsustainable. It is the single largest threat to our freedom and national security. Perhaps worst of all, we are doing it to ourselves. But we can and must address this problem to preserve our country for future generations. Later in the book I will discuss the sacrifices and actions required to confront this threat.

Our national debt is directly related to our trade imbalance. In 2007 communist China had the world's largest trade surplus at $371 billion (*Central Intelligence Agency*). In contrast, out of 196 nations, the U.S. had the world's largest trade deficit at negative $731 billion! That means the U.S. imported or purchased $731 billion more than it exported or sold, while China, on the other hand, exported or sold $371 billion more than it imported or purchased. (These numbers paint a pretty clear picture of where most of the lost U.S. manufacturing jobs have gone, don't they?) Simply put, we are buying much more from other countries than what we are selling to them and, in the process, we're transferring our nation's wealth to the countries we are buying from.

Furthermore, we are borrowing more and more money from the nations we are buying from the most, such as communist China, Japan, and the oil-exporting countries in the Middle East. This is a toxic combination that directly opposes the practices that built the wealth of America over the past 200 years. Almost fifty percent of our nation's debt is owned by foreign countries.

> ALMOST FIFTY PERCENT OF OUR NATION'S DEBT IS OWNED BY FOREIGN COUNTRIES.

To put this in perspective, after World War II one hundred percent of our nation's debt was owned by Americans. Foreign ownership of our national debt grew to about five percent by 1965. Since then it has been steadily increasing every year, along with our trade deficit. It is no coincidence that our main lenders—China, Japan, and the oil-exporting countries of the Middle East—are also the countries that export the most to us. With the passage of the economic stimulus and corporate bailout programs following the economic collapse of

2008, our foreign borrowing continues to rapidly increase, especially from communist China. This has serious economic and political consequences.

Communist China—Fleecing America

The capitalists will sell us the rope with which we will hang them.

—Vladimir Ilyich Lenin,
first leader of the Soviet Union

As previously mentioned, communist China has the world's largest trade surplus with the majority of its exports coming to the United States. They are also our largest banker, owning $1.1 trillion of the U.S. national debt! The irony of this defies belief since our country led the free world in the fight against communism after World War II and sacrificed countless American lives in Korea, Vietnam, and other conflicts around the world during the Cold War to defeat communism and bring down the former Soviet Union. Now we find ourselves enriching and borrowing from the world's largest communist nation! Worse yet, American corporations and our government are collaborating with the communist Chinese government to deny the Chinese people basic human rights! Why? We will explore this in-depth later, but the short answer is *greed*. The same greed that destroyed our financial markets and thrust our nation into the worst economic crisis since the Great Depression. I imagine Lenin would be pleased that his prediction is being fulfilled by the U.S. and China—we offered up the rope they're using to hang us. There are some who believe communist China is adopting American values and that political freedom will follow as a result of their newfound prosperity. As Eamonn Fingleton states in his book *In the Jaws of the Dragon: America's Fate in the Coming Era of Chinese Dominance*, this is a naïve and gross miscalculation with disastrous consequences for the U.S. and the rest of the free world if left unchallenged. Now, let's take a closer look at our trade relationship with communist China.

Predatory Trade Practices

In 2010 China exported $365 billion of goods to the U.S. and only imported $92 billion from us *(The U.S.-China Business Council)*. This imbalance gets even more exaggerated when you take into account that a large portion of what China imported from the U.S. were components or materials used to manufacture goods for resale back to the U.S. and other countries. In contrast, most of what we imported from China were finished goods consumed domestically. In fact, calling this "trade" is misleading. What is really happening between the U.S. and China is the transfer of American jobs to China to exploit low-cost labor and an artificially low currency exchange rate. Real trade would mean both the U.S. and China were engaged in the production of goods that were then sold to each other, and consumed in our respective countries by either individuals or businesses. Instead, we're experiencing a one-way production and sale of finished goods from communist China to the U.S. I will discuss this topic in more depth in chapter six.

China is following the same strategy that Japan, Korea, and other Asian nations have successfully deployed against the U.S. since the end of World War II. It is a fairly simple and highly effective strategy—exploit the world's largest and most open economy with low-priced exports while protecting your markets from U.S. imports. Now some who read this book will argue that communist China is opening up its markets. They will cite as evidence the tariffs they have lowered and other actions taken in recent years to meet the conditions they agreed to as part of joining the World Trade Organization (WTO). On the surface this appears true; however, to understand what is really going on you have to look deeper. China is playing the same cat-and-mouse game that Japan has been playing with the U.S. for over fifty years. It goes something like this: *Tell them what they want to hear and do the minimum to appear compliant while simultaneously stalling and deflecting as much as possible. Be gracious and flatter their egos continually. Entertain them, and tell them regularly how much you value your relationship with them. Since most Americans have relatively short attention spans, they will eventually get distracted and leave you alone. You just need to be patient and wait them out.*

My experiences with Asian culture suggest that they are extremely skilled at applying stall tactics and generating ambiguity. For example, a common observation of foreigners who have done business in Asia is that *yes* may not always mean *yes*, but sometimes be just an acknowledgement of understanding rather than an agreement. That may sometimes be the case. However, what is not as obvious is that in many cases our Asian counterparts are intentionally creating ambiguity to avoid being locked into an agreement. So how does this influence trade?

Well, one real-world example is communist China's admission into the WTO in November 2001. Their membership was contingent upon meeting certain commitments that would open up their markets to the rest of the world within five years. As of the writing of this book, it's been ten years and China still has not met the agreed-upon commitments which include: protection of intellectual property rights; enforcement of export restrictions; elimination of prohibited subsidies; discriminatory application of value-added taxes; continued restrictions on trading and distribution rights; agriculture; services; and overall transparency. One of the most harmful violations of international trade law is the continued manipulation of China's currency by their government. They have rebuffed repeated requests by the U.S. and other countries to allow the value of their currency to be determined like all other countries in the WTO. The communist Chinese government's artificial control of the value of their currency creates a significant unfair trading advantage and is a clear violation of trade law, yet it has gone unpunished by the WTO and the U.S. Meanwhile, China's effective use of this tactic is doing catastrophic damage to the U.S. economy. According to a 2007 report published by the Trade Lawyers Advisory Group and funded by the U.S. Small Business Administration *(Trade Lawyers Advisory Group)*:

> Many economists estimate that China continues to undervalue its currency by as much as 40 percent. As a result, Chinese goods continue to compete domestically and internationally at prices that are artificially low, hurting U.S. producers in the U.S.

market, in the Chinese market and in third country markets. It is argued that China's exchange rate intervention effectively acts as a tax on U.S. exports and a subsidy to China's exports, which causes the loss of U.S. manufacturing jobs. Despite these concerns, the Department of Treasury has declined to designate China as a currency manipulator under Section 3004 of the Omnibus Trade and Competitiveness Act of 1988, stating in its June 2007 report that it was "unable to determine that China's exchange rate policy was carried out for the purpose of preventing effective balance of payments adjustment or gaining unfair competitive advantage in international trade."

Since most of us are not economists and get bleary-eyed when people start talking about exchange rates, let me explain in familiar terms why this is so serious. Let's imagine Canada did the same thing as communist China. This would mean that when you went to Canada and exchanged US$1 you would always get back C$1.40. Sounds good until you try to sell a Ford Taurus in Canada that costs US$25,000 and C$35,000 because of the difference in the exchange rate. Conversely, if the Ford Taurus is built in Canada and priced at C$25,000 and then sold in the U.S., it would cost US$15,000. Which car would you buy?

Instead of following through on the commitments they made in 2001 when they were allowed to join the WTO, communist China is effectively using the deflect, stall, and wait-them-out strategies I mentioned earlier. Meanwhile they grow wealthier and more powerful as a result of their WTO membership. They are exploiting this membership and using the access it provides to the U.S. market to their advantage.

Ignoring Product Safety

In 2010 there were 220 U.S. safety recalls of Chinese-made products. I have difficulty writing about this topic without getting emotional. It is unbelievable to me that Americans aren't marching on Washington demanding that our government immediately stop all trade with communist China until this vital issue gets resolved—until we have undeniable proof that the communist Chinese government has a product-safety system that works, is not corrupt, and complies with U.S. law. This is a very serious issue that threatens all of us, and perhaps most importantly, our children. Imagine giving your child cold medicine made with the same chemicals used in antifreeze, and killing your child as a result. Or how about having a loved one die in surgery because the medication they are given is counterfeit. Unfortunately, these are not hypothetical situations; they are real human tragedies that have happened in the U.S. and other countries due to the total lack of concern for product safety and human life by Communist China, Inc. Here is a list of some of the China product safety issues over the past few years:

- lead paints used on children's toys
- sixty-two U.S. deaths related to counterfeit Heparin
- poisoned medicines around the world as a result of counterfeit ingredients from communist China are blamed for thousands of deaths, mostly children
- poisoned pet foods due to contaminated ingredients
- toxic tooth paste containing the chemicals used in antifreeze
- contaminated seafood
- defective tires
- infant deaths from contaminated infant formula
- contaminated dairy products used in the making of candy and other food products
- toxic drywall used in as many as one hundred thousand U.S. homes

So how has communist China responded? In short, denial. They argue that such problems are exaggerated. Case in point, after it was discovered that the same toxic chemicals used in antifreeze were found in toothpaste manufactured in China, Chinese government officials issued a statement calling the U.S. Food and Drug Administration's warnings against using this contaminated toothpaste "unscientific, irresponsible, and contradictory" *(Associated Press)*. They went on to assert that "low levels of the chemical have been deemed safe for consumption." This response is typical and consistent with the deflect, stall, and wait-them-out strategies. However, as though finally realizing that poisoning your customers and then appearing indifferent isn't good for business, the Chinese government hired a U.S.-based public relations firm to spin their product safety issues to convince us that there really isn't a significant problem—that China's product-safety errors are no worse than similar problems in the U.S. The real problem, they want to convince us, is that Americans are too demanding. What's the big deal if some of the products they sell us occasionally kill us or our children? After all, we are saving money! With the help of U.S. public relations firms, the Chinese government is sending us a well-scripted, carefully choreographed message intended to convince us that now they're very serious about product safety. They also continue to spend millions of dollars lobbying our elected representatives to ensure there is no disruption of Chinese exports to the U.S., regardless of safety concerns.

Their strategy must be working, since China's product-safety issues are now almost never talked about on the U.S. news and it is business as usual with Communist China, Inc. I recently went to a local grocery store and found a can of mandarin oranges on the shelf that was labeled "Made in China." Needless to say, I did not purchase this product. Thankfully the can was properly labeled and I had a choice. However, lately I have noticed that many food products do not list the country of origin—only the point of distribution. This is very concerning. Also, what about products labeled "Made in USA" or elsewhere that may include counterfeit or contaminated ingredients from China? Or what about the food being supplied to our restaurants? How much of it comes from China? Who is protecting us and our children? In November 2011 the WTO ruled that the U.S. could no longer require country-of-origin labels for food products being exported to the U.S. *(Food Safety News)*, which is insane and should be the cause of a major uproar. But I bet most people are unaware of this ruling since it hasn't been very well covered in the U.S. media. The PR firms and lobbyists hired by Communist China, Inc., are doing a great job of suppressing such issues and ensuring our government does nothing to prevent them from putting unsafe products on the shelves of U.S. stores—it's all about the money! Is anyone up for a road trip to Washington, D.C.? Perhaps if about five million or so of us gather in our nation's capital and demand action something will get done! Please visit my website at Selling-US-Out.com if you would like more information on this issue and the steps you can take to protect your family.

One-Party Rule

It is extremely troubling that we seem to have forgotten or chosen to ignore that one of our largest trading partners and primary lender is a communist totalitarian state. The freedoms we take for granted in this country do not exist in communist China. There is only one political party, the Communist Party, and they rule supreme and unchallenged. It is a dictatorship in the truest sense of the word, and it denies its citizens basic human rights. Our nation's silence on this issue is deafening! Our Founding Fathers would be ashamed at how we have chosen to put our business and financial interests above freedom, liberty, and human rights.

The most obvious example of this is the Tiananmen Square protests of 1989. Think back for a moment and recall how powerful and uplifting it was to see all those brave young Chinese students carrying images of Lady Liberty, one of America's most iconic symbols of freedom, in Tiananmen Square. They were protesting peacefully for the same universal Glorious Cause our Founding Fathers declared. The Chinese students were full of hope and optimism for their individual futures and the future of their country. They clearly never imagined that their fellow countrymen—soldiers to whom they were giving roses—would later murder them in cold blood! And what has our government done since? They've increased our trade with communist China and borrowed more money from them, despite the blood of innocent children staining the hands of the Chinese government. Even worse, we have collaborated with the communist Chinese government by ignoring and downplaying the brutality they showed in suppressing the uprising in Tiananmen Square. Much to their satisfaction, our political and business leaders act as if this never happened. They treat Tiananmen Square as a taboo subject not to be spoken of, lest we offend our largest banker and leading source of low-cost labor. What message does this send to the Chinese people and all people around the world yearning to be free? I find it hypocritical that some of our political leaders display such bravado in support of the recent uprisings in the Middle East, while ignoring the legacy of Tiananmen Square and the continuing human rights abuses in communist China. The protests in the Middle East are similar to those in Tiananmen Square and are being met with the same totalitarian brutality. During the uprising in Iran, I saw some of our political leaders on a Sunday talk show discussing these protests. They mentioned other similar past protests that took place around the world but never once mentioned Tiananmen Square. I found this very odd and can only speculate that they didn't want to offend our largest lender—communist China.

Tibet

As reported by Amnesty International, Human Rights Watch, and other related organizations, hundreds of Tibetans have been incarcerated for peacefully expressing their political and religious beliefs. Conditions in Tibetan prisons are reportedly dismal, with numerous accounts of torture and ill treatment. In particular, Chinese law-enforcement officials have perpetrated violent acts against Tibetan women in detention centers and prisons. Buddhist nuns and lay women have been subject to torture and other violent, degrading, and inhuman treatment, including assault, rape, and sexual abuse. Chinese authorities have also severely restricted religious practice; of the 6,000 Buddhist monasteries destroyed by the Chinese government since its 1949 invasion of Tibet, only a few hundred have been rebuilt. Communist Chinese policies, including population transfers of hundreds of thousands of Chinese into Tibet, threaten to make Tibetans a minority in their own land and to destroy Tibetans' distinct national religious and cultural life. Since March 2008 the Tibetan region has been sealed off to the rest of the world by the Chinese government. There was significant controversy surrounding Tibet prior to the 2008 Olympic Games since in their 2001 bid for the Olympics, Chinese officials argued that international attention would "improve" the country's human-rights policies (*Editorials: The Washington Post*). However, once again, the Chinese deceived the Western world and are continuing their human rights abuses in Tibet unabated.

Darfur, Sudan

China's motto for the 2008 Olympics was "One world, one dream." Meanwhile, they were actively supporting the genocidal nightmare taking place in Darfur. China denied visas to any Olympic athlete speaking out against their involvement in Darfur. What an outrage! Once again, the silence from the U.S. government over this issue was deafening.

The genocide in Darfur is one of the greatest humanitarian crises in recent history. As reported by the *Sudan Tribune*, with the financial assistance and support of communist China, over four hundred thousand people have been murdered and millions more have been displaced. China has provided Khartoum more than $10 billion in commercial and capital investments over the past decade, and has been the regime's primary supplier of weapons, weapons technology, and weapons engineering expertise. It is estimated that up to 90% of the weaponry used in Darfur is from China, or is of Chinese design and manufactured in Khartoum. China has also provided the criminals of Khartoum diplomatic cover at the United Nations, where it wields veto power on the Security Council. The simple fact is that China views Sudan through its own petroleum needs—it consumes almost two-thirds of Sudan's crude oil exports.

Beijing has shown callous disregard for human life in Sudan as it pursues its own economic and political interests. Despite these atrocities, it's been business as usual between the U.S. and communist China. Our government turned a blind eye toward China's involvement in this genocide. Why? Is this yet another example of us not wanting to upset our largest banker and primary source of low-cost labor?

The One-Child Policy

In 1978 the Communist Chinese Government enacted a policy of one child per family, which is strictly enforced through forced abortions and sterilizations. Imagine being told that you can have only one child. And if you do not comply a group of people from the local family planning organization show up at your house unannounced, takes you by force to a clinic, and injects you with poison to kill your baby. Then, after you give birth to your dead fetus, imagine receiving a forced operation to ensure you can't have any more children. This policy has also resulted in the killing and abandonment of baby girls, since families in China place a much higher value on having boys. This has been happening in communist China for over thirty years and continues today. I have a difficult time reconciling how U.S. political leaders who espouse their Christian faith and family values can also strongly support trading with and borrowing from a nation that has such a policy in place. What would our Founding Fathers say?

By now, some who are reading this book may be thinking that I am anti-Chinese. Nothing could be further from the truth. I spent much time in both China and Taiwan. I have a genuine appreciation and respect for the Chinese People, their culture, and history. However, while I respect and appreciate the Chinese people, I have absolutely no regard for their communist dictatorship that tortures and murders its own citizens and denies them their unalienable human rights. It is a national disgrace—and an insult to our ancestors who committed their Lives, Fortunes, and sacred Honor for the Glorious Cause of liberty—that the U.S. government and American corporations are collaborating with these communist dictators. The protestors in Tiananmen Square and, more recently, in Iran, Tunisia, Egypt, Syria, and Libya, remind us all how precious freedom is and echo Patrick Henry's rallying cry, "Give me liberty or give me death!"

Widespread Corruption

You don't have to go far in communist China to find corruption. It is common practice for companies to pay bribes to corrupt government officials to get them to issue required permits, licenses, and other similar documents. For companies doing business in China, these bribes are viewed as just another business expense. The corruption is severe and pervades all levels of Communist Chinese political and corporate life. For some recent examples, just go online and do a search for "China corruption" and you will see what I am talking about. This is a serious problem since most, if not all, of the product-safety issues discussed earlier involved bribes paid to government officials. What is most alarming is that U.S. companies doing business in China are adopting this behavior instead of opposing it. As a result, they are becoming tainted and compromised with these corrupt business practices, a concern I will discuss in more detail later.

Taiwan and Communist China

The history of Taiwan (known in the past as Formosa) and their relationship with mainland China is somewhat complex. The original inhabitants of this island were of Polynesian origin, not Chinese *(Wikipedia)*. In fact, the Chinese did not have any presence on the island until the seventeenth century, after they seized control from the Dutch. They maintained very loose control over the island for the next two hundred years and then gave it to Japan in 1895 as part of the Treaty of Shimonoseki, which ended the First Sino-Japanese War. Taiwan remained under Japanese control until it was liberated by U.S. Armed Forces near the end of World War II. China had absolutely no claim to Taiwan, however; President Franklin D. Roosevelt expressed his desire to have Taiwan "restored" to China. After WWII fighting broke out between the Nationalist and Communist forces on mainland China. Communist forces prevailed in 1949, forcing General Chiang Kai-shek and his Nationalist forces into exile on the island of Taiwan. Thus began the debate over the status of Taiwan that continues today, between the U.S. and the communist government of mainland China.

Selling Out Taiwan

Technically, mainland China has absolutely no claim over Taiwan since China gave Taiwan to Japan in 1895, and the U.S. liberated the people of Taiwan from Japan through the heroic sacrifices of our armed forces during

WWII. By all rights, Taiwan is and should be a U.S. territory just like Guam. However, with the Korean War starting shortly after WWII, President Truman decided to allow Chiang Kai-shek to govern Taiwan until the U.S. could decide on the status of the island at some future date. In 1971, Secretary of State Henry Kissinger went on a secret mission to communist China, which resulted in President Nixon's 1972 visit and the signing of a document stating that the U.S. agreed with communist China that there was only "one" China, meaning that we were ceding ownership of Taiwan to mainland China. In 1979 President Jimmy Carter took this much further by ending all official relations with Taiwan, withdrawing remaining U.S. military forces, and terminating our security treaty with Taiwan. This was the beginning of a complex and convoluted U.S. policy that can only be described as the U.S. selling out the people of Taiwan to establish trade relations with the communist government in mainland China.

Embracing Communist China

Over the past thirty-five years we have embraced communist China with U.S. policies driven by short-term economic interests with little or no regard for the long-term political, social, and economic consequences of these policies. Many proponents of these policies assume that liberalization of trade with communist China and opening our markets to them will eventually lead to the collapse of communism and the adoption of a democratic political system in mainland China. This is a very naïve and dangerous assumption. In fact, just the opposite is happening. As a result of U.S. trade and economic policies during the past thirty-five years, the communist Chinese government has greatly prospered and has increased its power, wealth, and control over its people, with a total disregard for human rights. China is gaining more influence and leverage in greater Asia and the rest of the world. They are becoming the dominant power in Asia and beginning to challenge U.S. power and influence in this region. The communist party is in firm control of mainland China, including Hong Kong, and shows no signs of moving toward a more democratic system.

A Growing Military Power

While we are all aware of China's growing economic power, many of us are totally unaware that they are using their prosperity to rapidly expand their military power far beyond what is required for defense. Over the past twenty years, China has been quietly expanding its military power, with double-digit increases in military spending. It is believed to have the largest armed forces in the world today, with an army of two-and-a-half million. This martial expansion has caused fear and concern in the region. The U.S. military is also becoming increasingly concerned, as expressed in a 2008 Pentagon report entitled *Military Power of the People's Republic of China* that details:

- China's military spending continues to increase by double-digit figures.

- China has deployed over one thousand short-range ballistic missiles to garrisons opposite Taiwan and is adding more than one hundred missiles per year.

- Chinese computer hackers have launched sophisticated strikes on computer networks around the world in the past year, including U.S. government networks, that might be the work of the Chinese government.

- China's strategy of defense includes conducting preemptive attacks "if the use of force protects or advances core interests, including territorial claims, for example, Taiwan and unresolved border or maritime claims."

- China's anti-satellite weapon test in January 2007 shows that the military's space warfare capability is more than theoretical. Additional space weapons include jammers, laser blinders, and microwave weapons to disable satellites and ground stations.

- China's "wide-ranging espionage" targeting officials, businessmen, and scientists has prompted more than four hundred U.S. investigations.

- China's military buildup is shifting the cross-Strait military balance in its favor, through a long-term expansion designed to fight "local wars" with high-tech weapons using speed, precision targeting, mobility, and information technology as force multipliers.

These same concerns are echoed in a 2009 Pentagon report *(Office of the Secretary of Defense)* which also notes that China continues to modernize its nuclear arsenal by improving its fleet of ballistic-missile submarines to give itself greater strategic strike capability. China's aircraft carrier research program supported its navy's intention to build multiple carriers by 2020, the report added. The 2009 report further states that "[r]isks to the United States and its allies in the Pacific region arise from incomplete Chinese defense spending figures and actions that appear inconsistent with declared policies." This is a very dangerous and volatile situation that is eerily similar to how the totalitarian regime in Japan behaved prior to the Pearl Harbor attack on December 7, 1941. Let us all hope and pray that history does not repeat itself.

The Coming Showdown over Taiwan

As previously discussed, communist China has over fourteen hundred ballistic missiles aimed at Taiwan and also has troops and equipment positioned across the Strait of Taiwan, prepared for invasion at any time it chooses. The threat of retaliatory action by the U.S. and Taiwan military forces are all that is keeping the Chinese military from invading Taiwan and taking it by force. The Chinese government has shown no interest in serious talks with Taiwan to settle their differences peacefully, despite the agreements and policies the U.S. has established with communist China since 1971. Instead, China claims that Taiwan is a renegade province that they will bring back under control by force, if necessary. Unless there is a democratic revolution on mainland China, which is highly unlikely, it is only a matter of time before the Communist People Liberation Army makes good on its promise and invades Taiwan. How will the U.S. respond when this happens? Will our government honor its treaties with Taiwan and go to war with China? Or will we allow our largest lender to enslave the people of Taiwan under a totalitarian communist dictatorship? Unless there is democratic political reform in mainland China, the question is not *if* we will face this reality—the question is *when*.

CHAPTER FOUR

Selling Our Freedom II

Japan Inc.—Paving the Way

So how did Japan rise from the defeat and devastation of WWII to become the second-largest economy in the world and the second-largest banker to the U.S. behind communist China? In short, they used protectionism and industrial policy, with the full cooperation and support of the U.S. government. They closed Japan's markets to foreign competition in industries they wished to enter, and only allowed imported goods that helped build up Japan's own industries. The U.S. allowed Japan to freely export to our markets, while protecting Japan's domestic markets from U.S. imports. Japan took full advantage of this policy by establishing predatory trade practices through government and business partnerships that enabled Japan Inc. to target and eventually dominate the steel, consumer electronics, automotive, computer, semiconductor, and many other industries. Japan developed a government-directed, export-driven economy and benefited greatly by becoming a member of the General Agreement on Tariffs and Trade (GATT), the forerunner of the WTO. This membership allowed Japan to purchase oil and the other raw materials necessary for its industrial development at low prices. Another key factor in Japan's economic development has been the money saved on defense spending. Since WWII, the U.S. has provided protection to Japan. As a result, defense spending in

Japan accounts for only 1 percent of their gross domestic product, compared to 4.7 percent in the U.S.

The Cold War, which began almost immediately after WWII, also provided Japan with a great opportunity to expand economically and further exploit U.S. trade policies. I was a frequent visitor to Japan when the former Soviet Union collapsed and the Cold War came to an end. I recall the concern expressed at the time by many Japanese business leaders that the U.S. would shift its focus to economics and the uneven trade relationship with Japan. This did not happen. Instead the Globalists and Free Traders pushed for trade policies and agreements that further weakened the U.S. economy while strengthening Japan and fueling the rise of communist China. At the same time, the U.S. became entangled in the so-called Global War on Terror. How convenient for both Japan and China that the U.S. is once again distracted with another war while they continue to exploit and benefit from the misguided trade policies that are destroying our country.

America's Second-Largest Banker

How ironic that a country the U.S. defeated militarily in 1945, and helped rebuild afterward, is now our second-largest banker, owning $885 billion of the U.S. national debt! The harsh reality is that while we may have defeated Japan militarily in WWII, they have since overtaken us economically. Worse yet, we helped them do it, just as we are now assisting China! The U.S. now owes a total of two trillion dollars to Japan and communist China. We also purchased $333 billion more in goods than we sold to Japan and China in 2010. This is unsustainable and poses a direct threat to our independence and national security. It is also a national disgrace, an insult to our ancestors, and a gross injustice to future generations! We are literally selling America and jeopardizing our freedom.

East Asian Economic Model and Trade Policy

While there is much discussion and promotion of free markets in the U.S., no such economic system exists in Japan or the rest of Asia. As explained by Eamonn Fingleton in his book *In the Jaws of the Dragon:*

America's Fate in the Coming Era of Chinese Dominance, it never has and most likely never will. It is a myth that Japan and the rest of Asia will someday "evolve" and adopt Western-style democracy and capitalism. The reality is that Japan and the rest of Asia have no interest in shifting to Western-style capitalism, a system they view as inferior. According to Fingleton, Japan and the rest of East Asia (China, Hong Kong, Taiwan, Singapore, Malaysia, Thailand, and Korea) are using an economic system that Japan initially developed during WWII and has since refined. He refers to this economic system as the East Asian Economic Model with the key attributes being:

- Focus on exports to the U.S. and other rich industrialized nations
- Impose high tariffs on imports and undervalue currencies to suppress domestic consumption and support exports
- Use a non-democratic and relatively authoritarian political system
- Force a high savings rate by suppressing domestic consumption
- Government and big business work together to manage and develop the economy via regulations and market rigging
- Allow monopolies or cartels and price fixing
- Produce sustainable double-digit growth rates for decades primarily through exports

This economic system was first developed and tested by the Japanese from 1931 to 1944 during their occupation of the Manchuria region of China. During this period, Manchuria experienced rapid economic growth while the rest of China was stagnant. Japan refined the system during the postwar years and it was subsequently adopted by Korea, Taiwan, Singapore, and other Asian countries in the 1960s. Communist China, convinced this system was superior to capitalism, adopted the economic model in late 1970s.

As Fingleton further explains in his book, all of these economies share the attributes described above and clearly depend upon government control and market rigging. Contrary to Western-style capitalism, the governments of East Asia manage and drive their economies—not the capitalists. In Japan, China, and the rest of East Asia, the government has an authoritarian role in economic policy. At the core of this economic system is suppressed consumption. This is what creates the unprecedented and historically high savings rates in Asia (China's savings rate is 40 percent!). The concept is relatively simple: the government puts policies in place that make it very difficult for people to spend money, which forces more savings. For instance, in China, the majority of people are confined to small living spaces, which means they don't need to buy much furniture and they don't consume much in the way of utilities. Also, credit is tightly controlled—most transactions are done using debit cards or cash—and mortgages are scarce. People must save their money for many years to buy a home. Prices for consumer goods in communist China and throughout Asia are kept artificially high—especially imported goods—through trade barriers and price fixing. This creates huge profits for favored companies, which also contributes to national savings. These national savings are controlled and invested through government-run banks and cartels. The government and cartels also control industrial capacity and work together to keep prices low for exports and high for domestic consumption. Their policies totally contradict the Western notions of free markets and free trade, and are the main reasons the U.S. continues to have record trade deficits with both China and Japan.

Orchestrated the Demise of Several U.S. Industries

Over the past sixty years, using the East Asian economic system, Japan Inc. has systematically targeted and orchestrated the demise of U.S. companies in the consumer electronics, automotive, steel, computer, semiconductor, and many other industries. There are those who would argue that the U.S. companies in these industries lost to Japanese or other Asian competitors simply because these competitors offered better products and services at competitive prices and therefore took market share. They would say that is how the free market works. This is an erroneous, yet commonly held view that has been aggressively promoted by Japan along with other Asian countries over the past sixty years as they have systematically attacked and overtaken industries once dominated by U.S. companies. Let's take a closer look at some of the industries the U.S. has lost to Japan and other Asian countries.

Consumer Electronics Industry

The global market for consumer electronics in 2010 was $873 billion with $181 billion in sales coming from the U.S. market. This market is dominated by Japanese and Korean companies with the top five consumer electronics companies worldwide being Sony, Toshiba, Panasonic, Samsung, and LG. The U.S. participation in this market has been relegated to marketing and distribution of products that are manufactured primarily in Asia. Even the extraordinarily popular Apple iPhone and iPad are manufactured in Asia, using components mostly provided by Asian suppliers.

The sad irony is that the consumer electronics industry was created by the U.S. with the invention of the electron tube in 1904, which led to the development of commercial radio in the 1920s and television in the 1930s. In 1947, the electronics industry made another important advance when John Bardeen, Walter Brattain, and William Shockley, scientists at the Bell Telephone Laboratories in Murray Hill, New Jersey, invented the transistor. This was followed in 1959 by the invention of the integrated circuit by Jack Kilby of Texas Instruments and Robert Noyce of Fairchild Semiconductor Corporation. These inventions laid the foundation for the consumer electronics industry, which was dominated by U.S. manufacturers, such as RCA, Westinghouse, General Electric, Motorola, Philco, Zenith, Emerson, and Curtis Mathis, from the first experimental radio and television broadcasts until the 1980s.

Television Manufacturing

In the 1950s several major Japanese manufacturers formed the Home Electronic Appliance Market Stabilization Council. This cartel worked closely with Japan's Ministry of International Trade and Industry (MITI) to maintain high prices for televisions sold in Japan while ensuring government tariff policy kept the Japanese market closed to foreign competition. This produced huge profits in their guaranteed home market, enabling Japanese manufacturers to sell exported televisions at very aggressive prices—often below cost. To make matters worse, U.S. companies, who were locked out of the Japanese market, tried to penetrate it by partnering with Japanese companies, and began licensing advanced technology to these firms. In 1962, RCA Corporation became the first company to license color technology to Japanese manufacturers. In 1963, Japanese manufacturers began exporting televisions to the U.S. They used the huge profits being made from sales in their protected home market to subsidize below-cost sales in the U.S., which was a clear violation of U.S. trade laws. In addition, Japanese manufacturers gave American importers, including Sears, Roebuck & Co., illegal rebates (kickbacks) on every Japanese television they sold in the U.S. Sales of Japanese-made televisions soared while U.S. companies suffered *(Reference for Business)*.

The United States Electronic Industry Association filed a complaint about the illegal "dumping" in 1968. However, Japanese manufacturers stonewalled the investigation for more than three years. In addition, the U.S. government was not eager to upset trade negotiations with Japan and proceeded with the investigation reluctantly. In 1971, the Treasury Department ruled that the Japanese companies had violated U.S. law and owed millions of dollars in antidumping levies. Nine years passed before a settlement was reached, however, and the Japanese paid about one-tenth of what they owed. The damage to U.S. television manufacturers was catastrophic and irreversible. In 1968, there were twenty-eight U.S.-owned companies manufacturing televisions domestically. By 1976, only six remained. More than seventy thousand U.S. jobs were eliminated. Several financially strapped U.S. companies were purchased by Japanese or European competitors, while others simply went out of business. Matsushita Electric Industrial Company, the largest consumer-electronics company in the world, purchased Motorola's Consumer Products Division. Magnavox was purchased by N.V. Philips, S.A., a Dutch manufacturer. Among the brand names to disappear were Admiral and Dumont. In addition, dozens of smaller manufacturers making parts for U.S.-made televisions also failed (*Reference for Business*).

In 1977, Japanese electronics manufacturers signed an agreement limiting exports to the U.S. However, this agreement had little meaning since it allowed the Japanese to manufacture televisions in the U.S. in excess of the quotas. Three of the five largest Japanese companies—Matsushita, Sony Corporation, and Sanyo Electric Company—had already established manufacturing facilities in the U.S., and Hitachi and Tokyo Shibaura Electric soon followed suit. The Japanese also established manufacturing facilities in other countries (such as Mexico, Brazil, and Argentina) with abundant, low-cost labor to circumvent the U.S. limits on imports from Japan. An investigation later revealed that Robert Strauss, the former Democratic Party chairman who was appointed by President Carter as special trade representative to Japan, signed a secret agreement in which he promised the U.S. would settle financial claims against the Japanese manufacturers "expeditiously," and would limit an International Trade Commission investigation into further allegations of illegal dumping. Strauss also promised that the Carter administration would appeal a court decision in favor of Zenith, which had won a $400 million predatory pricing suit against Matsushita. The award would have been trebled under U.S. antitrust law to $1.2 billion. Finally, Strauss agreed to ignore official Japanese government policies that prevented U.S. companies from competing in the protected Japanese home electronics market (*Reference for Business*). It is hard to imagine why Strauss and the Carter administration would have made such an agreement with the Japanese, since it so patently opposed U.S. economic interests. Congress did not learn of this secret agreement until 1979. Then, instead of being outraged and reversing this action, they simply agreed to honor the commitments made in secret by Strauss. Under the agreement, the Japanese eventually paid about $66 million of the $500 million the Treasury Department said they owed for illegal dumping, and the antitrust suit filed by Zenith was eventually dismissed by the Supreme Court. In addition, Taiwan and South Korea began exporting televisions to the U.S. Using the same predatory trade practices as Japan Inc., Taiwanese imports more than doubled in 1977, increasing that country's share of the U.S. market from 7 percent to 14 percent.

Meanwhile, the Japanese solidified their hold on the U.S. television market and, through continued use of predatory trade practices, forced U.S. companies to exit this business by the end of the 1980s. This was a coordinated attack on the U.S. television manufacturing industry led by the Japanese government through use of preferential low-cost loans via large banks, by condoning de facto cartels, the Ministry of International Trade and Industry's guided investment coordination, and various forms of non-tariff trade barriers. These factors, coupled with the lack of support provided by the U.S. government to U.S. manufacturers, led to the total collapse of the U.S. consumer electronics industry and was the beginning of the decline in U.S. manufacturing that continues unabated today. In 1995 LG Electronics acquired a controlling share of Zenith, the last major U.S. television manufacturer, and took complete control of the company by 1999. Zenith was founded in 1918, pioneered subscription television, offered up the modern remote control, and was the first to develop HDTV in North America.

Audio Equipment

The experience of the U.S. audio equipment manufacturing industry was similar to that of television manufacturers. Until the mid-1960s, most of the leading manufacturers in the world were U.S.-owned companies with well-known brand names like Fisher, Bose, Sherwood, and Marantz. The first Japanese brand to appear in the annual *Stereo/Hi-Fi Directory and Buyers' Guide* was Kenwood, in 1965 *(High Beam Business)*. However, over the next five years, the number of Japanese brands sold in the U.S. increased dramatically. Sony, Pioneer, and Sansui were introduced in 1968; JVC was introduced in 1970. By 1980, most U.S.-owned companies had either moved their manufacturing facilities offshore to take advantage of cheap labor, or had licensed their brand names to Japanese companies and became distributors for foreign manufacturers. Many Japanese companies eventually built manufacturing facilities in the U.S. It soon became difficult to distinguish U.S.-made from foreign-made products. In the early 1980s, a lingering recession was affecting the industry. Ironically, many of the same Japanese companies that established U.S. manufacturing facilities in the 1970s to avoid restrictions on imports were beginning to move their operations to Mexico, where labor costs were considerably lower. Televisions and audio equipment made in Mexico by foreign companies went almost exclusively into the U.S. market. The North American Free Trade Agreement (NAFTA), endorsed by President Clinton in 1993, hastened this movement to Mexico.

VCRs, Camcorders, and CD Players

With the exception of RCA, major U.S. manufacturers did not enter the market for VCRs, camcorders, and CD players. Looking at what had transpired over the previous twenty-five years in the television and audio markets, who could blame them! Japan Inc. had successfully divided and conquered the U.S. consumer electronics industry. The few demoralized U.S.-owned companies remaining had neither the infrastructure, resources, government support, nor technological capabilities to effectively compete against Japan Inc. in these markets. The loss of U.S. television manufacturing dealt a severe blow to the ability of U.S.-owned companies to compete in the consumer electronics market. Instead, U.S. companies were relegated to a marketing role, rather than manufacturing, which helped create a huge trade deficit in consumer electronics in the 1980s that continues today.

Automotive Industry

While the Japanese are shipping us Toyotas, they are really exporting

something more important than cars. They are sending us

unemployment. . . . Now, I don't want to give anyone the wrong

impression about my attitude toward the Japanese. Yes, I'm angry about

the tilted playing field. And, I'm angry that we're sitting passively while

all this is going on. But Japan is really doing nothing wrong. As Kubo

said, they're simply dealing in their own self-interest. It's up to us to start

dealing in ours. Because I speak out on these inequities, while many of my

colleagues are silent, people get the impression that I'm anti-Japanese.

—LEE IACOCCA, 1984

There is probably no better illustration of the predatory trade practices of Japan Inc. and the damage done to the U.S. manufacturing base and overall economy than what has transpired in the automotive industry. Prior to WWII, the U.S. Big Three automakers dominated the Japanese domestic automobile market. The Ford Motor Company of Japan was established in 1925 and a production plant was set up in Yokohama. General Motors established operations in Osaka in 1927. Chrysler also came to Japan and set up Kyoritsu Motors. Between 1925 and 1936, the U.S. Big Three automakers' Japanese subsidiaries produced a total of 208,967 vehicles, compared to the Japanese domestic producer's total of 12,127 vehicles. By 1939, foreign automobile manufacturers were forced out of Japan and never allowed to return *(Wikipedia)*. After the war ended, Japan Inc. designated the creation of a world-class automotive industry as its number-one national industrial policy strategy. The government provided every benefit, incentive, and protection from competition that it could. This is clearly illustrated in the following account of the negotiation of the first post-occupation trade agreement between the U.S. and Japan in 1955 *(Fletcher, "Japan, the Forgotten Protectionist Threat," Economy in Crisis)*. In the course of this negotiation, the head of the American delegation, C. Thayer White, told the Japanese that they must cut their tariff on imported cars because, in his words:

1. The United States industry is the largest and most efficient in the world.

2. The industry is strongly in favor of expanding the opportunities for world trade.

3. Its access to foreign markets in recent years has been limited by import controls.

4. Although the United States Government appreciates that it is necessary for some countries to impose import restrictions for balance of payments reasons . . . it would be in Japan's interest to import automobiles from the United States and export items in which Japan could excel.

The Japanese trade negotiator, Kenichi Otabe, replied as follows:

1. If the theory of international trade (you propose) were pursued to its ultimate conclusion, the United States would specialize in the production of automobiles and Japan in the production of tuna.

2. Such a division of labor does not take place . . . because each government encourages and protects those industries which it believes important for reasons of national policy.

Japan used the same strategy to cripple and overtake U.S. automotive manufacturers in the U.S. market that it used in the consumer electronics industry. After 1955 Japanese auto corporations began to produce more cars than before. At the same time, the Japanese government restricted car imports to protect their domestic auto industry. Other countries seldom criticized Japan's protectionism in those days, since the car market in Japan was very small. Under the guidance of the Ministry of International Trade and Industry, the Japanese auto industry began to weed out small companies through mergers, eventually reaching its current state.

Japan's annual car production and exports gradually increased. In 1961 annual exports exceeded ten thousand for the first time. In the early 1970s Japan exported more than one million cars, most of them to the U.S. By 1990, Japan was producing over thirteen million cars and exporting just under six million, mostly to the U.S. That same year, Japan imported just thirty thousand cars from U.S. manufacturers. In 2008, Japan produced over eleven million cars and exported just under seven million (or 58 percent) of them, mostly to the U.S. market. That same year, Japan imported twelve thousand cars from U.S. manufacturers. In fact, the combined share of all foreign makes in Japan totaled a mere 4 percent in 2008. Even Volkswagen, which outsells Toyota in many markets around the world, is nowhere in the Japanese market. Then there is Renault, which in 1999, via a major stake in Nissan, acquired ostensible control of Japan's second-largest car distribution system. But even Renault cannot get its own cars into Japanese showrooms. Meanwhile, Japan auto manufactures have fully exploited the U.S. open market, capturing a total of 54.5 percent in 2008. Of this, 15 percent were imported directly from Japan and 39.5 percent were supplied by the U.S. transplant factories. There are many who think these transplant factories do nothing but help the U.S. Thanks to the aggressive PR campaign orchestrated by Japan Inc., most Americans now believe that it makes no difference if they buy a Japanese car or a GM, Ford, or Chrysler. After all, most Japanese cars sold in America are now made in America, right? And the parts used to build these cars are made in America too, right? Well, not exactly . . . . These factories are Trojan horses that are doing more damage than good as they destroy the U.S. automobile manufacturing industry. We explore this further in chapter seven.

U.S. Auto Industry Bailout

In December 2008 the Big Three U.S. auto companies asked the government for a $34 billion bailout to avoid bankruptcy. They argued that their demise would trigger three million layoffs within a year, plunging the economy further into recession. In January 2009, the government used

$24.9 billion of the $700 billion bank bailout fund to assist GM and Chrysler:

- $17.4 billion for General Motors and Chrysler
- $6 billion for GMAC
- $1.5 billion for Chrysler Financial

The purpose of the loans was to provide operating cash for GM and Chrysler, and allow them to keep making auto loans available to car buyers.

Though some opposed the bailout, what was the alternative? Concede defeat to Japanese and Korean auto manufacturers? Allow the U.S. auto manufacturing companies to fold like the consumer electronics industry? As explained in a CNN Money article published in July 2011 *(Valdes-Dapena, Peter)*, if GM and Chrysler collapsed, it would have destroyed families and communities across America and cost the federal government at least $28.6 billion in lost tax revenues and unemployment-related assistance in just the first two years alone, according to the Michigan-based Center for Automotive Research. This $28.6 billion figure is a conservative estimate, since it doesn't include the business taxes the federal, state, and local governments would have lost from GM, Chrysler, and their suppliers, who are returning to profitability. The Big Three are pillars of American industry and vital to our economic and national security. Having said this, I don't support more bailouts, but instead strongly suggest that we address the underlying issues that drove two of the Big Three U.S. auto manufacturers into bankruptcy. We should start with our trade policies and the creation of a carefully considered and coordinated U.S. industrial policy. If we choose to do nothing other than throw money at the problem and then leave it up to the auto manufacturers to continue to fend for themselves, we will witness the continued decline of these companies and the U.S. taxpayer will be asked to provide more bailouts. If you agree, then let your voice be heard by visiting the take action section at Selling-US-Out.com.

Steel Industry

For most of the twentieth century, the U.S. led the world in steel production. United States Steel Corporation, which was founded in 1901 and headquartered in Pittsburgh, Pennsylvania, was the largest producer in the world followed by Bethlehem Steel, based in Bethlehem, Pennsylvania. After WWII the U.S. provided both technical and financial assistance to Japan to rebuild its steel industry, which had been destroyed during the war. In 1949 and 1950, a team of American engineers from U.S. Steel and Bethlehem Steel arrived in Japan and offered technical guidance to the industry in steelmaking, heat control, and operating techniques for open-hearth and reheating furnaces. A team of Japanese engineers also toured the U.S. to learn the latest in American techniques *(Shorrock)*. The Japanese took full advantage of this type of assistance as well as the U.S.'s postwar liberal trade policies. Japan followed the same strategy in building up their steel industry as in the other examples I've discussed. The Japanese government supported the formation of a cartel among steel producers, which was closely linked to the banks, automotive, construction, and other related industries. This cartel worked closely with Japan's Ministry of International Trade and Industry (MITI) to maintain high prices for steel sold in Japan while ensuring a government tariff policy kept the market closed to foreign competition. This monopoly in the domestic market produced huge profits and enabled Japanese manufacturers to sell exported steel at aggressive prices—often below cost. Since the steel industry is closely linked to the automotive industry, Japanese steel producers have also played a key role in helping Toyota, Honda, and other Japanese car manufacturers attack the U.S. car market. U.S. steel manufacturers have been shut out of supplying both the Japanese domestic car market and the transplant factories in the U.S. As the Japanese automakers continue to gain market share in the U.S., not only do U.S. auto manufacturers shut down factories and eliminate jobs, but so do the U.S. steel manufacturers that supply them.

In 2001, Bethlehem Steel, who helped rebuild the Japanese steel industry, filed for bankruptcy after one hundred and forty years of continuous operation. Their closure was due, in large part, to the predatory trade practices of Japan Inc. and the irreparable harm Japanese steel manufacturers and the policies that support them have done to the U.S. Steel Industry. In 2003 Bethlehem Steel was dissolved and its remaining assets were sold to International Steel Group (ISG), a company formed by Wilbur L. Ross, Jr., a wealthy U.S. investor known for restructuring failed companies. In 2005 ISG was sold to Mittal Steel, an Indian-owned company based in Luxembourg, ending U.S. ownership of the assets of Bethlehem Steel. This was the loss of not only a U.S.-owned steel manufacturer, but a national treasure. Bethlehem Steel produced steel for many iconic U.S. landmarks, including the George Washington Bridge, the Golden Gate Bridge, the Chrysler Building, Madison Square Garden, the Merchandise Mart, Rockefeller Center, Alcatraz Island, Bonneville Dam, Grand Coulee Dam, and Hoover Dam.

In 2001, U.S. Steel was reorganized and spun off from USX Corporation. The new company is much smaller, employing 42,000, which is only 12 percent of the 340,000 employed at its peak. U.S. Steel also has a storied past, including financing and constructing the Unisphere in Corona Park, in Queens, New York, for the 1964 World's Fair. It is the largest globe ever made and is one of the world's largest freestanding sculptures. U.S. Steel fabricated the Chicago Picasso sculpture, and donated the steel for Chicago's Polish Cathedral of St. Michael's, where 90 percent of the parishioners worked at its mills. They built Disney's Contemporary Resort at Walt Disney World, and erected the U.S. Steel building in Pittsburgh, Pennsylvania.

The U.S.-owned steel industry is battered, bruised, and barely surviving. Meanwhile, Japanese steel companies are doing quite well as they still enjoy the protection offered by the closed markets provided by their government and the Japanese cartels. In 2009, Japan was the second-largest producer of steel worldwide while the U.S. was fourth and continues to decline. The once-mighty U.S. Steel Corporation is now ranked eleventh among steel manufacturers worldwide, and no U.S.-owned companies made the list's top ten. Some argue that steel is a commodity, and that it doesn't matter if we lose this industry. They could not be more wrong since steel is essential for virtually every aspect of our economic and national security. It is used to make roads, buildings, bridges, cars, trucks, planes, trains, ships, tanks, missiles . . . the list goes on and on. Japan's "big four" steelmakers recently announced that they were investing $7.8 billion over the next four years to boost capacity and solidify Japan's position ahead of Russia as the world's biggest exporter of steel. Why do you think the Japanese (and others, such as India and China) are making huge investments in this industry? Because they understand the economic and strategic value of the steel industry.

Semiconductor Industry

Semiconductors were invented in the U.S. in the late 1950s by Robert N. Noyce at Fairchild Semiconductor and Jack Kilby at Texas Instruments. Noyce later went on to found Intel along with Gordon Moore. As the undisputed leader in semiconductor technology, Intel eventually became the dominant company in the industry. They developed the first memory chips and pioneered the development of microprocessors, which are the brains powering personal computers, iPads, smart phones, and many other similar types of electronic products. Jerry Sanders, who founded the U.S. company Advanced Micro Devices, once called semiconductors "the crude oil of industry." His metaphor is apt because semiconductors are such a pervasive, but generally unseen, aspect of everyday life *(Reference for Business)*. These devices are critical to the operation of virtually all electronics, from automatic coffeemakers and antilock braking systems to cellular phones and supercomputers.

The global market for semiconductors in 2010 was $298.3 billion with $53.7 billion (or 18 percent) of the total sales coming from the U.S. market, while $206.7 billion (or 69 percent) came from Asia. This industry was invented and dominated by U.S. manufacturers until the 1980s, when foreign industrial targeting and illegal dumping practices led by Japan Inc. combined to erode U.S. worldwide market share. This is reflected in the fact that of the forty new semiconductor foundries (factories) built in 2007, thirty-five were in Asia and only three were in the U.S. The U.S. companies that once dominated this industry include Intel, Motorola, Texas Instruments, National Semiconductor, Advanced Micro Devices, Mostek, Fairchild Semiconductor, Analog Devices, Monolithic Memories, AMI, Micron, and many others. Of these companies, only Intel and Texas Instruments are now in the top five (based on sales in 2010) and Micron is the only U.S.-owned manufacturer of memory products. With the exception of Intel and Texas Instruments, this industry is now dominated by Japanese, Korean, and Taiwanese companies, with communist China making huge investments to catch up and eventually take the lead.

In 1957 Japan enacted "The Extraordinary Measures Law for Promotion of the Electronics Industry." Under the law, Japan's Ministry of International Trade and Industry (MITI), in collaboration with Japanese industry, developed a plan to catch up with and overtake the U.S. in the design, production, and sale of semiconductors. It authorized the creation of cartels where MITI deemed them useful, and also established an Electronics Industry Deliberation Council consisting of workers from Japanese industry, academics, and members of the press to develop plans on how to best target the semiconductor industry. Only Japanese companies were allowed to participate in this council—no foreign companies, their subsidiaries, or joint ventures in which a foreign company had a majority ownership. MITI restricted the purchase of equity in Japanese firms by foreigners. MITI imposed high import duties, restrictive import quotas, and implemented "approval registration" requirements to control the importation of semiconductors and other electronics. This enabled MITI and the cartels to control domestic pricing. Approval from MITI was also required for all patent, technical assistance, and licensing agreements. The agency used this requirement to "extort" trade secrets and intellectual property from foreign companies wishing to do business in Japan. They then shared the information with Japanese companies to accelerate their development of competing products. For example, in the early 1960s, Texas Instruments, who was then the world's largest semiconductor manufacturer, applied to MITI for permission to begin production in Japan. They withheld approval until Texas Instruments agreed to license its patents. They also had to agree that they would not take more than ten percent of the Japanese semiconductor market. In another case, IBM had to agree to license its basic patents to fifteen Japanese companies before MITI would permit them to begin production in Japan. In the 1970s MITI organized a government-funded cooperative called the Very Large Scale Integration, a research and development program. The Japanese government provided $200 million in funding over four years, and interest-free loans, to major manufacturers of semiconductors, including NEC, Toshiba, Hitachi, Fujitsu, and Mitsubishi *(Irwin)*. These firms formed cooperative laboratories for the joint development of basic semiconductor design and manufacturing technology. In the early 1980s, Japan Inc. executed its plan to enter and take over the U.S. semiconductor market. The result was the total collapse of the U.S. semiconductor memory market. In 1975, U.S. manufacturers had one hundred percent of the U.S. digital random-access memory (DRAM) market. By 1986, they had only five percent of this market! This "blood bath," as it was referred to in industry publications at the time, drove Intel, Motorola, National Semiconductor, Advanced Micro Devices, and Mostek out of the DRAM market altogether. As a result, U.S. semiconductor manufacturers began to refocus their development efforts on proprietary products during the early 1990s, capitalizing on their well-known strengths in design and innovation and moving away from commodity products. They also sought and received assistance from the U.S. government to challenge Japan Inc.'s illegal and predatory trade practices.

> IBM HAD TO AGREE TO LICENSE ITS BASIC PATENTS TO FIFTEEN JAPANESE COMPANIES BEFORE MITI WOULD PERMIT THEM TO BEGIN PRODUCTION IN JAPAN.

It's Still Groundhog Day

Our trade relationship with Japan is much like the popular 1993 Bill Murray movie *Groundhog Day*—we keep doing the same things over and over again. Unlike the movie, though, this is no laughing matter. Entire industries have been lost, the U.S. auto industry is on life support, and towns and families have been devastated by our country's failure to effectively respond to and deal with Japan's predatory trade practices. The U.S. has spent five decades complaining to Japan about their predatory trade practices. We have negotiated a building full of meaningless legal agreements, while the Japanese continue to wage economic warfare against us. Not one of the major U.S.–Japan trade disputes of the 1980s was ever resolved—not cars, not financial services, not even rice. The rest of Asia, especially China, are following Japan's example and using the same stonewalling tactics in dealing with U.S. trade disputes. Meanwhile, as so eloquently stated by Eamonn Fingleton, the U.S. continues to run record trade deficits and owes more money to foreign creditors than any major power since the late-era Ottoman Empire, which no longer exists. If we do not change course soon, our fate will be the same.

As Lee Iacocca said, we should not blame the Japanese or any other country for acting in their own self-interest; instead, we should begin doing the same. The Japanese think our society and government are weak and on the decline because, in their view, we are constantly complaining about "fairness," and expecting them to change how they think and behave. It is time to stop complaining and start doing what is in America's best interest!

CHAPTER FIVE

Selling Our Freedom III

It's a shame when the White House's top economic adviser says
outsourcing of American jobs is inevitable, or even that it benefits our
economy . . . . I believe Americans know that our country gains when we
export American goods—not American jobs.

—Nick Lampson, Former U.S. Congressman, Texas

India—Quietly Destroying American Industry and Taking Millions of Jobs

It is with mixed emotions that I begin this chapter discussing India, since I have many former business associates and friends from India whom I admire and respect. Having also spent most of my childhood living in poverty and working my way through both high school and college, I feel a kinship with ordinary people in India, China, Japan, Mexico, and other parts of the world who are simply working as hard as they can to make a better life for themselves and their children. Recent history has not been kind to India. For 1,700 years, until the eighteenth century, India was one of the wealthiest nations in the world *(Wikipedia)*. Starting in the late eighteenth and early nineteenth centuries, India began to plunge into desperate poverty as a result of colonization and free trade imposed upon her by the British Empire. During the eighty years from 1780 to 1860, India shifted from being an exporter of processed goods for which it received payment in bullion, to being an exporter of raw materials and a buyer of manufactured goods. Sound familiar? America's fate will be the same if we do not change course soon. Unlike communist China, India does not deny its citizens freedom—it is the world's largest democracy. However, like China, poverty and corruption are rampant.

India is a very complex and diverse society that has been struggling with internal armed conflicts and a hostile relationship with its neighbor Pakistan. Both Pakistan and Bangladesh were once part of India and separated due to differences in religion—India is primarily Hindu, while Pakistan and Bangladesh are primarily Muslim. This is a very important lesson on the importance of religious tolerance, another value that seems to be on the decline in our country. After achieving independence from Britain in 1947, India developed a close relationship with the Soviet Union. India's strategic and military relations with Moscow and strong socialist policies had a dampening effect on its relations with the U.S. Soon after the fall of the Iron Curtain and collapse of the Soviet Union, India began developing closer ties with both the U.S. and the European Union. This was followed by a move away from socialism and toward capitalism and economic liberalization in the 1990s.

The Exporting of U.S. Jobs to India

As part of its shift toward capitalism and economic liberalization, India created a national economic strategy. India was determined not to miss out on the digital revolution of the twenty-first century as it had on the industrial revolution in the eighteenth century due to British imposition of free trade. At the center of its national economic strategy was the development of information technology (IT) and business process outsourcing (BPO) industries by primarily targeting U.S. corporations and government entities—replacing their American workforce with lower-cost Indian workers. They executed this plan with extreme precision—growing their IT and BPO industries from $100 million in 1990, to $88 billion in 2011 *(NASSCOM)*. According to India's National Association of Software and Services Companies (NASSCOM), these industries are expected to reach more than $200 billion by 2020. Since sixty percent of their business originates from U.S. outsourcing, the result has been huge high-wage job losses in the U.S., which has eroded our middle class and achieved the opposite effect in India, as illustrated below.

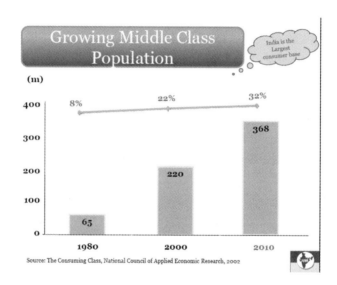

Source: The Consuming Class, National Council of Applied Economic Research, 2002

America's Middle Class is Shrinking

More of the Employed Have Low-Income Jobs

Middle-income jobs are disappearing from the economy.

The share of middle-income jobs in the United States has fallen from 52% in 1980 to 42% in 2010.

Middle-income jobs have been replaced by low-income jobs, which now make up 41% of total employment.

Share of Total Employment

Private Sector Middle-Income

Private Sector Low-Income

Government Jobs

Source: Bureau of Labor Statistics, Westwood Capital

Source: New America Foundation Report – The American Middle Class Under Stress

Education is **NOT** the Issue ....The cause is outsourcing and off-shoring of American jobs!

The Under-Employed American

The problem is not lack of skills, but the structure of the job market.

17 million Americans with college degrees are doing jobs that require less than the skill levels associated with a bachelor's degree.

Just under 30% of flight attendants and 16% of telemarketers have bachelor's degrees even though this credential is not necessary for these jobs.

Source: New America Foundation Report – The American Middle Class Under Stress

Occupation	Percent with BA/BS	Number
Waiter/Waitress	13.4	317,759
Flight Attendants	29.8	29,645
Laborers	5.07	118,441
Janitors	5.01	107,457
Truck Drivers	5.09	85,205
Bartenders	16	80,542
Food Preparation	7.24	63,737
Telemarketers	15.85	54,713
Postmen/women	13.95	49,452
Parking Lot Attendants	13.74	18,749

Source: Bureau of Labor Statistics

In 2012, the Indian IT and BPO industries are expected to add 230,000 jobs, providing direct employment to about 2.8 million people, and indirectly employing 8.9 million others. This translates to a loss of approximately 1.68 million direct and 5.34 million indirect IT and BPO jobs in the U.S. While these are large numbers, they are only the tip of the iceberg. These numbers do not include U.S. job losses from:

- Major U.S. corporations moving IT and BPO operations to India, such as:

U.S. Corporations Operating in India		
Agilent	EDS	MetLife India
Agro Tech	Eli Lilly	Microsoft
American Express	Emerson Electric	Morgan Stanley
Amway	FedEx	New York Life
Avaya	Ford	Ogilvy and Mather
Caltex	Franklin Templeton	Oracle
Caterpillar	GE	Pfizer
CB Richard Ellis	General Motors	Sun Microsystems
Cisco	Gillette	Texas Instruments

U.S. Corporations Operating in India		
Citigroup	Honeywell India	Tecumseh
Cognizant	IBM	Timex
Colgate Palmolive	Intel	Tyco
CSC	Johnson & Johnson	Visteon
Cummins	J.P. Morgan	Whirlpool
Discovery	Kimberly Clark	Xerox Modicorp
DuPont	Kodak	

- Outsourcing of other jobs to India such as hardware design, radiology, accounting, aeronautical engineering, software design, stock analysis, research and development, and many other occupations from numerous industries including automotive, financial services, pharmaceutical, semiconductor, medical device and diagnostic, book publishing, and countless others.

- The 2.7 million Indian citizens living and working in America (compared to sixty thousand U.S. citizens living and working in India).

- Indian-owned companies operating in the U.S. that hire predominately foreign workers.

Unlike the U.S. "trade" with China, the majority of jobs being outsourced to India are in professional services—not manufacturing. According to a 2011 report issued by the U.S. Congressional Research Service, as many as thirty million high-paying U.S. jobs are susceptible to outsourcing (*Levine*). However, this is only an estimate since nobody in the U.S. government has any real idea of how many U.S. jobs have been lost due to outsourcing to India or any other country. Companies are not required to report this data and the U.S. government makes no attempt to track it. In my opinion, this is outrageous; and, I believe it is by design. The global capitalists, corporations, special interests, and lobbyists—who are financing the U.S.'s two major political parties and profiting enormously from selling out America and American workers—want to keep us all in the dark when it comes to the catastrophic damage that outsourcing and offshoring are doing to the U.S. economy. If the American public clearly understood how many U.S. jobs were being lost to offshoring and outsourcing, there would be a rebellion rivaling the American Revolution of 1776. I believe those who are profiting from offshoring and outsourcing realize the inflammatory nature of the problem, and that is why this information is not being collected or reported.

L-1 and H-1B Visas—Destroying U.S. Wages and Jobs

[The H-1B] has become the outsourcing visa. If at one point you had X amount of outsourcing, and now you have a much higher quantum of outsourcing, you need that many more visas.

—KAMAL NATH, FORMER INDIAN COMMERCE MINISTER

Many of you are probably asking, what in the world are L-1 and H-1B visas? In short, they are the golden tickets to America for low-cost foreign workers and they are easily obtained by U.S. and foreign-owned corporations from the U.S. government. Corporations use these visas as a tool to replace millions of American workers with low-cost foreign workers. Despite record unemployment and the deepest and longest U.S. recession since the Great Depression, our government continues to issue these job-killing visas, allowing corporations to continue giving away American jobs to foreign workers on American soil!

Both the L-1 and H-1B programs were created for legitimate reasons, but they are not being used as intended and are doing serious harm to American workers and the U.S. economy. The H-1B visa law was created to allow skilled, specialized foreigners to work in America for up to six years and then pursue permanent residency. The L-1 visa was created to allow intra-company transfers of executives or highly skilled employees. However, the H-1B and L-1 visas are now being used as a tool by Indian outsourcing vendors to gain expertise and win contracts from U.S. companies so critical business operations can be outsourced to India *(Wikipedia)*, eliminating millions of American jobs, as shown below.

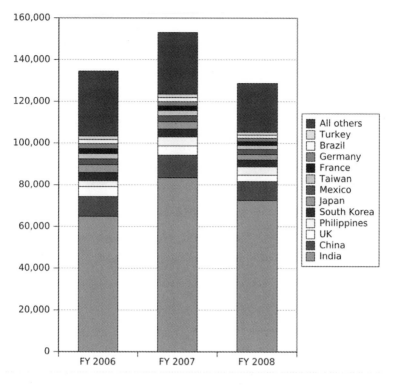

H-1B Visas Issued by Nation, 2006–2008
Source: Wikipedia

H-1B and L-1 visas are an essential and critical part of the Indian outsourcing business model as evidenced by this statement in a 2010 U.S. Securities and Exchange Commission financial statement filed by Infosys, a leading Indian IT and BPO outsourcing firm. Infosys states that any constraint on its access to H-1B and L-1 visas would pose a significant risk to its business model:

> The vast majority of our employees are Indian nationals. Most of our projects require a portion of the work to be completed at the client's location. The ability of our technology professionals to work in the United States, Europe, and in other countries depends upon the ability to obtain the necessary visas and work permits.

As of March 31, 2010, the majority of our technology professionals in the United States had either H-1B visas (approximately 8,900 persons, not including Infosys BPO employees or employees of our wholly owned subsidiaries), which allow the employees to remain in the United States for up to 6 years during the term of the work permit and work as long as he or she remains an employee of the sponsoring firm, or L-1 visas (approximately 1,800 persons, not including Infosys BPO employees or employees of our wholly owned subsidiaries), which allow employees to stay in the United States only temporarily.

As Dr. Ron Hira points out in his Economic Policy Institute (EPI) briefing paper "The H-1B and L-1 Visa Programs—Out of Control," there is a direct correlation between U.S. outsourcing and the number of H-1B and L-1 visas issued to Indian companies such as Infosys. Infosys reported revenues for 2010 that were more than twenty times its revenues from 2000 (an increase from $203 million to $4.8 billion), while its workforce increased from 5,400 to 113,800. In the same timeframe its employment of H-1B and L-1 visa holders increased more than tenfold from 963 to 10,700. Hira also wrote a book in 2005, along with his brother Anil Hira, entitled *Outsourcing America: What's Behind Our National Crisis and How We Can Reclaim American Jobs*. In a separate but related EPI briefing paper "ABUSES IN THE L-VISA PROGRAM—Undermining the U.S. Labor Market," Dr. Daniel Costa states the following:

- The use of the L visa has dramatically increased since 1990. In 2008, nearly 84,000 L-1 visas were granted, along with more than 72,000 L-2 visas. This is one of the least-regulated visa categories with no number cap or significant educational or skill requirements.

- The L-1 visa can and has been used, legally, by employers to replace U.S. workers with lower-paid temporary foreign workers, and to avoid basic requirements that are a part of other work visa categories, such as paying the prevailing wage and requiring U.S.

employers to attest that there are no U.S. workers available for the position.

- Neither the public nor the government knows how many L-1 and L-2 visa beneficiaries are present in the U.S. or may have returned to their country of origin, nor does it possess or share data on how many of them are working, what occupations they hold, and what their wages are.

- The L-1 visa is being used by Indian offshoring companies to train their workers while they are in the U.S., and those workers export that knowledge and training, along with the job itself, back to their home country where the work is performed at a lower cost to the company.

Both Hira and Costa have provided their findings and recommendations to fix the H-1B and L-1 visa programs to Congress and the Obama administration. Their recommendations were:

Reform of the H-1B Visa Program:

- Rewrite law to prevent U.S. workers from being replaced by "guest" workers.

- Require employers to demonstrate that they have looked for and could not find qualified U.S. workers to fill open positions.

- Perform random audits on employers using guest workers to ensure they are in compliance with the law.

- Provide resources and proper authority to the agencies responsible for this program—Departments of Homeland Security, Labor, and State.

- When there is more than one temporary shortage of skilled workers and foreign workers are truly needed, we should bring them in permanently.

Reform of the L Visa Program:

- U.S. government must compile and publish accurate data on all of the L visa categories, and do a much better job keeping track of L visa beneficiaries.

- Enact legislation that clearly establishes the specific meaning of "manager" and "executive" for L-1A petitions, and develop a narrowly tailored definition and consistent, clear administrative policy guidance for "specialized knowledge" applications for L-1B visas.

- Set an annual numerical cap on L-1 and L-2 visas.

- Forbid multinational companies from transferring employees to U.S. offices on L-1 visas *unless* no qualified U.S. workers can be found to fill the position. In order to determine that no qualified U.S. worker is available, a reliable and effective labor market test should be developed and implemented, which includes independent shortage analyses of particular occupations and industries in the U.S.

- Require L-1 transferees to possess extensive post-secondary education, training, or experience.

- Require employers to pay L-1 and L-2 workers at least the market wage for U.S. workers similarly situated, and no less than the prevailing wage, to ensure that wages are not depressed for U.S. workers in similar occupations with comparable skill levels.

- Empower the Department of Labor with significant authority to audit firms and enforce any new rules created to protect against U.S. worker replacement, adverse working conditions, and downward pressure on wages caused by L-1 or L-2 temporary workers.

- Give U.S. workers the right to an administrative proceeding and remedy, and standing to sue an employer in federal court if they have been replaced by a specific employee with an L-1 visa, or if an employer pays an L-1 worker less than the prevailing wage.

- Introduce employment requirements for L-2 dependent spouses, such as a labor market test to determine if employment of an L-2 worker would adversely affect U.S. workers, and give U.S. workers the right to an administrative proceeding and remedy, and standing to sue an employer in federal court if they have been replaced by a specific employee with an L-2 visa, or if an employer pays an L-2 worker less than the prevailing wage.

- Require L-1 employees to work only at the worksite of their original petitioner-employer or at their parent, subsidiary, and affiliate site and do not permit any waivers under any circumstances, in order to prevent the outsourcing and subcontracting of these workers to other firms.

- Determine the appropriate maximum allowable percentage of temporary foreign workers that companies may hire as a portion of their total U.S. workforce—but not to exceed 20 percent—unless a bona fide labor shortage in a particular sector of the economy has been identified by the Department of Labor or a Foreign Worker Adjustment Commission.

- Reduce the amount of time that an L-1 beneficiary is authorized to stay and work in the U.S.

- Suspend the blanket petition procedure (allowing companies to extend the expiration date on multiple L-1 visas at the same time).

- Review and reform the criteria and proof required in the L-1 petition process for applicants wishing to enter the U.S. for the purpose of opening a new office.

- Impose an "antifraud" fee of at least $5,000 for every L visa granted.

So what has our government done to address the problems with H-1B and L-1 visa programs since receiving all of this information? Absolutely nothing! Outsourcing and offshoring aren't even being discussed in the 2012 election cycle. Instead, the politicians are discussing gay marriage, contraception, and taxes, with no mentions of trade policy or outsourcing.

This is no accident. Those who profit from outsourcing and offshoring are also financing both major political parties and want to suppress all discussion of the issue. We must break the silence and demand that our government either immediately fix or cancel these visa programs. Please join me in this call to action by signing an online petition to Congress and the White House. Go to Selling-US-Out.com.

Acquisition of Strategic U.S. Industries

In the course of researching and writing about the decline of the U.S. steel industry, I was surprised to learn that the vast majority of what was the U.S. Steel Industry is now owned and operated by the richest man in India, Asia, and the United Kingdom—Lakshmi Niwas Mittal. As the twenty-first-century Andrew Carnegie, he is also the sixth richest man in the world. Like Carnegie, he created his vast fortune through the merger and acquisition of steel companies around the world. However, his biggest prize was buying International Steel Group (ISG) from WL Ross & Co. in 2002. ISG was formed by the merger of Bethlehem Steel, LTV Corp. (formerly J&L Steel and Republic Steel), Weirton Steel Corporation, and several other smaller U.S. producers. At the time of its sale, ISG was the leading steel producer in the U.S. After the purchase deal was announced *(Nevers)*, ISG chairman Wilbur Ross said,

> "This transaction achieves all of our financial and business objectives. It provides our shareholders with an excellent rate of return and the potential for strong future appreciation. It accelerates by several years our strategy to become a leading global steelmaker. By joining with Mittal Steel, respected in the global steel industry for both its strategic vision and operational excellence, we have provided our shareholders immediate value, as well as participation in a new, financially strong, profitable global enterprise with excellent growth prospects."

A few things that I noticed about this quote:

- It was all about giving shareholders "an excellent rate of return"—nothing is mentioned about the impact on ISG employees or the American communities in which most of its plants operated.

- "It accelerates by several years our strategy to become a global steelmaker." Was part of the ISG "global" strategy to transfer ownership of the largest U.S. steel producer to foreign ownership?

- "This sale achieves all of our financial and business objectives . . . .We have provided our shareholders immediate value"—what about U.S. economic and national security?

This sale was obviously good for WL Ross & Co. and the other ISG shareholders, but was it beneficial to U.S. long-term economic and strategic interests? How about our national security? When Defense Secretary Robert Gates decided to increase production of armored trucks for the Iraq counterinsurgency campaign in 2007, the Department of Defense discovered there was only one steel plant in the nation producing steel of sufficient strength to meet military needs. That plant—the old Lukens Steel Company facility in Coatesville, Pennsylvania—was part of the ISG sale to Mittal, which already had weapons makers waiting in line for its limited-capacity output. Our soldiers in battle did not have the protection they needed, but at least the shareholders of ISG got "an excellent rate of return" when the factory was sold to Mittal. Hopefully these former ISG shareholders were also wearing their flag pins in 2007 to display their patriotism! After purchasing ISG, Mittal then merged with Arcelor, a Dutch Steel company, to become ArcelorMittal, the world's largest producer of steel *(Wikipedia)*. Here is how the global steel industry looked in 2010:

Top steelmakers 2010

Ranking 10	09	Company	Country of origin/ main domicile	2010 output	2009 output
1	1	**ArcelorMittal** Luxembourg		**90.50**	**73.20**
● 2	2	**Hebei Steel**	China	**52.86**	**40.24**
● 3	3	**Baosteel**	China	**44.50**	**38.87**
● 4	4	**Wuhan**	China	**36.55**	**30.34**
▲ 5	6	**Nippon Steel**	Japan	**36.14**	**27.61**
▼ 6	5	**Posco**	South Korea	**33.72**	**29.53**
▲ 7	9	**JFE Steel**	Japan	**32.66**	**26.28**
▼ 8	7	**Shagang Group**	China	**30.12**	**26.39**
▲ 9	12	**Shougang**	China	**25.84**	**17.29**
● 10	10	**Tata Steel**	India	**23.50**	**21.90**
▼ 11	8	**Shandong**	China	**23.15**	**26.38**
▲ 12	15	**US Steel**	USA	**22.26**	**15.24**
▼ 13	11	**Anshan Steel**	China	**21.00**	**20.13**
▲ 14	17	**Gerdau**	Brazil	**17.80**	**13.50**
▲ 15	31	**Benxi Steel**	China	**16.80**	**9.06**
▲ 16	22	**ThyssenKrupp**	Germany	**16.70**	**11.00**
▲ 17	19	**Nucor**	USA	**16.56**	**12.70**
▼ 18	14	**Evraz**	Russia	**16.29**	**15.28**
▼ 19	16	**Maanshan**	China	**15.40**	**14.83**
● 20	20	**Valin Group**	China	**15.11**	**11.81**
▼ 21	13	**Severstal**	Russia	**14.70**	**16.74**
▼ 22	21	**Riva Group**	Italy	**14.01**	**11.32**
▲ 23	38	**Metinvest**	Ukraine	**13.83**	**7.03**
▼ 24	18	**SAIL**	India	**13.58**	**12.69**
▼ 25	23	**Sumitomo Metal**	Japan	**13.10**	**10.81**

Source: Metal Bulletin

This strategic industry, that was once was dominated by U.S. companies, has been taken over by communist China, Japan, and India. ArcelorMittal, the number-one steel company in the world, is headquartered in Luxembourg, but is actually an Indian-owned company. The U.S. doesn't even have a company in the top ten. U.S. Steel, which was once the largest steel producer in the world, is now ranked number twelve, behind even Posco of South Korea, which is ranked fifth. So why are India, China,

Korea, and Japan focusing on the steel industry? Primarily because of its direct link to the automobile industry. We are kidding ourselves if we believe U.S. companies can remain dominate players in automobile manufacturing by relying on steel purchased from Japanese, Indian, Korean, and Chinese suppliers. These countries will use their ownership position in steel and other materials related to automobile manufacturing to crush American car manufacturers. The billions poured into the automobile industry by the U.S. government did nothing except buy us some more time to change course. If we do not use the time wisely, I assure you that once Japan fully recovers from the tsunami of 2011, they will reestablish their position as a dominant automobile manufacturer. Korean companies will also continue to gain U.S. market share, and in the not-too-distant future China and India will begin manufacturing and exporting automobiles to the U.S. Once this happens, goodbye U.S. auto industry! The only way we can prevent this from happening is by fixing our international trade policies and creating a national economic strategy, which I will explore in more depth later.

Another thing I find interesting about the Mittal acquisition of ISG, and the many other acquisitions accomplished by Indian companies in the U.S. over the past ten years, is how quietly the sales are being executed. It seems Indian companies are wary of drawing attention to their business activities in the U.S. Why is this? I believe it is because they want to avoid U.S. public scrutiny of their business acquisitions, which have substantially increased in the past several years and are doing major damage to the U.S. economy by transferring millions of high-wage jobs from the U.S. to India. Here is a chart showing the types of U.S. businesses Indian companies are acquiring along with a partial list of U.S. companies acquired.

Indian Acquisition of U.S. Companies
Jan - Jun 2010

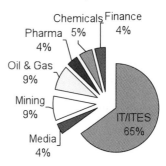

Chemicals 5%
Finance 4%
Pharma 4%
Oil & Gas 9%
Mining 9%
Media 4%
IT/ITES 65%

Source: IVG Global Partners Brochure – July 2010

Industry	U.S. Company Sold	Indian Buyer
Auto	Ford-Jaguar and Land Rover	Tata Motors
Chemical	Columbian Chemicals	Aditya Birla Group
Chemical	El du Pont de Nemours's non-mixture mancozeb fungicide business	United Phosphorus Ltd
Finance	Northgate Capital Group, LLC	Religare Enterprises Ltd
IT/ITES	Fortify Infrastructure Services	MphasiS Ltd
IT/ITES	ASTUS Tech Inc.	Comp-U-Learn Tech India Ltd
IT/ITES	Bureau of Collection Recovery	Aditya Birla Minacs
IT/ITES	DecisionOne Inc.	Glodyne Technoserve Ltd
IT/ITES	DenMed Transcription Service	Accentia Technologies Ltd
IT/ITES	Dynamic Test Solutions, Inc.	Tessolve Services Pvt Ltd
IT/ITES	GSR Physicians Billing, Inc./GSR Systems	Accentia Technologies Ltd
IT/ITES	Infocrossing, Inc.	Wipro Ltd
IT/ITES	Jass & Associates Inc./SDG Corporation	Mascon Global Ltd
IT/ITES	Pacific Crest Technology	Prodapt Solutions Pvt Ltd
IT/ITES	Percentix, Inc.	Prithvi Info Solutions Ltd
IT/ITES	Pyramid Healthcare Solutions	Avantha Group
IT/ITES	Regulus Group LLC	3i Infotech Ltd
IT/ITES	Vox Holdings Inc.	Cambridge Tech Ent Ltd
IT/ITES	OneGIS, Inc.	Rolta India Ltd
IT/ITES	Silver Editions, Inc.	Integra Software Svcs Ltd
IT/ITES	SLM Corp—Back Office Unit, TX	Aegis Ltd
IT/ITES	StudyPlaces Inc.	Educomp Solutions Ltd
IT/ITES	American Solutions Inc. and United Consultancy Services	Spectacle Industries Ltd
Media	IM Global LLC	Reliance Big Ent Pvt Ltd
Mining	Trinity Coal Corporation	Essar Group
Oil & Gas	Pioneer Natural Resources	Reliance Industries Ltd
Oil & Gas	Atlas Energy Inc.-Marcellus	Reliance Industries Ltd
Pharma	Allen S.p.A, a division of GlaxoSmithKline (GSK)	Ranbaxy Laboratories (RLL)
Pharma	Karalex Pharma LLC	Orchid Chem & Pharm Ltd

Source: IVG Global Partners Brochure, July 2010/siliconindia News, June 2011/Global Atlanta, March 2011

I find the patterns in these charts interesting. For example, India is building on its IT and BPO outsourcing success by acquiring numerous U.S.-based IT and BPO companies. This enables penetration into new markets as well as the ability to set up satellite operations in the U.S. that can transfer the bulk of the work to staff in India. They are also focusing on becoming a major player in the pharmaceutical industry, as evidenced by their acquisitions in this area and the following slides, which were taken from a 2010 Organization of Pharmaceutical Producers of India strategy presentation given at a life science conference in India *(Ray)*.

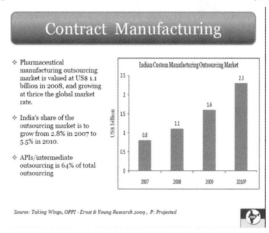

Key point:

India is a major player in the pharmaceutical outsourcing business, more than doubling its global share from 2007 to 2010.

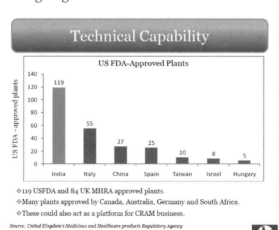

Key points:

- India has the most U.S. FDA-approved pharmaceutical drug manufacturing facilities outside of the U.S.

- India plans to leverage its U.S. FDA facilities to significantly increase its contract research and manufacturing (CRAM) business—meaning outsourcing. Their target is the U.S., which is currently the largest pharmaceutical supplier in the world.

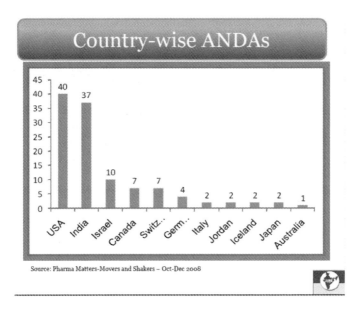

Source: Pharma Matters-Movers and Shakers – Oct-Dec 2008

Key point:

India is heavily targeting the U.S. generic drug market—this is what Abbreviated New Drug Application (ANDA) is all about. ANDA refers to the paperwork drug companies are required to file with the U.S. FDA to get approval to manufacture and sell generic drugs. This is significant. It will mean that India will be able to take significant business away from U.S. pharmaceutical companies, potentially crippling them and the U.S. pharmaceutical industry as a whole. We cannot allow this to happen. Here is an excerpt from an Indian investment report published in 2012 *(IHS Global Insight)*:

Indian Companies Garner 33% of ANDA Approvals in 2011 (Published: 1/3/2012)

The United States continues to be a key market for Indian generic firms, which garnered over 30% of approvals awarded in 2011, with the number of approvals growing by 1% from 2010.

IHS Global Insight Perspective	
Significance	Indian generic firms received over 190 Abbreviated New Drug Application (ANDA) approvals from the US FDA during 2011. With 21 such approvals, Sun Pharma (India) beat its domestic counterparts to receive the highest number of marketing authorisations in the US over the year.
Implications	The number of generic approvals received by Indian firms during 2011 increased by 1% from 2010 figures, compared with 15% growth in 2010 versus 2009, showing increased scrutiny from the US FDA in regards to manufacturing compliance. Despite this slowing growth, firms continue to look to the US to file ANDAs in order to grow presence.
Outlook	The US will continue to be one of the leading countries for Indian generic firms' investment, with several blockbuster molecules set to go off-patent and an intensified drive to increase generics use.

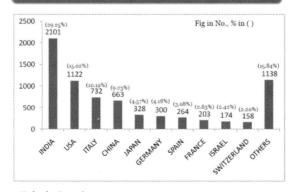

Global DMF with U.S. FDA

Updated to September 2009

Source: Pharmexcil Research on CDER US-FDA data base

Key point:

In 2009, India submitted twice as many Drug Master Files (DMFs) to the FDA as U.S. manufacturers. DMFs are the paperwork drug companies must submit to the FDA for approval to manufacture and distribute new drugs.

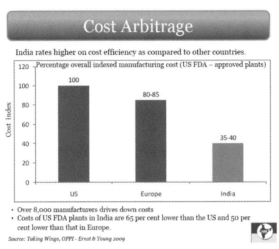

Cost Arbitrage

India rates higher on cost efficiency as compared to other countries.

Percentage overall indexed manufacturing cost (US FDA – approved plants)

- Over 8,000 manufacturers drives down costs
- Costs of US FDA plants in India are 65 per cent lower than the US and 50 per cent lower than that in Europe.

Source: Taking Wings, OPPI - Ernst & Young 2009

Key point:

India's pharmaceutical manufacturing cost structure is 60–65 percent lower than the U.S. This is due primarily to differences in labor costs and currency valuations.

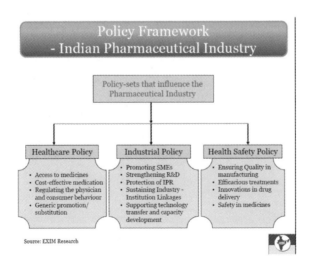

Policy Framework
- Indian Pharmaceutical Industry

Policy-sets that influence the Pharmaceutical Industry

Healthcare Policy	Industrial Policy	Health Safety Policy
• Access to medicines • Cost-effective medication • Regulating the physician and consumer behaviour • Generic promotion/ substitution	• Promoting SMEs • Strengthening R&D • Protection of IPR • Sustaining Industry - Institution Linkages • Supporting technology transfer and capacity development	• Ensuring Quality in manufacturing • Efficacious treatments • Innovations in drug delivery • Safety in medicines

Source: EXIM Research

Key point:

India has a national economic strategy to significantly grow their pharmaceutical business, and it includes a well-planned industrial policy. There is close coordination between industry and government to formulate and execute the strategy and its supporting policies.

The targeting of the U.S. Pharmaceutical industry by India should be a major concern for U.S. policy makers, but it doesn't appear to even be on their radar. Instead, the U.S. FDA and pharmaceutical industry are assisting in this process by enabling the outsourcing of drug research and manufacturing to India. This is extremely short-sighted and a further testament to our lack of a national economic strategy and industrial policy. For the sake of increased profits today, the U.S. pharmaceutical industry and FDA are sowing the seeds for the destruction of this industry tomorrow.

Another very interesting Indian acquisition is that of Jaguar and Land Rover from Ford *(Carty)*. The purchase sends a clear signal of India's strategy to become a major player in the automotive industry and should serve as a wake-up call to America. However, it happened so quietly, I am sure most Americans have no idea the transaction occurred. This acquisition coupled with those in the U.S. steel, mining, chemical, and energy industries is positioning India to compete effectively with U.S. and Japanese auto manufacturers. They are building a complete Indian-owned supply chain for this and other industries they are targeting. It's very smart strategy. Along with their U.S. steel, mining, and energy acquisitions they are also acquiring large parcels of U.S. land and mineral rights. For instance, along with the steel plants Mittal acquired with the purchase of ISG, they also gained ownership of iron ore mines in Minnesota and coal properties in Pennsylvania. Essar Group, which purchased Trinity Coal, also owns about $4 billion in other related mineral businesses throughout the U.S. These operations are supplying U.S. coal and other minerals to India to run their power plants and steel mills. This is good for India and bad for the United States of America. Wouldn't it be better to export steel made by an American company to India, instead of sending American minerals to make steel? We are allowing India to do to the U.S. what Britain did to them in the eighteenth and nineteenth centuries. If we do not change course, the result will be the same!

Predatory Trade Practices

In 2011 India exported $36.1 billion in goods to the U.S. and imported $21.6 billion from us. This $14.5 billion trade deficit tripled from 2010 *(U.S. Census Bureau)*. While this should be cause for concern, an even greater concern is the billions of dollars India is siphoning out of the U.S. economy, through outsourcing of professional services and its acquisition of American companies, which together could represent tens of billions or hundreds of billions. We have absolutely no idea since nobody is tracking this. Also, like China, the $14.5 billion trade imbalance gets even worse when you take into account that a large portion of what India imported from the U.S. were components or raw materials used to manufacture goods for resale back to the U.S. and other countries. Our "trade" relationship with India is based on outsourcing and the transfer of technology and American jobs to India to exploit low-cost labor. Like China, India is using the same proven strategy developed by Japan—exploitation of the world's largest and most open economy with low-priced exports while protecting its markets from U.S. imports. However, India has adapted this model to include professional services as well as manufactured goods. This is a lethal combination that, combined with the offshoring of manufacturing to communist China, has brought the U.S. economy to its knees. India is also cleverly using membership in the World Trade Organization to gain and exploit full access to the U.S. market while protecting its home markets. They abide by the WTO rules that benefit them and ignore those that don't. They are also playing the same cat-and-mouse game on trade that Japan has been playing with the U.S. for more than fifty years. Why not? It is a proven

> IN 2011 INDIA EXPORTED $36.1 BILLION IN GOODS TO THE U.S. AND IMPORTED $21.6 BILLION FROM US. THIS $14.5 BILLION TRADE DEFICIT TRIPLED FROM 2010

business strategy that has worked well for Japan and is now working very well for China. Why reinvent the wheel?

India uses numerous trade barriers to protect its home markets. A full list and description of these trade barriers is contained in a 2011 U.S. Trade Representative report located at: http://www.ustr.gov/sites/default/files/ India_0.pdf. This thirteen-page report is extremely interesting. I will do my best to summarize here, but I encourage you to go online to read the full report. It is unbelievable.

India's Foreign Trade Barriers

Tariffs and Other Charges on Imports

- The structure of India's customs tariff and fees system is complex and lacks transparency. This makes it very difficult to determine rates of customs tariff, excise duty, and other duties and charges on imports into India. No single official publication is available to traders that includes all relevant information on tariffs, fees, and tax rates on imports, making it very difficult for importers.

- Tariff rates range from 12 percent to more than 300 percent! India has not reduced the basic customs duty in the past four years and maintains very high tariff rates on a number of goods, including flowers (60 percent), natural rubber (70 percent), automobiles and motorcycles (60 percent on new products, 100 percent on used products), coffee (100 percent), poultry (30–100 percent), textiles (some rates exceed 300 percent), agricultural products (maximum rates ranging from 100–300 percent, with an average of 118.3 percent), and wine and distilled spirits (150 percent). Imports also are subject to state-level value-added or sales taxes, the Central Sales Tax, and various local taxes and charges.

Import Licensing

- India maintains a "negative list" of imported products subject to various forms of non-tariff regulation. The negative list is currently divided into three categories: banned or prohibited items (e.g., tallow, fat, and oils of animal origin); restricted items that require an import license (e.g., livestock products and certain chemicals); and "canalized" items (e.g., petroleum products and some pharmaceuticals) importable only by government trading monopolies subject to cabinet approval regarding timing and quantity.

- India has required import licenses for all remanufactured goods since 2006. As with licensing requirements on other products, the requirement is onerous as implemented: the license application requires excessive details; quantity limitations are set on specific part numbers; the delay between application and grant of the license is long and creates uncertainty. In some cases, licenses are never issued for no apparent reason.

Customs Procedures

- India's valuation procedures allow its customs officials to reject the declared transaction value of an import when a sale is deemed to involve a lower price compared to the ordinary competitive price. U.S. exporters have reported that India's customs valuation methodologies do not reflect actual transaction values and raise the cost of exporting to India beyond applied tariff rates.

- U.S. companies have faced extensive investigations related to their use of certain valuation methodologies when importing computer equipment. Companies have reported being subjected to excessive searches and seizures.

- India does not assess the basic customs duty, additional duty, and special additional duty separately on the customs value of a given imported product. Rather, India assesses each of these duties cumulatively; that is, the additional duty is assessed on the sum of the actual (or transaction) value and the basic customs duty, while the special additional duty is assessed on the sum of the actual (or transaction) value, the basic customs duty, and the additional duty. This can result in importers paying higher duties than they should be liable for on the basis of the actual value of their imported product.

- India's customs officials generally require extensive documentation, which inhibits the free flow of trade and leads to frequent and lengthy processing delays.

- Motor vehicles may be imported through only three specific ports and only from the country of manufacture.

Government Procurement

- India applies sector-specific procurement policies in certain areas, such as defense procurement. India's defense "offsets" program requires companies to invest 30 percent or more of the value of contracts above Rs300 crores ($67 million) in Indian-produced parts, equipment, or services. Recently, offsets were expanded to include civil aviation. Offset requirements are often so onerous that they dissuade foreign companies from bidding. In addition, it is not uncommon for the Defense Ministry to request significant changes to previously accepted offset proposals.

- India's government procurement practices and procedures are not transparent. Foreign firms rarely win Indian government contracts due to the preference afforded to the numerous Indian state-owned enterprises. Similarly, the 2006 Micro, Small, and Medium Enterprise (MSME) Act authorizes the government to provide procurement preferences to MSMEs.

- India is not a signatory to the WTO's Agreement on Government Procurement.

Export Subsidies

- India provides tax holidays for certain export-oriented enterprises and exporters in special economic zones. This acts as a government subsidy for exports.

- India continues to maintain several other export subsidy programs, including duty drawback programs that appear to allow for drawback in excess of duties levied on imported inputs. India also provides pre-and post-shipment financing to exporters at a preferential rate.

- India's textile industry enjoys government subsidies through various modernization schemes, such as the Technology Upgradation Fund Scheme and the Scheme for Integrated Textile Parks.

- Numerous other sectors, including paper, rubber, toys, leather goods, and wood products receive government subsidies tied to export performance.

- After several consecutive years of not submitting a subsidies notification, India recently submitted two notifications to the WTO Committee on Subsidies and Countervailing Measures (SCM Committee), both of which notify only one central government program of preferential tax incentives related to Free Trade Zones, Special Economic Zones, and Export Processing Zones covering the 2003–09 time period. These notifications failed to mention several well-known subsidies, including export subsidy programs maintained by India. (Surely this was just an honest oversight with no intention of "gaming" the WTO or the United States . . . !)

Intellectual Property Rights Protection

- India remained on the Priority Watch List in 2011 because of concerns regarding weak protection and enforcement of intellectual property rights (IPR).

- India needs to provide stronger protection for copyrights, trademarks, and patents. India also needs to provide effective protection against unfair commercial use of undisclosed test and other data generated to obtain marketing approval for pharmaceutical and agrochemical products. India is using outsourcing to steal science and technology. What is the U.S. doing about this? Filing complaints with the WTO?! Unless we take quick and substantive action, you can say goodbye to the U.S. Pharmaceutical Industry.

- Large-scale copyright piracy, especially in the software, optical media, and publishing industries, continues to be a major problem. In addition, India's criminal enforcement in this area remains weak.

Services Barriers

- The Indian government has a strong ownership presence in major services industries such as banking and insurance, while private firms play a preponderant to exclusive role in some of the fastest growing areas of the services sector, such as information technology and business consulting.

- Key sectors such as telecommunications, financial services, and legal services remain either closed to foreign investment or are subject to restrictions on foreign participation. Meanwhile, Indian companies have complete access to the U.S. market!

Insurance—Foreign equity in the insurance sector is currently limited to 26 percent of paid-up capital.

Banking—Although India allows privately held banks to operate in the country, the banking system is dominated by government-owned banks, and direct investment by foreign banks is subject to restrictions. State-owned banks account for roughly 72 percent of the assets and 86 percent of all bank branches in the banking system. Foreign banks are not authorized to own more than 5 percent of on-balance-sheet assets of an Indian private bank without government approval, while individual investors, including foreign investors, cannot own more than 10 percent of any private bank. In addition, voting rights are capped at 10 percent.

Audiovisual Services—U.S. companies continue to experience difficulty importing film and video publicity materials and are unable to license merchandise in connection with movies due to royalty remittance restrictions. The industry has difficulty importing digital masters of films loaded on electronic media, as opposed to those imported on cinematographic film, because of a different customs duty structure. U.S. companies also continue to face difficulties with India's downlink policy. Under this policy, international content providers that downlink programming from a satellite into India must establish a registered office in India or designate a local agent. U.S. companies have reported that this policy is overly burdensome and can result in having a taxable presence in India. Additionally, India requires that foreign investors have a net worth of $1 million (up from the previous amount of $300,000) in order to be allowed to downlink an initial content channel, and an additional $500,000 (up from the previous amount of $200,000) of net worth to downlink each additional channel.

Accounting—Foreign accounting firms encounter several hurdles to entering the Indian accounting services sector. Before an accountant can practice in India, the accountant must become a member of the Institute of Chartered Accountants of India (ICAI), which requires taking ICAI courses, undergoing practical training at an ICAI-accredited organization, and passing an examination. Foreign accounting firms may only practice in India if their home country provides reciprocity to Indian firms. Only firms established as a partnership may provide financial auditing services, and foreign-licensed accountants may not be equity partners in an Indian accounting firm. Foreign accounting firms are also concerned with proposed amendments to the Indian Companies Act in the Companies Bill 2011. The Companies Bill 2011, which has been cleared by the Indian Cabinet, will replace a fifty-year-old law, and is expected to be brought before Parliament in 2012. The proposed amendments include provisions that would require clients to rotate audit firms every five years and increase third-party liability. Foreign firms are concerned that these changes will disrupt business continuity and represent a departure from the practices employed by most G-20 countries.

Legal Services—The Bar Council of India (BCI) is the governing body for the legal profession in India. Membership in the BCI is mandatory to practice law in India, and is limited to Indian citizens. Foreign law firms are not allowed to open offices in India.

Telecommunications and Broadcasting—Foreign investment in wireless and fixed telecommunications in India is limited to 74 percent, and U.S. companies have noted that India's initial licensing fee (approximately $500,000 per service) for telecommunications providers serves as a barrier to market entry for smaller market players. Foreign investment in cable networks and direct-to-home (DTH) broadcasting is limited to 49 percent. TV channels, irrespective of ownership or management control, are required to transmit from ground stations (i.e., uplinks) located in India; while full foreign ownership is permitted for entertainment and general interest channels, foreign investment in news and current affairs channels uplinking from India is limited to 26 percent.

India issued a new telecommunications security policy in May 2011. There is concern about certain provisions of this policy, such as: (1) the requirement of telecommunications equipment vendors to test all imported information and communications technology (ICT) equipment in labs in India; (2) the requirement to allow the telecommunications service provider and government agencies to inspect a vendor's manufacturing facilities and supply chain, and to

ALL OF THIS ADDS UP TO INDIA USING GOVERNMENT REGULATIONS TO ACQUIRE FOREIGN-OWNED INTELLECTUAL PROPERTY.

perform security checks for the duration of the contract to supply the equipment; and (3) the imposition of strict liability and possible "blacklisting" of a vendor for taking "inadequate" precautionary security measures, without the right to appeal and other due process guarantees. All of this adds up to

India using government regulations to acquire foreign-owned intellectual property.

The government of India continues to hold equity in three telecommunications firms: a 26 percent interest in the international carrier VSNL; a 56 percent stake in MTNL, which primarily serves Delhi and Mumbai; and full ownership of BSNL, which provides domestic services throughout the rest of India. These ownership stakes have caused private carriers to express concern about the fairness of India's general telecommunications policies. India does not allow companies to provide Internet telephony over networks connected to the publicly switched telecommunications network unless they obtain a telecommunications license.

U.S. satellite operators have long raised concerns about the closed and protected satellite services market in India. Even though current Indian regulations do not preclude the use of foreign satellites, in practice, foreign satellite capacity must be provided through the Indian Space Research Organization (ISRO), effectively requiring foreign operators to sell capacity to a direct competitor. U.S. companies have noted that this requirement creates additional costs, allows ISRO to negotiate contract terms with the goal of moving the service to one of its satellites once capacity is available, and puts ISRO in a position of being able to determine the market growth rate.

Distribution Services—While full foreign ownership is permitted in wholesale cash-and-carry services, the retail sector in India is largely closed to foreign investment. Foreign investment in single-brand retailing (e.g., a Stride Rite Shoe Store) is limited to 51 percent, while foreign investment in multi-brand retailing (e.g., Target or Kohl's) is prohibited outright.

Postal and Express Delivery—In 2011, the Department of Posts announced a proposed bill to replace the 1898 Post Office Act. This bill may establish a monopoly on express delivery of items weighing up to fifty grams (1.76 ounces) and require that private operators charge twice the express mail service rate to provide services falling within the government monopoly. The bill would also establish a new licensing and registration scheme, potentially granting India Post regulatory authority over its private sector competitors.

Education—Foreign providers of higher education services interested in establishing themselves in India face a number of market access barriers, including a requirement that representatives of Indian states sit on university governing boards; quotas limiting enrollment; caps on tuition and fees; policies that create the potential for double taxation; and difficulties repatriating salaries and income from research.

Investment Barriers

Equity Restrictions

- India continues to prohibit or severely restrict foreign investment in certain sectors, such as agriculture, multi-brand retail trade, railways, and real estate.

  - Foreign shareholding is counted as domestic shareholding, so long as the investment is transacted via a company "controlled" by Indian residents and is less than 50 percent foreign-owned.

  - India had allowed 100 percent FDI in the pharmaceutical sector for several years with no requirement of government approval. In October 2011, India appeared to have moved away from this openness, adopting a requirement that foreign acquisition of pharmaceutical firms ("brownfield investments") be approved by the Competition Commission of India (CCI).

  - India's stringent and nontransparent regulations and procedures governing local shareholding inhibit inbound investment and increase risk to new entrants. Attempts by non-Indians to acquire full ownership of locally traded companies often face regulatory hurdles that may render ownership unobtainable, even though such acquisitions are legal. Price control regulations in some sectors, such as the pharmaceutical sector, have further undermined incentives for foreign investors to increase their equity holdings in India.

Other Barriers

- India has an unwritten policy that favors linking imports and exports in individual transactions (counter trade). India issued guidelines that require solar project developers to exclusively source photovoltaic cells and modules used in solar projects that are manufactured in India. These restrictions effectively blocked imports of U.S. equipment based on crystalline silicon technology, impacting a large segment of U.S. solar manufacturers.

- India issued a number of policy proposals in 2011 aimed at encouraging domestic manufacturing in the telecommunications equipment, electronic products, and information technology areas. These proposals include procurement preference guidelines for electronic products that, if implemented, would impose significant barriers to trade in the information technology and communications industries.

- India has steadily increased export duties on iron ore and its derivatives ranging from 10 to 30 percent.

- Several Indian states have banned the export of iron ore. Such restrictions affect international markets for raw materials used in steel production. India also requires that exports of high-grade iron ore (ore with greater than 64 percent iron content) pass through state trading enterprises, with the state-owned Minerals and Metals Trading Company acting as a clearing house. Perhaps the U.S. should implement similar policies governing the mines owned by India in the U.S. Better yet, perhaps we should restrict Indian ownership of these mines.

- In 2010 India became the world's sixth-largest steel producing economy, and it appears the Indian government is using these measures to improve supply and lower prices of inputs used by India's rapidly growing steel industry.

- India implemented export restrictions and bans on cotton and yarn during 2010 and 2011. These restrictions contributed to significant volatility on world cotton markets and appear to have provided India's textile and apparel producers with more affordable cotton during a period of record-high global cotton prices.

So, you might ask, what are U.S. political leaders doing about India's predatory trade practices? Not much. Republicans keep preaching their *free trade* and *free markets* dogma while President Obama and his administration are going full speed ahead with expanding our so-called trade relationship with India. Recently, the Obama administration did impose duties on steel imports from India. The Indian government responded by filing a complaint with the WTO *(Reuters)*. This is absurd, given the trade barriers I've just listed. However, I also question the timing of the Obama administration's motives. Is this just a symptom of election-year politics, designed to pacify American workers? Or does this signal a shift in our approach to trade with India? In either case, it isn't enough. We must switch from a reactionary to a proactive trade and economic strategy that includes other well-thought-out and pragmatic actions to get our trading relationship with India, China, Japan, and others under control and balanced. For now, though, let's continue focusing on India.

Establishing a Strategic and Mutually Beneficial Trade Relationship

In spite of all that we just covered, I do believe that, if properly structured and managed, our trade relationship with India can be mutually beneficial and propel both of our economies into a positive and productive future. This partnership could very well be the most important and positive trading relationship in U.S. history. There is much we can learn from India, and much we can share in return. I also do not blame India for the problems the U.S. economy is having. In fact I don't blame China, Japan, or any other nation either. Why? Well, let me explain it this way. My wife and I are both huge American football fans. I grew up in Pittsburgh and am a loyal Steelers fan, but my favorite NFL quarterback is Peyton Manning (famous for his years with the Indianapolis Colts, and now with the Denver Broncos). Why, you ask? Because Manning understands all aspects of the game and comes prepared—both mentally and physically—to play and win each one. His preparations not only include knowing his team's game plan, but also what the opposing team may do. Manning approaches football like chess—always strategizing and thinking ahead.

How does this relate to our trade relationship with India (or China, Japan, etc.)? Think of the United States and India as professional American football teams. India has a game plan and has done its homework about how to compete with and win against the U.S. They take the Manning approach. The U.S. has no game plan and hasn't done any pre-game preparation. Who do you expect will win? So we play the game, and India wallops the U.S. Afterward the coach for the U.S. team complains that the playing field wasn't level, that India didn't play fair, and so on and so forth. Was it India's responsibility to create a game plan for the U.S. and ensure that we came prepared to play? Of course not!

U.S. trade and economic policy is an analogous situation. The U.S. needs to stop complaining about fairness and a level playing field, and put some energy into creating a game plan. The game plan needs to be a national economic strategy that includes sensible and mutually beneficial trade policies. This is our responsibility—not India's, China's, Japan's, or any other nation. We also need to stop trying to control the behavior of other countries and focus instead on what we can control—our own behavior and responses. We have much in common with India as well as many cultural differences. We need to honestly acknowledge both and find ways to operate in an open and honest way that lifts both countries up and moves both societies forward. As the two largest democracies in the world, we have a solemn responsibility to support and promote human rights and liberty—not only for our nations, but for all mankind.

CHAPTER SIX

The Free Trade Myth

Reciprocity must be treated as the handmaiden of protection. Our first duty is to see that the protection granted by the tariff in every case where it is needed is maintained, and that reciprocity be sought for so far as it can safely be done without injury to our home industries. Just how far this is must be determined according to the individual case, remembering always that every application of our tariff policy to meet our shifting national needs must be conditioned upon the cardinal fact that the duties must never be reduced below the point that will cover the difference between the labor cost here and abroad. The well-being of the wage-worker is a prime consideration of our entire policy of economic legislation.

—THEODORE ROOSEVELT

The American economy has gone away. It is not coming back until free trade myths are buried six feet under.

—PAUL CRAIG ROBERTS,
FORMER ASSISTANT SECRETARY OF THE TREASURY

It's Not Trade and It's Not Free

What is commonly referred to as *free trade* is not trade—it is outsourcing disguised as trade, and it is not free. The numerous so-called free-trade agreements negotiated by both Republicans and Democrats over the past forty years have resulted in the U.S. economy losing more than $7 trillion to international commerce, with the majority of those losses coming in the past ten years alone *(Harrington)*. The losses continue to mount, with roughly $700 billion in commerce continuing to leave the U.S. each year. What is not commonly understood is that the primary purpose of these agreements is to provide U.S. and foreign corporations with the opportunity to outsource the production of goods for sale into the U.S. market—not to promote bilateral trade by making it easier for each country to export what it does best. As stated by Jeff Faux in an Economics Policy Institute article published in 2010 *(Faux and Orr)*, these agreements have destroyed U.S. manufacturing and the U.S. economy by effectively giving other countries a free pass to flood American markets with low-priced goods and services produced under labor conditions we would not tolerate for American workers. To satisfy Wall Street, boost shareholder returns, and generate management bonuses, U.S. corporations have moved production off-shore under the cover of free trade. This was well understood by Peru's president when, after signing a free-trade agreement, he told the U.S. Chamber of Commerce, "Come and open your factories in my country so we can sell your own products back to the U.S."

What was once produced in cities like Pittsburgh, Pennsylvania, or Greenwood, South Carolina, is now produced in communist China, Mexico, Peru, Argentina or some other off-shore location and then sold back to the U.S. This is not trade—it's the looting of the American economy! The impact has been devastating on families and communities across our nation. High-wage manufacturing jobs have been replaced with low-wage retail and service jobs. Coupled with the loss of the corporate income realized from onshore manufacturing, this has led to a steep decline in the tax base of America's city, state, and federal governments. As Paul Craig Roberts makes clear in his essay *Doomed by the Myths of Free Trade—How the Economy was Lost,* for many years, economists and ideologues espousing so-called free trade covered up the damage being done to the U.S. economy through outsourcing by preaching that we no longer needed manufacturing and were transitioning to a new economy based on services and innovation. They convinced us that America pulled a fast one on China, sending them those dirty, grimy manufacturing jobs. Freed from these "old economy" jobs, we could all now become information technology workers (IT), software engineers, innovators, and entrepreneurs. However, U.S. corporations then discovered that by falsely declaring "shortages" of skilled Americans, they could get H-1B work visas for lower-paid foreigners to replace their higher-cost American work force. As a result, millions of the supposed "new economy" jobs in the U.S. have also been filled by low-wage foreign workers, or simply outsourced to India, China, and other off-shore locations—all under the banner of free trade.

The free trade myth has been propagated by Wall Street, U.S. corporations, both major political parties, lobbyists, and well-paid academics. The reason is simple—greed. Over the past forty years, the super-rich, Wall Street, and large corporations have made trillions of dollars selling out America and American jobs under the free-trade banner. Over this same period, campaign contributions from Wall Street and corporations to both major parties have increased dramatically—as have the number of ex-administration officials and members of Congress who go to work for corporations as employees, consultants, and lobbyists. Together, they insisted that more trade with communist China, in particular, would produce many more high-paying jobs here in America in advanced sectors, such as electronics, computers, and silicon chips. This is another myth that I can personally testify to, and will explore in more depth later.

My wife and I both hold engineering degrees and are refugees from the once-thriving (now dying) U.S. semiconductor and computer industries. I served for nine years in the U.S. Navy working in cryptology and satellite communications prior to entering the semiconductor industry. My wife graduated cum laude with a degree in engineering physics from a top university. She now owns and runs a successful direct-mail advertising business but would much rather be using her engineering physics degree. We also have many former colleagues in similar situations. U.S. corporations deserted their American workforce in pursuit of low-cost labor with the full support and cooperation of the U.S. government. The leaders of these corporations were heavily incentivized to invest where the cost of labor and environmental regulation was cheapest. Corporate leaders have not been shy about admitting this. This is what Jeffrey R. Immelt, CEO of General Electric, said in a shareholder meeting in December 2002 *(Stumo)*:

> "When I am talking to GE managers, I talk China, China, China, China, China. You need to be there. You need to change the way people talk about it and how they get there. I am a nut on China. Outsourcing from China is going to grow to five billion. We are building a tech center in China. Every discussion today has to center on China. The cost basis is extremely attractive. You can take an 18-cubic-foot refrigerator, make it in China, land it in the United States, and land it for less than we can make an 18-cubic-foot refrigerator ourselves."

Senator Bernie Sanders shared this quote in a speech he gave opposing President Obama's appointment of Immelt as chair of a White House jobs panel tasked with finding ways to grow private-sector jobs. Senator Sanders went on to comment:

> "Gee! When GE had, a couple of years ago, some really difficult economic times, they needed $16 billion to bail them out, I didn't hear Mr. Immelt going to China, China, China, China, China. I didn't hear that. I heard Mr. Immelt going to the taxpayers of the United States for his welfare check. So I say to Mr. Immelt, and I say to all these CEOs that have been so quick to run to China, that maybe it's time to start reinvesting in the United States of America."

In 1995, Alexander James Trotman, a British citizen and the first foreign-born CEO of Ford Motor Co. stated, "Ford is not an American company." Yet, in September 2009, the Obama Administration awarded Ford a $5.9 billion loan to upgrade their manufacturing facilities to improve fuel efficiency, as part of something called the Advanced Technology Manufacturing (AVTM) program. If it's not an American company, then why is it asking for and receiving subsidies from American taxpayers? In 2004, John Chambers, CEO of Cisco Systems, Inc., was quoted as saying "What we're trying to do is outline an entire strategy of becoming a Chinese company" (Lemon). I guess this explains their cooperation with the Chinese communist party to suppress human rights in China. (I will explore that more later.) If this is really how Chambers, and any other CEO in America, feels, then I invite them to surrender their U.S. passports. I'm sure we'd all be more than happy to arrange for them to change their citizenship to communist China. It is time that we reminded CEOs of companies incorporated in the U.S. of their civic duties and responsibilities. Such disloyalty is an insult to the many Americans who have served and sacrificed to preserve and protect the United States of America so that companies like GE, Cisco, Ford, and countless others could prosper and enjoy the benefits and privilege of operating in a free society. As Theodore Roosevelt put it, the prime consideration of our entire policy of economic and trade legislation should be to ensure the well-being of America, our home industries, and our workers.

The World Trade Organization and Communist China

The World Trade Organization (WTO), which was established in 1994, is part of the international trading system that has its roots in agreements made among the Allied nations after World War II. The purpose of the WTO is to settle disagreements (trade disputes) among nations regarding the rules agreed upon in the General Agreement on Tariffs and Trade (GATT). The GATT treaty regulates trade among 153 countries and was originally negotiated and signed in 1947 *(Wikipedia)*. According to its preamble, the purpose of the GATT is the "substantial reduction of tariffs and other trade barriers and the elimination of preferences, on a reciprocal and mutually advantageous basis." Notice that the purpose of GATT is to establish conditions for "reciprocal and mutually advantageous" trade—not outsourcing of jobs or offshoring of manufacturing. This is an important distinction. I am confident that those representing the U.S. in 1947 did not intend for GATT to be used by American and other foreign corporations to off-shore the manufacturing of goods for sale to the U.S. market and destroy the U.S. manufacturing base and economy in the process, but this is precisely what has happened. I am also confident that those who negotiated the agreement in 1947 never intended for the U.S. to surrender its economic sovereignty to GATT and the WTO, but that has happened as well. The WTO rulings supersede national laws covering everything from food-safety standards, the environment, social service policies, intellectual property standards, government procurement rules, and more. Since its creation in 1995, the WTO has been a major impediment to America's ability to effectively compete in the world market. In nine out of every ten cases, the WTO rules against the U.S.—requiring changes to laws, and further damaging the American economy. Here are some examples of WTO rulings against the U.S. *(Ensinger)*:

- In 2002 Brazil challenged U.S. federal subsidies on its imported Brazilian cotton. The WTO ruled against the U.S., and eventually gave Brazil permission to impose tariffs totaling nearly $830 million on American-made products such as cars, textiles, electronics, and media.

- In 2010 the U.S. attempted to ban uninspected chicken products from China, out of concerns that they may be harmful or toxic. The WTO ruled against the U.S., stating that the ban was not in accordance with its regulations, which put U.S. consumers in harm's way.

- In 1995 Venezuela challenged U.S. regulations on imported gasoline. The WTO ruled against the U.S., preventing us from protecting our own oil manufacturers.

- In 2004 two Caribbean states challenged U.S. prohibitions on cross-border gambling, a ban put in place to protect against money laundering and other dangerous exposures. The WTO ruled against the U.S., stating the ban breached a global deal that liberalized trade in services (the sale and delivery of an intangible product)—in this case, online casinos.

- In 2010 anti-dumping duties imposed by the U.S. on Brazilian orange juice were challenged. The WTO ruled against the U.S., opening the door for around $400 million in Brazilian orange juice to be shipped here each year.

What do you think Washington, Adams, or Jefferson would say about the United States of America surrendering its economic sovereignty to the WTO and jeopardizing the health and safety of its citizens?

Of course, such rulings are only a concern to a country like the U.S., which respects the rule of law. For countries such as communist China, Japan, and many others that are much less concerned about the rule of law, this is a non-issue. They pick and choose which WTO rules they want to follow and to what extent they will abide by them. The communist Chinese government uses every policy tool it can to drive its economic development. They have absolutely no concern about the fairness or unfairness of such policies or whether they are allowed under the rules of the WTO. Communist China, like Japan, and many other countries, game the international trading system by using GATT and the WTO to gain improved access to the U.S. market for their goods at lower tariff levels, while blocking such access to their home markets. They aggressively pursue development of their export industries, to the detriment of U.S. industries. Let's take a closer look at China and their entry into the WTO.

In 2000 the U.S. government opened up the domestic market to communist China by granting it, on a permanent basis, what used to be called Most Favored Nation trade status. This means that Congress surrendered its right to an annual review and renewal of the U.S. trade relationship with China. In exchange, the Chinese loosened restrictions on U.S. investment in China. By granting this trade status and opening up the U.S. market to China, the U.S. gave up the most important nonmilitary leverage it had in its relationship with this totalitarian communist government. In December 2001 a U.S. trade delegation, led by Charlene Barshefsky, negotiated China's entry into the WTO *(Eckert and Dawson)*. This gave China even greater access to the U.S. market and heralded unprecedented economic growth for China, vaulting it in a decade to the second-largest economy in the world. In 2011, Barshefsky was quoted as saying, "The Chinese consider WTO entry the most historic achievement in U.S.-China relations since [U.S. President Richard] Nixon's visit to China, in 1972."

Photo: Nelson Ching, Bloomberg

Unfortunately, it is a different story in the U.S. According to a study published by the Economic Policy Institute in 2011 *(Scott, GROWING U.S. TRADE DEFICIT WITH CHINA COST 2.8 MILLION JOBS BETWEEN 2001 AND 2010)*, communist China's entry into the WTO in 2001 has had a devastating impact on U.S. workers and the U.S. economy. Here are some highlights:

- The U.S. trade deficit with communist China grew from $84 billion in 2001 to $278 billion in 2010.

- This trade deficit has eliminated or displaced nearly 2.8 million U.S. jobs, or about 2 percent of total U.S. employment.

- Most of the jobs lost or displaced by trade with China between 2001 and 2010 were in manufacturing industries (1.93 million jobs, or 69.2 percent).

- Computer and electronic parts (including computers, parts, semiconductors, and audio-video equipment) accounted for $124.3 billion of the $278 billion U.S. trade deficit with China in 2010.

- Rapidly growing imports of computer and electronic parts accounted for more than 44 percent of the increased U.S. trade deficit with China between 2001 and 2010. This contributed to the elimination of 909,400 U.S. jobs in computer and electronic products.

- Global trade in advanced technology products (ATP)—often discussed as a source of comparative advantage for the U.S.—is instead dominated by communist China. This includes the advanced computer and electronic parts industry and other industries such as biotechnology, life sciences, aerospace, and nuclear. In 2010 the U.S. had a $94.2 billion deficit in ATP with China, which was responsible for 34 percent of the total U.S.–China trade deficit. In contrast, the U.S. had a $13.3 billion surplus in ATP with the rest of the world in 2010.

- Other industrial sectors hit hard by growing trade deficits with China between 2001 and 2010 include: apparel and accessories (178,700 jobs), textile fabrics and products (92,300 jobs), fabricated metal products (123,900 jobs), plastic and rubber products (62,000 jobs), motor vehicles and parts (49,300 jobs), and miscellaneous manufactured goods (119,700 jobs). Several service sectors were also hit hard by indirect losses including administrative, support, and waste management services (204,300 jobs) and professional, scientific, and technical services (173,100 jobs).

- The 2.8 million U.S. jobs lost or displaced by the trade deficit with China between 2001 and 2010 were distributed among all fifty states, as shown in the accompanying chart.

- Jobs displaced due to growing deficits with China exceeded 2.2 percent of total employment in the ten hardest-hit states: New Hampshire (19,700 jobs, 2.84 percent), California (454,600 jobs, 2.74 percent), Massachusetts (88,600 jobs, 2.73 percent), Oregon (47,900 jobs, 2.71 percent), North Carolina (107,800 jobs, 2.61 percent), Minnesota (70,700 jobs, 2.61 percent), Idaho (17,400 jobs, 2.54 percent), Vermont (7,800 jobs, 2.37 percent), Colorado (55,800 jobs, 2.30 percent), and Rhode Island (11,800, 2.24 percent).

U.S. Jobs lost and gained due to trade with Communist China 2001-10							
State	Import jobs	Export jobs	Net job change	State	Import jobs	Export jobs	Net job change
Alabama	-51,700	7,400	-44,300	Nebraska	-16,000	4,400	-11,500
Alaska	-3,100	800	-2,300	Nevada	-17,300	2,400	-14,800
Arizona	-59,000	8,900	-50,000	New Hampshire	-22,500	2,800	-19,700
Arkansas	-25,700	5,300	-20,300	New Jersey	-90,300	11,400	-78,800
California	-519,000	64,300	-454,600	New Mexico	-15,100	2,700	-12,300
Colorado	-63,600	7,700	-55,800	New York	-183,300	21,900	-161,400
Connect-icut	-37,200	5,500	-31,600	North Carolina	-122,400	14,600	-107,800
Delaware	-6,900	1,200	-5,600	North Dakota	-5,000	1,900	-3,000
District of Columbia	-3,800	500	-3,300	Ohio	-124,100	20,500	-103,500
Florida	-134,500	20,100	-114,400	Oklahoma	-27,800	5,900	-21,900
Georgia	-101,200	13,500	-87,700	Oregon	-56,900	9,000	-47,900
Hawaii	-6,400	1,200	-5,200	Pennsylvania	-127,200	20,200	-107,000
Idaho	-21,300	3,800	-17,400	Puerto Rico	-24,900	3,500	-21,400
Illinois	-139,400	21,200	-118,200	Rhode Island	-13,400	1,600	-11,800
Indiana	-74,500	12,800	-61,600	South Carolina	-48,900	7,000	-41,900
Iowa	-29,200	7,400	-21,800	South Dakota	-7,900	2,400	-5,500
Kansas	-24,800	5,900	-18,800	Tennessee	-67,700	9,700	-57,900
Kentucky	-43,700	7,300	-36,400	Texas	-269,300	36,400	-232,800

| U.S. Jobs lost and gained due to trade with Communist China 2001-10 ||||||||
State	Import jobs	Export jobs	Net job change	State	Import jobs	Export jobs	Net job change
Louisiana	-23,000	5,200	-17,700	Utah	-25,200	3,800	-21,400
Maine	-11,800	2,200	-9,500	Vermont	-9,200	1,300	-7,800
Maryland	-46,700	6,200	-40,500	Virginia	-67,500	10,100	-57,400
Massachu-setts	-99,300	10,700	-88,600	Washington	-63,900	11,900	-52,000
Michigan	-97,400	17,600	-79,800	West Virginia	-10,500	2,200	-8,200
Minnesota	-82,400	11,700	-70,700	Wisconsin	-70,600	13,700	-56,900
Mississippi	-24,600	4,100	-20,500	Wyoming	-2,800	1,000	-1,700
Missouri	-51,000	9,500	-41,500	United States			
Montana	-5,300	2,100	-3,200	& Puerto Rico*	-3,278,900	488,800	-2,790,100
Source: EPI Briefing Paper #323				* Totals vary slightly due to rounding			

Advocates of communist China's entry into the WTO frequently claimed that it would create jobs in the U.S., increase U.S. exports, and improve the trade deficit with China. In 2000 President Clinton claimed that the agreement then under negotiation to allow China into the WTO "creates a win-win result for both countries." Exports to China "now support hundreds of thousands of American jobs," and these figures "can grow substantially with the new access to the Chinese market the WTO agreement creates," he said. Obviously, he was misinformed, lying, or engaged in wishful thinking. Proponents also claimed that communist China's entry into the WTO would bring it into compliance with an enforceable, rules-based regime that would require China to open its markets to imports from the U.S. and other nations by reducing tariffs and addressing non-tariff barriers to trade. This never happened—instead they broke the promises made when they joined the WTO and chose to follow only the rules that benefit communist China.

The U.S. also negotiated a series of special safeguard measures designed to limit the disruptive effects of surging imports from China on domestic producers. My guess is that the Chinese are storing these agreements in the same warehouse where the Japanese keep the numerous trade agreements they have negotiated with the U.S. and ignored for the past fifty-plus years.

Finally, promoters of liberalized U.S.–China trade argued that the U.S. would benefit because of increased exports to a large and growing consumer market in China. The truth is that the much-anticipated U.S. exports to communist China never happened, and never will, because China has absolutely no serious interest in establishing a "reciprocal and mutually advantageous" trade relationship with the U.S. This is clearly evidenced by their continued currency manipulation and other trade-distorting practices, including extensive subsidies, legal and illegal barriers to imports, dumping, suppression of wages and labor rights, ongoing piracy of intellectual property, continued expansion of state-owned corporations, and corporate espionage.

The plain and painful truth is that support for communist China's entry into the WTO was never about trade—it has always been about offshoring and outsourcing. This is well understood by both major U.S. political parties, which have been handsomely rewarded for their support by Wall Street, corporate interests, Japan, China, and other foreign interests. Why do you think neither the Democrats nor the Republicans are talking about trade policy even though it's at the core of our economic collapse? The U.S. political establishment has been paid to keep its mouth shut and maintain the status quo when it comes to international trade. Trillions of dollars are being made by American and other first-world capitalists, who have formed an unholy alliance with the Chinese communist party. They supply the money and technology, and the Chinese provide cheap labor. The U.S. political establishment ensures easy access to the U.S. market through its membership in the WTO and the numerous so-called free-trade agreements. It is time that we put a stop to this and demand that American capitalists and companies put loyalty to their country first. As Senator Bernie Sanders, an Independent from Vermont, has said, "The time for playing nice with corporate turncoats and their enablers in government is over. It's time to name names and demand that American companies act like they actually give a damn about the land of the free and the home of the brave." Let's join together and put an end to offshoring and outsourcing that is masquerading as "free trade"!

North American Free Trade Agreement

If you're paying $12–$14 an hour to factory workers and you can move your factory south of the border, pay $1 [an hour] for labor, . . . have no health care (cost), . . . have no environmental controls, no pollution controls, and no retirement, and you don't care about anything but making money—there will be a giant sucking sound going south.

—Ross Perot, during a 1992 presidential debate

When Ross Perot made this statement during a 1992 presidential debate, he was ridiculed by the supporters of the North American Free Trade Agreement (NAFTA), including George H. W. Bush and Bill Clinton, who claimed that NAFTA would create jobs for the U.S. economy and a trade surplus for the U.S. with Mexico. President George H. W. Bush, along with Canadian Prime Minister Brian Mulroney, spearheaded the negotiations of NAFTA. President Clinton inherited this agreement from the first Bush administration and made its final ratification and passage a top priority of his new administration. While signing the agreement, Clinton remarked, "NAFTA means jobs. American jobs, and good-paying American jobs. If I didn't believe that, I wouldn't support this agreement" *(Wikipedia).* The Clinton administration confidently predicted that NAFTA would result in a rising trade surplus with Mexico, and that therefore it would be a net U.S. job creator.

Newt Gingrich was also a strong supporter of NAFTA. As Speaker of the House of Representatives, he was instrumental in its passage. NAFTA was very controversial and only narrowly passed the House of Representatives. It most likely would have failed to pass without Gingrich's support. He was critical of those who claimed it would result in jobs moving from the U.S. to Mexico. In 1993, Gingrich spoke on the House floor and called the idea that Mexico would hijack our industrial base a myth. He said that any impact on U.S. jobs would be small, and that whatever effects were felt would be beneficial ones. He also stated that the U.S. could see large financial benefits from NAFTA within ten to fifteen years (from 1993). He asserted that a prosperous, stable, and democratic Mexico would simply be a better neighbor than a poor, unstable, and undemocratic Mexico, since higher economic growth would ultimately reduce illegal immigration into the U.S. According to his argument, NAFTA would mean that Mexicans could stay home and get jobs. Here we are, seventeen years later, and it turns out Perot was the only one who got it right! NAFTA has been a colossal failure that has helped destroy the U.S. economy.

According to a report by Economic Policy Institute (EPI) economist Robert Scott titled "Heading South: U.S.–Mexico Trade and Job Displacement after NAFTA," an estimated 682,900 U.S. jobs have been lost or displaced because of NAFTA and the resulting trade deficit. The EPI's calculation of 682,900 jobs lost to NAFTA takes into account those jobs created as well. In 2010, for example, U.S. exports to Mexico supported 791,900 jobs. However, those jobs are far fewer than the 1.47 million U.S. jobs that would be necessary without the imports resulting from NAFTA. Jobs continue to be lost to NAFTA today. In the years 2007–10, the U.S. economy lost 116,400 as a result of the trade deficit created by NAFTA. And in 2010, the growth of Mexican auto exports to the U.S. alone created more Mexican jobs—30,400 of them—than the entire U.S. auto industry.

> AN ESTIMATED 682,900 U.S. JOBS HAVE BEEN LOST OR DISPLACED BECAUSE OF NAFTA AND THE RESULTING TRADE DEFICIT.

In 1993, before NAFTA was signed, the U.S. had a $1.6 billion trade surplus with Mexico. This surplus supported 29,400 U.S. jobs. By 1997, the U.S. had a trade deficit with Mexico of $16.6 billion, and as of 2010 that deficit had grown to $97.2 billion. So much for the surplus forecast by the Clinton administration. Instead, NAFTA created a trade deficit that is approximately sixty-two times the trade surplus that existed with Mexico before NAFTA.

As Perot predicted and Gingrich ridiculed, NAFTA did indeed play a significant role in hijacking our industrial base. As a result of NAFTA, 415,000 U.S. manufacturing jobs have been eliminated, which is 60.8

percent of the total lost overall due to the agreement. Specifically, those making computer or electronic parts account for 22 percent of all job losses, and motor vehicle and parts workers accounted for 15 percent of job losses. Job losses haven't been limited to certain geographic regions, either, as all fifty states have lost jobs as a result. And while some of the states with the largest total number of job losses (California and Texas, for example), share a border with Mexico, it's actually manufacturing-heavy states to the north, such as Michigan, Indiana, and Kentucky, that have lost the largest share of jobs due to NAFTA. The chart below illustrates U.S. job displacement due to trade with Mexico under NAFTA.

So, Mexico is the big winner, right? Not exactly. Though NAFTA is considered a boon for Mexico, the country's economy grew only 1.6 percent per capita on average between 1992 and 2007, according to a study released by the Carnegie Endowment for International Peace in 2009 (*Zepeda, Wise, and Gallagher*).

Net jobs displaced due to trade with Mexico, 2010
(ranked by share of total jobs displaced)

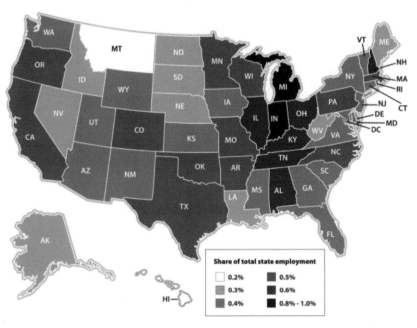

Share of total state employment
0.2%	0.5%
0.3%	0.6%
0.4%	0.8% - 1.0%

The trade deficit with Mexico has resulted in 682,900 U.S. jobs lost or displaced. Source: EPI Report.

So who is benefiting from NAFTA? The same group that is profiting from the trade with communist China—Wall Street, U.S. corporations, and American, Canadian, Mexican, and other first-world capitalists. Like the other free-trade agreements and the U.S. trade relationship with China, NAFTA isn't about trade at all—it is about removing tariffs so U.S. and foreign corporations can use Mexico as a low-cost outsourcing platform to manufacture products sold to the U.S. market. It is outsourcing and offshoring masquerading as free trade! Even the Japanese Trojan-horse consumer electronics factories that invaded the U.S. in the 1970s relocated to Mexico after NAFTA was signed. And they made the move for the same reasons that U.S. corporations did: unabated exploitation of low-cost Mexican workers, no regulatory requirements, and free access to the U.S. market! Communist China is also using Mexico as a port of entry for products sold into the U.S. market.

The NAFTA Superhighway

Many Americans (until recently I was one of them) had most likely never heard of the North America SuperCorridor Coalition (NASCO). You can find them on the web at NASCOCORRIDOR.com. This group was formed as a part of NAFTA and exists to promote the development of transportation infrastructure (highways, railroads, ports, etc.) to support the movement of goods between Mexico, Canada, and the U.S. Sounds pretty harmless until you look closer at what has been called their NAFTA superhighway proposal (the official name is the International Mid-Continent Trade Corridor). This proposed superhighway was to consist of a two-mile wide $184 billion transit system of toll roads, rail lines, and utilities from the Texas–Mexico border all the way up to the Minnesota–Canada border. It was conceived as a way to substantially increase the volume of foreign goods shipped into the U.S. from China and other countries. It became so unpopular in Texas that the Texas portion of it, called the Trans-Texas Corridor, was renamed and mostly abandoned a couple of years ago (*Alexander*). This massive project would have cut right through the heartland of America, following what is now the Interstate 35 corridor. Below is a NASCO illustration of the proposed NAFTA superhighway.

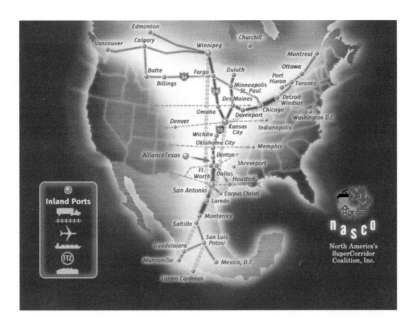

It should be no surprise that a substantial portion of the funding for this project was coming from China and other overseas investors. The inland ports called for in the plan would essentially eliminate the border between Mexico and the U.S., allowing goods and people to move freely. It would also allow illegal immigrants and drugs to flood into the U.S. and Canada. However, of even greater concern, is the easy access this would give communist China, or any other potential adversary, to the heartland of the United States. If such a system had existed in 1941, the Japanese would probably have not only bombed Pearl Harbor, but also sent an invasion force to Mexico and used this transportation and logistics network to quickly move their armies and supplies into the heartland of America. Such an invading force could also use the extra-wide superhighway as a runway to land military jets and cargo planes. These are not farfetched notions. A similar highway already exists in Singapore. It's called the East Coast Parkway and it is designed for use as both a highway and an emergency runway in the event Singapore comes under attack. I have been on the East Coast Parkway many times in my travels to Singapore and it looks like a standard U.S. interstate highway—not an extra-wide superhighway, as proposed by NASCO. Communist China has an army of two-and-a-half million, and is in the process of building and deploying a blue-water naval force that will rival the U.S. Navy. This means that, in the not too distant future, they will have the capability of sending an invasion force to North America. If they choose to do so, they could use this transportation and logistics system to quickly deploy and supply their invasion force. Hopefully this will never happen—but hope is not a strategy, and hope alone will not protect our freedom.

Why would any of our business or political leaders support a super-highway proposal given the obvious national security risks and the damage already inflicted on the U.S. economy by NAFTA? The answer—again—is *greed*! Those who profit from outsourcing and offshoring via the China trade, NAFTA, and other so-called free-trade agreements only care about lining their pockets with more gold—even if it means selling out America and jeopardizing our freedom.

Tax-free Trade—Robbing the U.S. Treasury and Destroying the U.S. Economy

The citizens of the United States must effectively control the mighty

commercial forces which they have themselves called into being. . . .

The State must be made efficient for the work which concerns only the

people of the State; and the nation for that which concerns all the people.

There must remain no neutral ground to serve as a refuge for lawbreakers,

and especially for lawbreakers of great wealth, who can hire the vulpine

legal cunning which will teach them how to avoid both jurisdictions . . . .

The immediate necessity in dealing with trusts [corporations] is to place

them under the real, not the nominal, control of some sovereign to which,

as its creatures, the trusts owe allegiance, and in whose courts the

sovereign's orders may be enforced . . . .

—THEODORE ROOSEVELT

Both U.S. and foreign corporations are gaming the U.S. tax system, robbing the U.S. Treasury of trillions of dollars, and destroying the U.S. economy. A General Accountability Office (GAO) study of corporate tax returns for the years 1998 to 2005 offers ample evidence. The report found that in any given year the number of large, foreign-controlled domestic corporations that reported no income-tax liability ranged as high as 54 percent *(U.S. GAO)*. This means one of every two big foreign-owned corporations operating in the U.S. paid no taxes. As for large U.S.-owned corporations, 38 percent reported they owed no federal income tax. How is that possible? They are cleverly exploiting what Roosevelt described as "neutral ground to serve as a refuge for lawbreakers, and especially for lawbreakers of great wealth, who can hire the vulpine legal cunning which will teach them how to avoid both jurisdictions." In Roosevelt's time the "neutral ground" that corporations were exploiting was between the federal and state governments. Today the neutral ground exists between nations and is being fully exploited by U.S. and foreign corporations with the full support of both major political parties under the free-trade banner. Corporations avoid paying taxes primarily by hiding profits in off-shore tax shelters or by simply changing their incorporation to another country, even though the majority of their business, plants, and employees are in the United States. All of this is legal thanks to a rigged U.S. corporate tax system that U.S. and foreign corporate lobbyists helped create. I was totally unaware of these facts (as are most Americans) until I experienced them firsthand while working with a company based in Singapore, manufacturing in communist China, and selling most of its products in the U.S. market. What I learned during this experience opened my eyes to the myth of free trade, and inspired me to write this book. Here's my story.

A few years ago I engaged with a foreign-owned company that had factories in China. They were referred to me by a former colleague and said that they wanted my assistance establishing a U.S. operation. Prior to that, I had resigned as Corporate Director of Worldwide Sales and Marketing from a U.S.-based company that was engaged in a similar business to help my wife expand a franchise we had purchased. After engaging this foreign-owned company, I discovered they were already doing tens of millions of dollars of business in the U.S.—unincorporated and tax-free. At first I thought, well, this is why they engaged me—to help them set up a proper business structure. I assumed that once I explained to the president and CEO the need to incorporate a subsidiary company and set up a proper business structure that was fully compliant with U.S. laws, he would do the right thing. Unfortunately, that was not the case. He resisted, and I refused to back down. Shortly afterward we parted ways. He seemed genuinely surprised and confused by my insistence on setting up a business structure that complied with U.S. laws. Under the contract we had in place, I could have made a lot of money if I had played along and simply kept my mouth shut. What he failed to understand was that there is absolutely no amount of money that anyone could pay me to sell out my country and my fellow countrymen. I am first and foremost an American patriot!

Concerned about what I had discovered and the broader implications, I consulted with a highly respected corporate tax attorney. After explaining how this company was set up and operating in the U.S., he advised me that what they were doing may or may not be legal—it was in a gray area, or as President Roosevelt called it the "neutral ground" of the law. He further advised me that it appeared the company was fully aware of what it was doing. It seemed they were exploiting loopholes in the U.S.–China tax treaty signed by the Reagan administration in 1986. Based on how they were set up in the U.S., there was a possibility that what they were doing was illegal, but that could not be determined without further investigation.

The catch was that if I turned them into the Internal Revenue Service (IRS) for further investigation, I could be sued by the company since the IRS whistle-blower laws, as they currently stand, offer no protection from civil suits. This being the case, I wondered about the purpose of having an IRS whistle-blower law at all. Obviously, I did not want to expose my family to such a risk, so I opted instead to contact my representatives in the U.S. Senate and House of Representatives to make them aware of this situation and gain their support.

Up to that point in my life, I had never contacted any member of congress. I chose to do so not because of the activities of this relatively small company, but because of the broader implications. Surely if they had figured out how to game the U.S. tax system, other much larger companies were doing the same thing. If their tactics were legal, the laws needed to be changed. If their actions were illegal, the laws needed to be enforced. Contacting my congressional representatives on this matter was quite a learning experience and a huge disappointment. Of the three U.S. congressional offices I contacted, only one responded with an offer to meet with me. Unfortunately, the person they sent to the meeting was very junior and had absolutely no idea of what I was talking about. He had no understanding of, or experience in, business. He had only worked in the senator's office since college. He was very nice and professional, but trying to explain the situation to him was like speaking Greek to someone who only understands English. Expecting that might happen, I came prepared with the slides shown below, hoping he would pass them along to someone on the senator's staff more knowledgeable about such important issues, and they would contact me for follow-up discussions.

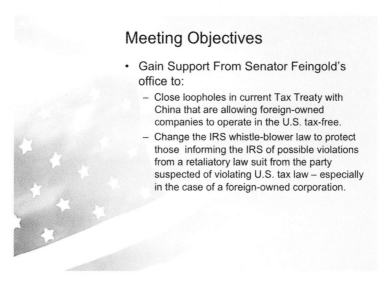

Meeting Objectives

- Gain Support From Senator Feingold's office to:
    - Close loopholes in current Tax Treaty with China that are allowing foreign-owned companies to operate in the U.S. tax-free.
    - Change the IRS whistle-blower law to protect those informing the IRS of possible violations from a retaliatory law suit from the party suspected of violating U.S. tax law – especially in the case of a foreign-owned corporation.

Foreign Companies Operating in U.S. Tax-Free

- Foreign companies are operating in the U.S. without paying any taxes using the Tax Agreement with China as cover. This agreement was ratified by the U.S. and China in 1986 under the Reagan administration.
- Enables foreign companies to compete, unfairly destroying U.S. companies, jobs, and our overall tax base.
- Foreign companies are using "shell companies" to import products and avoid detection by the IRS.

Here's How It Works...

- Company is incorporated in a country such as Singapore.
- Establishes operations and an affiliated company in China.
- Establishes "shell companies" in Malaysia and Hong Kong.
- Indirectly sets up a "shell company" in U.S. to handle import/export.
- Uses agents, who by IRS rules are really employees, to operate on its behalf in the U.S.

Product and Money Flow

Product Manufactured In China

Shipped to U.S. Through a "Shell Company"

Payment Made to an off-shore Trust in Malaysia

Possible Solutions....

- Revisit our tax agreement with China; update and amend it, with special emphasis on Article 5.
- Add language to differentiate between companies owned and operated in China from those owned by foreign entities operating in China.
- Set up a special IRS task force and recruit experienced international business executives to audit foreign companies to ensure they are complying with U.S. tax laws.

Much to my disappointment, I never heard from anyone else in Senator Feingold's office. Instead, I received the following letter, which, in my opinion, amounted to sweeping the issue under the rug and doing absolutely nothing!

RUSSELL D. FEINGOLD
WISCONSIN

506 HART SENATE OFFICE BUILDING
WASHINGTON, DC 20510
(202) 224-5323
(202) 224-1280 (TDD)
feingold.senate.gov

COMMITTEE ON THE BUDGET
COMMITTEE ON FOREIGN RELATIONS
COMMITTEE ON THE JUDICIARY
SELECT COMMITTEE ON INTELLIGENCE
DEMOCRATIC POLICY COMMITTEE

United States Senate

WASHINGTON, DC 20510-4904

April 20, 2009

John Martin

Dear Mr. Martin:

As you know, my office wrote to the Internal Revenue Service (IRS) regarding the tax avoidance and whistleblower issues you discussed with my staff.

Enclosed is a copy of the response from IRS which addresses the concerns you raised. I also enclosed some information from the Congressional Research Service (CRS) which may be of interest to you, including legislative initiatives.

Thank you for bringing this matter to my attention. I will certainly keep your situation in mind should legislation to amend these matters come before the U.S. Senate. Feel free to contact me in the future on any federal issue. All the best.

Sincerely,

Russell D. Feingold
United States Senator

RDF/mjn

enclosure

1800 ASPEN COMMONS
ROOM 100
MIDDLETON, WI 53562
(608) 828-1200
(608) 828-1215 (TDD)

517 EAST WISCONSIN AVENUE
ROOM 408
MILWAUKEE, WI 53202
(414) 276-7282

401 5TH STREET
ROOM 410
WAUSAU, WI 54403
(715) 848-5660

425 STATE STREET
ROOM 225
LA CROSSE, WI 54601
(608) 782-5585

1640 MAIN STREET
GREEN BAY, WI 54302
(920) 465-7508

PRINTED ON RECYCLED PAPER

LARGE AND MID-SIZE
BUSINESS DIVISION

DEPARTMENT OF THE TREASURY
INTERNAL REVENUE SERVICE
WASHINGTON, D.C. 20224

APR 17 2009

The Honorable Russell D. Feingold
United States Senator
425 State Street, Room 225
LA Crosse, WI 54601

Dear Senator Feingold:

I am responding to your letter of March 10, 2009, on behalf of two of your constituents. They wrote about allegations of tax avoidance through shell corporations under an international tax treaty and whistleblower protection.

We have experienced international examiners who are aware of tax issues associated with "treaty shopping" and both international and domestic "shell corporations." We have seen structures like the one you described, but each examination depends on the unique facts and circumstances of an individual case. A slight change in the facts can result in a different tax liability. In some cases, a corporation may have legitimate business motives, other than U.S. tax savings, for setting up shell corporations. We would need additional information to determine whether noncompliance has occurred in a specific case.

We take compliance with tax laws seriously, and welcome information about possible tax violations under our Whistleblower Program. This program provides rewards to a taxpayer for information that leads to additional tax collections. We protect the identity of the whistleblower to the fullest extent possible under the law. In some circumstances, such as when the whistleblower is an essential witness in a judicial proceeding, we may not be able to pursue the investigation without revealing the whistleblower's identity. We inform the whistleblower before deciding whether to proceed in such cases. The statute for this program does not include provisions to protect whistleblowers from litigation brought by their employers or through any other form of retaliation.

I hope this information is helpful. If you have any questions, please contact me at (202) 435-5000.

Sincerely,

Douglas W. O'Donnell

FOR Barry B. Shott
Deputy Commissioner (International)

I was stunned by Senator Feingold's lack of follow-up with me and the canned response I received from his office. I wondered, how could this be? Isn't my government concerned about our tax system being taken advantage of by foreign corporations? What about the damage this is doing to the U.S. economy and U.S. companies that play by the rules? Why aren't my elected representatives more interested in at least speaking with me to gain a deeper understanding of this issue? Perhaps then they could be convinced to take concrete steps to address it. Ironically, during this same period, the business my wife and I own was audited by the local IRS office. This was the first time we had ever been audited. It went well and, honestly, I was extremely impressed with the professionalism of our local IRS office. However, I did have a hard time reconciling why our small family business was being audited while foreign corporations were operating in the U.S. tax-free. That's just wrong—but it's not the fault of the IRS. Referring this matter to the IRS was not what I was asking Senator Feingold or his staff to do. I was asking that Congress close the loopholes in our laws that allow foreign corporations to game the U.S. tax system and that they change the IRS whistle-blower law to protect those informing the IRS of possible violations from a retaliatory lawsuit from the party suspected of violating U.S. tax law—especially in the case of foreign-owned corporations. Finally, I was asking the senator to ensure that the IRS has the resources necessary to enforce our international and domestic corporate tax laws. I was shocked and angered by the lack of interest shown by Senator Feingold and my other congressional representatives for this extremely important issue. I turned my shock and anger into action, and began the research that eventually led to this book. My hope is that those who read it will be motivated, as I am, to take positive action.

U.S. Corporations Operating Tax-Free

In 1909 Congress enacted an excise tax on corporations based on income. After ratification of the Sixteenth Amendment to the U.S. Constitution, this became the corporate provisions of the federal income tax. Up until that time, there was no federal income tax, except for a brief period during and after the Civil War. Prior to passage of the Sixteenth Amendment, the federal government was mostly funded by tariffs and excise taxes (like those on alcohol and tobacco products today), as illustrated in the chart below.

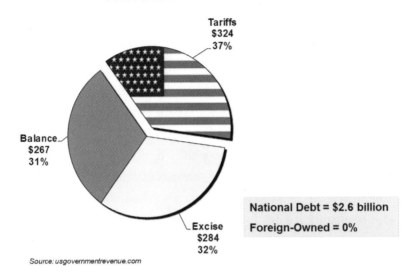

U.S. Federal Tax Receipts Fiscal Year 1910
Dollars in millions

Tariffs
$324
37%

Balance
$267
31%

Excise
$284
32%

National Debt = $2.6 billion
Foreign-Owned = 0%

Source: usgovernmentrevenue.com

Since the founding of our nation, Tariffs were used not only as the primary means of government funding, but also to protect American industry from low-cost foreign goods *(Wikipedia)*. Ironically, unlike today, it was the Republican Party that strongly supported tariffs and opposed free trade. (Theodore Roosevelt once wrote, "Thank God I am not a free trader," and the Republican Party platform of 1904 stated: "Protection, which guards and develops our industries, is a cardinal policy of the Republican Party. The measure of protection should always at least equal the difference in the cost of production at home and abroad.") Tariffs were vital to allowing American manufacturing to take root and develop. There were, however, serious abuses of the tariff system that angered many U.S. citizens at the turn of the twentieth century. Public demands for reform of the tariff system resulted in the passage of the Sixteenth Amendment and enactment of the Revenue Act of 1913 (also known as the Tariff Act, Underwood Tariff, Underwood Tariff Act, or Underwood-Simmons Act). The act lowered basic tariff rates from 40 percent to 25 percent, and established the federal income tax. The purpose of the federal income tax was to offset the tax revenues lost by reducing the tariff rates. This strategy worked better than intended, as the revenues generated by the federal income tax soon dwarfed those generated from tariffs. When the federal income tax was first implemented, the majority of the revenues generated came from corporate taxes. For instance, of the $4 billion in total income taxes paid in 1920, 53 percent came from corporations and 47 percent from individuals. The dominance of corporate income taxes remained true through the 1940s. As you can see on the accompanying chart, by 1950 the tables had turned and the percentage of tax revenues paid by corporations had dropped to 25 percent as compared to 37 percent coming from individuals.

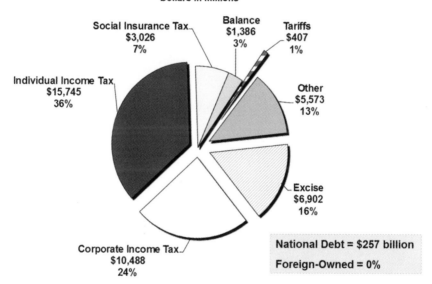

U.S. Federal Tax Receipts Fiscal Year 1950
Dollars in millions

Social Insurance Tax $3,026 7%

Balance $1,386 3%

Tariffs $407 1%

Individual Income Tax $15,745 36%

Other $5,573 13%

Excise $6,902 16%

National Debt = $257 billion
Foreign-Owned = 0%

Corporate Income Tax $10,488 24%

Source: usgovernmentrevenue.com

But Americans in the 1950s didn't seem to mind since the nation was booming economically. Also, even though individuals were contributing more in income taxes, corporations were still paying their fair share through fees, excise, and other forms of taxation. Collectively, Americans viewed paying taxes as their civic duty. Nobody enjoyed paying taxes but it was understood that it was necessary to ensure our society had the resources needed to serve the common good. This attitude began to unravel in the 1960s and only accelerated in the 1970s and 1980s. U.S. corporations began finding ways to avoid both federal and state taxes. They employed high-powered Washington lobbyists and contributed heavily to the campaigns of both major political parties to get loopholes added to the tax code that allowed corporations to legally avoid paying taxes. Many of the largest U.S. corporations no longer viewed paying taxes as their civic duty, but instead looked for ways to outwit the system and avoid paying taxes altogether. By 2010 the corporate income tax share fell to 8.9 percent—the lowest in seventy-five years—as illustrated in the following charts.

In the 1950s, corporate taxes accounted for 27% of U.S. revenue. By 2010, that percentage decreased to less than 10%.

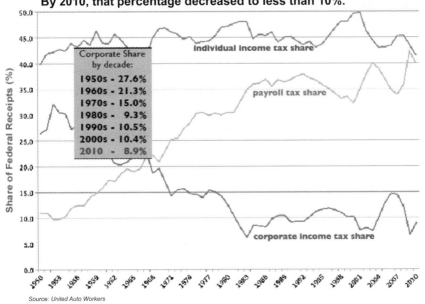

Corporate Share
by decade:

1950s - 27.6%
1960s - 21.3%
1970s - 15.0%
1980s - 9.3%
1990s - 10.5%
2000s - 10.4%
2010 - 8.9%

Source: United Auto Workers

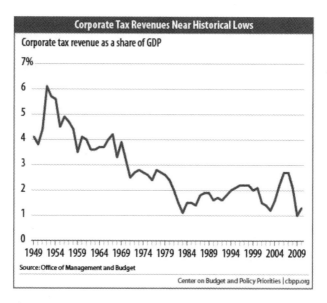

This reduction in corporate taxes was not due to a decrease in earnings. On the contrary, in 2010 U.S. corporations were registering record profits. At the end of that year, U.S. corporations posted an annualized profit of $1.65 trillion in the fourth quarter *(Huffington Post)*.

According to a report published by Citizens for Tax Justice in November 2011 *(McIntyre, Gardner, and Wilkins)*, thirty companies including General Electric, Verizon Communications, and The Boeing Company didn't pay federal income tax between 2008 and 2010, though they earned a combined $160.3 billion in pretax U.S. profits during that period. The report analyzed the taxes paid by Fortune 500 companies that were profitable between 2008 and 2010. Of the 280 companies analyzed, 40 percent—or 111 firms—paid an effective tax rate of less than 17.5 percent, which is half of the top U.S. corporate tax rate of 35 percent . Also, of the 280 companies studied, 78 paid a tax rate of zero or less during at least one year of the three-year period. Even worse, many of these same companies spent more on lobbying than they paid in taxes, as detailed in another report published in late 2011 by Public Campaign *(Public Campaign)*, a nonprofit, nonpartisan organization that seeks widespread campaign reform to reduce the impact of special-interest money on our political system. Here is a list of these companies.

30 U.S. Corporations That Paid More For Lobbying Than Taxes

All figures in millions. Cumulative from 2008-10				All figures in millions. Cumulative from 2008-10			
Company	Profits	Taxes	Paid Lobbying	Company	Profits	Taxes	Paid Lobbying
General Electric	$10,460	($4,737)	$84.35	Wisconsin Energy	$1,725	($85)	$2.45
PG&E Corp	$4,855	($1,027)	$78.99	DuPont	$2,124	($72)	$13.75
Verizon Communications	$32,518	($951)	$52.34	Baxter International	$926	($66)	$10.45
Wells Fargo	$49,370	($681)	$11.04	Tenet Healthcare	$415	($48)	$3.43
American Electric Power	$5,899	($545)	$28.85	Ryder System	$627	($46)	$0.96
Pepco Holdings	$882	($508)	$3.76	El Paso	$4,105	($41)	$2.94
Computer Sciences	$1,666	($305)	$4.39	Honeywell International	$4,903	($34)	$18.30
CenterPoint Energy	$1,931	($284)	$2.65	CMS Energy	$1,292	($29)	$3.48
NiSource	$1,385	($227)	$17.47	ConLway	$286	($26)	$2.29
Duke Energy	$5,475	($216)	$17.47	Navistar International	$896	($18)	$6.31
Boeing	$9,735	($178)	$52.29	DTE Energy	$2,551	($17)	$4.37
NextEra Energy	$6,403	($139)	$9.99	Interpublic Group	$571	($15)	$1.30
Consolidated Edison	$4,263	($127)	$1.79	Mattel	$1,020	($4)	$2.81
Paccar	$365	($112)	$0.76	Corning	$1,977	($4)	$2.81
Integrys Energy Group	$818	($92)	$2.45	FedEx	$4,247	$37	$50.81

Source: *Public Campaign Report, December 2011*

Not only have U.S. and foreign corporations rigged our income tax system in their favor, they have also totally destroyed our tariff system so that foreign-produced goods are allowed to enter the U.S. unabated and relatively tax-free. Recall for a moment that back in 1913, tariffs were reduced from 40 percent to 25 percent in favor of a more liberalized trading policy. In 2011 the average U.S. tariff rate is 1.3 percent ! In effect, there is no U.S. tariff. This outcome is a direct result of lobbying by U.S. and foreign corporate interests to fully exploit low-cost labor in communist China, India, Mexico, and other parts of the world to off-shore and outsource the production of goods for sale in the U.S. market. All of this is being done under the cover of free trade. I am confident that this was not the intent of either the Democrats or Republicans in 1913 when they passed the Sixteenth Amendment. The combination of U.S. and foreign corporations gaming our tax system along with the elimination of tariffs under the myth of free trade is bankrupting our treasury and destroying American manufacturing and our overall economy. This destruction is driving the collapse of middle-class America and causing our national debt to skyrocket.

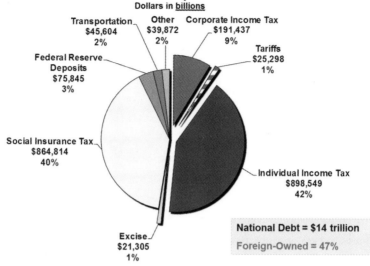

U.S. Federal Tax Receipts Fiscal Year 2010
Dollars in <u>billions</u>

Transportation $45,604 2%

Other $39,872 2%

Corporate Income Tax $191,437 9%

Tariffs $25,298 1%

Federal Reserve Deposits $75,845 3%

Social Insurance Tax $864,814 40%

Individual Income Tax $898,549 42%

Excise $21,305 1%

National Debt = $14 trillion
Foreign-Owned = 47%

Source: usgovernmentrevenue.com

If you compare the 2010 chart to those showing tax receipts in 1910 and 1950, a few things become apparent:

- A drastic decline in the share of taxes paid by corporations.

- A steep decline in tariffs being collected by U.S. customs.

- A significant decline in excise taxes collected.

- A growth of social insurance taxes.

- The skyrocketing national debt.

- The high percentage of U.S. debt now owned by foreign interests.

The significant decline in the share of taxes paid by corporations has added significantly to our national debt. In 2010, while the U.S. had not one, but two wars in progress (in Iraq and Afghanistan, which have both lasted twice as long as World War II), corporate tax collections averaged 1.3 percent of our gross domestic product. During WWII it was 5.7 percent, three times the 2010 rate. This is significant, since each percentage point equals roughly $150 billion in uncollected taxes *(Barlett and Steele)*. Imagine how far that money would have gone toward paying for these wars. Instead, we borrowed money from communist China and simply added it to our skyrocketing national debt.

Those who say U.S. corporations face one of the highest income tax rates in the world are speaking in half-truths and propagating another myth. That kind of political speak is intentionally designed to mislead the public into believing U.S. corporations pay too much in taxes and that we are uncompetitive compared to corporations based elsewhere. This is simply not true. While the 35 percent corporate income tax rate is high by comparison, the actual rate paid by U.S. corporations is among the lowest in the world. In 2007, U.S. companies paid an average of 13.4 percent in taxes, the fifth-lowest rate in the developed world.

U.S. corporations have become experts at hiding profits in tax havens overseas. Many smaller corporations avoid paying taxes by simply passing through their income to owners, who then report it on their personal returns. According to a 2008 Government Accountability Office report *(U.S. GAO)*, eighty-

U.S. Average Corporate Taxes Low By International Standards

Average Corporate Tax Rates (2000-2005)

Australia	30.5%
United Kingdom	27.7%
France	20.0%
Portugal	17.2%
Belgium	17.1%
Spain	16.7%
Japan	16.4%
Finland	16.2%
Czech Republic	15.7%
Denmark	15.0%
Greece	15.0%
Canada	14.5%
Switzerland	14.4%
Korea	14.3%
United States	13.4%
Slovak Republic	11.5%
Poland	11.3%
Austria	11.2%
Germany	7.2%

Source: Treasury Department (2007)
Center on Budget and Policy Priorities | cbpp.org

three of the one hundred largest publicly traded U.S. corporations reported having subsidiaries in countries that don't tax corporate profits. They use the subsidiaries to hide profits and avoid U.S. taxes. The giant drug company Abbott Laboratories reported thirty-six such tax-haven subsidiaries; ExxonMobil has thirty-two, and the banking giant Citigroup has four hundred twenty-seven! Countless other companies such as GE, Apple, Google, Cisco, HP, Pfizer, Lilly, Oracle, Facebook, and Microsoft use the same tax strategies—reducing their tax rates by hundreds of millions, and in some cases, billions of dollars. GE employs an entire team of former IRS and Treasury officials, dubbed the "world's best tax law firm" *(Kocieniewski)*, to make sure profits are recorded in tax havens, tax breaks are maximized, and laws passed on Capitol Hill are favorable to its interests.

In early 2011, it was estimated that U.S. corporations had $1.2 trillion of profits tucked away in their overseas accounts. This is earned income these companies are supposed to pay U.S. taxes on, less a credit for any income taxes already paid overseas, when the money is brought back home. However, corporations use a number of techniques to bring back their profits without paying any U.S. tax, or they leave them overseas and borrow against them to avoid paying U.S. taxes. Many of these same corporations are lobbying Congress to pass a tax loophole known as a repatriation tax holiday, which would allow them to bring their overseas money back into the U.S. at a greatly reduced tax rate. In exchange, the companies argue, companies would invest those dollars in the U.S. and create jobs. On the surface this sounds good, but a similar "tax holiday" was passed in 2004 and it did little to boost employment growth. In fact, the corporations that benefited most from the 2004 tax holiday cut nearly half a million jobs in the following years. Most of the money repatriated in 2004 was used to buy back company stock—not to create new jobs *(Bradford)*.

We, the citizens of the United States, must end this perversion of our tax system and as Theodore Roosevelt said, "effectively control the mighty commercial forces which [we] have called into being." Furthermore, we must eliminate the "neutral ground" he identified, that "serve[s] as a refuge for lawbreakers, and especially for lawbreakers of great wealth, who can hire the vulpine legal cunning which will teach them how to avoid both jurisdictions." We need to eliminate the havens of "neutral ground" for both U.S. and foreign-owned corporations. We must also revitalize our tariff system so that it once again provides significant revenues and does not support the offshoring and outsourcing of U.S. manufacturing. Finally, it is time to remind U.S. corporations of their civic duties—which include paying taxes—and place them firmly again "under the real, not the nominal, control of some sovereign to which, as its creatures, the trusts owe allegiance, and in whose courts the sovereign's orders may be enforced." We must change our tax laws to ensure that foreign corporations operating in the U.S. are also paying taxes comparable to those paid by U.S. corporations. This is our country and it is time to restore it by putting America and Americans first again! The final chapter of this book discusses these issues further along with actions that we can take.

A Conspiracy of Silence

Have you noticed that the 2012 election cycle has included little or no talk about our trade policies? Neither major political party is talking about the damage these policies have done and are continuing to do to the U.S. economy. Despite the dismal failure of NAFTA, both the Democrats and Republicans apparently remain committed to this approach and are proceeding with additional free-trade agreements. There is no discussion of our record trade deficits—only our national debt—even though the two are directly linked. It is as though the record U.S. trade deficits either don't exist or don't matter. Why do you think that is? I believe it's because the wealthiest among us are profiting handsomely from the outsourcing and offshoring we are doing with China, India, Mexico, and other countries that are masquerading as free trade. The establishment, including our media, has fully bought into the free-trade myth because they are profiting as well.

The Republicans and the Democrats are using their propaganda machines to suppress all discussions of our trade policies. They want to avoid such a discussion at all costs, because those with the money and power to fund their campaigns are profiting from selling out America. They fear a backlash from the American public if they figure out what is really going on. This is also why the unemployment numbers in the U.S. are being grossly underreported and why there is absolutely no reporting of the number of underemployed Americans (i.e., working less than forty hours a week and/or in jobs that pay much less than what they previously earned or are qualified to earn). By some estimates, the real unemployment rate in January 2012 was over 20 percent, not the 8.5 percent illustrated below.

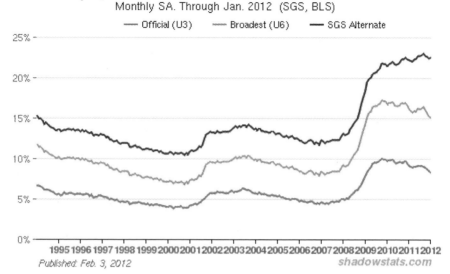

Unemployment Rate - Official (U-3 & U-6) vs SGS Alternate
Monthly SA. Through Jan. 2012 (SGS, BLS)

—— Official (U3) ——— Broadest (U6) —— SGS Alternate

Published: Feb. 3, 2012   *shadowstats.com*

When you add the underemployment rate, which is estimated to be at least 21 percent, it becomes clear that the U.S. economy is in much worse shape than acknowledged by either major political party. There is also very little discussion now about the collapse of Wall Street and the resulting Great Recession, a term I believe is a misnomer, a semantic flourish that avoids using the more accurate term *depression*. Both of these crises are directly linked to our failed trade policies. I am convinced that Wal-Mart, the world's largest corporation, Wall Street banks, and other large U.S. and foreign corporations are playing a very active role behind the scenes funding the propaganda machines to suppress these discussions. These corporations are reaping huge profits from our misguided trade policies and they do not want any changes that would disrupt their supply of cheap labor and goods from China, India, Mexico, and other low-cost foreign countries. Let's raise up our voices together to break this damaging silence at Selling-US-Out.com!

CHAPTER SEVEN

The Decline of U.S. Manufacturing

A Government-and Wall Street–Sponsored Exodus of U.S. Manufacturing

Our nation's industrial base and economy has been devastated over the past three decades as financial engineering has replaced the invention, design, and manufacturing of products. This has been driven by America's political and economic elite who argue the country does not need an industrial base. It is no coincidence that the same people who are telling us we don't need an industrial base are lining their pockets with gold as more factories and jobs are shipped overseas and the de-industrialization of America accelerates.

Worse yet, our government has been actively promoting and participating in the de-industrialization process with misguided, ill-advised, and weak-willed trade and globalization policies that are driven by ideology rather than sound business principles and common sense. Despite decades of so-called free-trade agreements, foreign markets still remain closed to U.S. exports while the U.S. market is wide open and being fully exploited. The U.S. government has also failed miserably at combating predatory foreign trade practices aimed at undermining U.S. manufacturers in their home market. Instead, the government's solution has been to encourage and support U.S. manufacturers in moving their factories, and supplying the U.S. market, from low-cost third-world countries such as Mexico, India, and China. This approach has also been driven by greedy Wall Street financial institutions and venture capital firms with no regard for the long-term impact on the U.S. economy. U.S. multinational corporations, and many of their suppliers, have responded by closing tens of thousands of U.S. factories and relocating to China, Mexico, India, and other third-world countries. The products of these factories are then exported back to the United States. U.S. factory closures as a result of problematic trade policies are reflected in the U.S. manufacturing employment numbers and the continuing decline

THE LAST TIME FEWER THAN 12 MILLION PEOPLE WORKED IN THE MANUFACTURING SECTOR WAS 1941

of family incomes. Manufacturing jobs tallied to 11.6 million in January 2011, a loss of 7.7 million or 40 percent of all manufacturing jobs since January 1980. The last time fewer than 12 million people worked in the manufacturing sector was 1941. In January 2011 more people were officially unemployed (13.9 million) than were working in manufacturing *(McCormack)*.

When a factory closes, not only are manufacturing jobs eliminated but also jobs in companies supplying goods and services to the factory. According to a study done by the Milken Institute, every computer-manufacturing job in California creates an estimated fifteen jobs outside the factory *(DeVol, Wong, and Bedroussian)*. This means that when computer manufacturers close a factory with 10,000 employees they are eliminating up to 150,000 jobs! The closures hurt dozens of companies such as those supplying design and business software; automation and robotics equipment; packaging, office equipment, and supplies; telecommunications services; energy and water utilities; research and development, marketing, and sales support; building and equipment maintenance; and janitorial services. The economic pain of factory closures is also spread to local businesses like restaurants, theaters, and shopping outlets—and diminishes the tax base that supports police, firemen, schoolteachers, and libraries. This is not theoretical; the evidence can be seen in cities and towns across America such as Detroit, Michigan, where the poverty and crime rates are the highest in the nation. People in Detroit are now cultivating urban farms in abandoned city lots and around foreclosed homes because these properties are so numerous and cannot be sold. This shrinking tax base and loss of tax revenue has prompted vigorous debate on taxes and spending in the 2012 election cycle. Unfortunately, there is little to no discussion about our failed trade policies, which are the root cause of the shrinking tax base. Hopefully this book will play a small role in helping bring this important issue to the forefront of our national consciousness.

Unless drastic measures are taken quickly to reverse the decline of U.S. manufacturing, the United States will turn into a second-class manufacturing power, with a drastically lower standard of living for all but the wealthiest among us. Also, our nation's ability to defend itself will be severely compromised, as will our influence around the world. Increased consumer spending alone will not put Americans back to work. Without U.S. manufacturing:

1. Our nation's trade deficit will continue to grow along with our national debt.

2. The middle class will shrink and perhaps disappear.

3. Our nation will be increasingly dependent on foreign manufacturers even for its key military technology.

4. The U.S. will eventually lose its position as the world's largest economy and its power and influence will diminish.

5. There will be no economic ladder stretching upward for those stranded in low-paying service-sector jobs.

A former Asian business associate once told me he could not believe how naïve the U.S. was in allowing such open access to our markets. He said no Asian country would ever do the same. However, he also admitted the reason his company and Asia overall was doing so well is that they were taking full advantage of this situation. I don't believe naïveté is driving U.S. trade policy. No, what's driving our trade policy is a combination of misguided political ideology and greed. It sickens me that many who make a show of wearing U.S. flag pins on their lapels to display their supposed patriotism are at the same time promoting and profiting from the misguided trade policies that are destroying our industrial base and the country they claim to love!

As my former business associate attested, export-driven Asian countries view trade as a strictly competitive game, with a piece of the American domestic market as the prize. They also view our promotion of free trade since 1945 as foolishness, but are happy to exploit the agreements to their advantage. Ironically, our country had the same opinion of free trade for our first 160 years, as illustrated by Teddy Roosevelt's 1904 campaign platform, which read: "Protection, which guards and develops our industries, is a cardinal policy of the Republican Party. The measure of protection should always at least equal the difference in the cost of production at home and abroad." It was upon this foundation that the U.S. built its wealth and became the world's largest and most successful economy.

U.S. De-Industrialization—Not a Recent Phenomenon

For American manufacturers, the bad years didn't begin with the banking crisis of 2008. The seeds for the decline of American manufacturing were sown after World War II when the U.S. government adopted free-trade principles and began working with the British government to create a global free-trading system. Free trade was not a new idea. On the contrary, the British Empire had been pushing their former American colony to adopt free trade since the end of the Revolutionary War. The British used free trade throughout the nineteenth century to control their colonies, and they were intent on undermining American independence using the same tactics. In a speech delivered by England's Lord Henry Brougham to the British Parliament, on April 9, 1816, he stated that "it is well worth while to incur a loss upon the first exportation [of English manufactures], in order, by the glut, TO STIFLE IN THE CRADLE

THOSE RISING MANUFACTURES IN THE UNITED STATES"
(Clark). Lord Brougham was advocating destroying America's infant industries by flooding the U.S. market with low-cost goods through "free trade."
The U.S. resisted pressure from Britain to adopt free trade until 1945. The
reason was simple: we understood that America's political independence
was directly linked to our economic independence. As Alexander
Hamilton wrote:

> "Not only the wealth, but the independence and security of
> a country, appear to be materially connected with the prosperity
> of manufactures. Every nation. . . ought to endeavor to posses
> within itself all the essentials of a national supply. These comprise
> the means of subsistence, habitation, clothing and defense."

America's political independence, Hamilton was saying, could not
survive without economic independence. This is as true today as it was over
two hundred years ago. However, in 1945 the U.S. was feeling invincible; the
Democratic Party, which supported free trade, was in power; and our government assumed that we no longer needed to protect our markets or industries
as we had during the previous 160 years. At first, this seemed like a valid
assumption, as U.S. manufacturers were able to prosper in the postwar global
economy. However, this started to change in the 1960s as Japan, Germany,
and other countries that rebuilt themselves after the war, with our assistance,
began exporting to the U.S. While our government opened up the U.S.
market to imports under free-trade agreements, other countries, such as
Japan, Korea, and China, kept their markets closed to U.S. manufacturers
while fully exploiting openness to their exports. This continues today and the
result has been catastrophic! Here are some quick facts:

1. In 1959 manufacturing represented 28 percent of all U.S.
   economic output. In 2008 it represented only 11.5 percent, and it
   continues to fall.

2. In 1970 25 percent of all jobs in the U.S. were manufacturing jobs.
   Today only 9 percent of jobs in the U.S. are manufacturing jobs.

3. More than 42,000 U.S. factories have closed since 2001.

4. The U.S. has lost a staggering 32 percent of its manufacturing jobs since the year 2000.

5. Between 1999 and 2008 U.S. multinational companies added 2.4 million jobs at their foreign affiliates, while eliminating 2.8 million jobs in the U.S.

6. The Bureau of Labor Statistics predicted that the U.S. economy would create 22 million jobs between 2000 and 2010. The U.S. economy created only 7 million jobs during that period, which represents the lowest rate of U.S. job growth since the 1940s.

7. China is now the world's largest exporter of high-technology products. In 1998, the U.S. had 25 percent of the world's high-tech export market and China had just 10 percent. In 2008, the U.S. had less than 15 percent and China's share soared to 20 percent.

8. Manufacturing employment in the U.S. computer industry is lower in 2010 than it was in 1975.

9. Japan is now the world's largest manufacturer of automobiles, producing about five million more than American manufacturers in 2009.

10. For most of the twentieth century the U.S. dominated the global automotive industry. In 2008 the U.S. was the third-largest manufacturer of automobiles, behind China and Japan.

11. The cell phone was invented in the U.S. by Motorola. In 2008, 1.2 billion cell phones were sold worldwide—none were manufactured in the U.S.

12. The U.S. steel industry produced 91.5 million tons of steel in 2008, down from 97.4 million tons in 1999. By comparison, China's steel industry produced 500 million tons in 2008, more than five times the amount of U.S. producers and up from the 124 million tons it produced in 1999, despite the far greater efficiency of U.S. steel production.

Long before the banking collapse of 2008, such important U.S. industries as machine tools, consumer electronics, auto parts, appliances, furniture, telecommunications equipment, and many others that had once dominated the global marketplace suffered their own economic collapse *(McCormack)*. The proponents of free trade argue that these industries collapsed as a result of the free-market forces because American industry could not compete globally. This is nonsense. American companies are among the most efficient in the world. The nation's steel industry, for instance, produces a ton of steel in two man-hours. A comparable ton of steel in China is produced with twelve man-hours. The same kinds of comparisons are true in other industries.

So why are so many American companies having difficulty? Because they are competing against foreign companies based in countries that undervalue their currencies; provide health care for their workers; provide subsidies for energy, land, buildings, and equipment; grant tax holidays and rebates; provide zero-interest loans; pay their workers poverty wages that would be illegal in the U.S.; and don't enforce safety or environmental regulations. U.S. multinational companies have taken the "if you can't beat 'em, join 'em" approach, which is why they have shut down factories and eliminated jobs in the U.S. and opened factories and created millions of jobs in China, India, and other countries. In fairness, this is partly due to a lack of a U.S. manufacturing strategy and industrial policy that fosters collaboration between government and industry, similar to the approach used in East Asia since World War II. In the absence of such policies and support, U.S. companies have had to go it alone, and do their best to survive against foreign competition in a so-called free market that is only free in the U.S. and nowhere else. As a result, many U.S. multinational companies are acting against the economic interests of the United States to ensure their own survival. This dynamic is being fully exploited by foreign governments and foreign-owned corporations that are waging an economic war against the U.S. Those who deny that economic war is being waged against America are either ignoring or distorting the facts.

The list of U.S. industries lost to foreign countries—primarily the countries of Asia—over the past sixty years is extensive, and it continues to grow at an unprecedented rate. As these industries have left our shores, so have the high-wage jobs and the tax revenues they provided. The list of industries and resulting job losses include the consumer electronics, automotive, steel, semiconductor, and computer industries. In 1978, the U.S. was home to seven of the world's top ten companies. These companies employed 2.3 million people, with more than half being employed by GM and Ford. GM was the leading company worldwide, both in terms of revenue and number of employees.

Top 20 Global Companies in 1978

COUNTRY	COMPANY	RANK	EMPLOYEES	SALES ($ billions)
US	GM	1	839,000	63
US	Exxon	2	130,000	60
Neth	Royal Dutch/Shell	3	158,000	44
US	Ford	4	506,531	43
US	Mobil	5	407,700	35
US	Texaco	6	67,841	29
UK	BP	7	109,000	27
US	Standard Oil	8	37,575	23
IR	National Iran Oil	9	67,000	23
US	IBM	10	325,517	21
US	GE	11	401,000	20
UK	Unilever	12	318,000	19
US	Gulf Oil	13	58,300	18
US	Chrysler	14	157,958	16
US	IT&T	15	379,000	15
Neth	Philips	16	387,900	15
US	Standard Oil (Indiana)	17	47,011	15
GR	Siemens	18	322,000	14
GR	Volkswagen	19	206,948	13
JP	Toyota	20	60,846	13
Source: *Fortune* Magazine, May 15, 1979.				

Moving ahead to 2011, we see that the U.S. is now home to only three of the world's top ten companies. These three companies also employ a total of 2.3 million people. However, 2.1 million are employed by Wal-Mart alone (1.4 million in the U.S.), with the balance employed by Exxon and Chevron.

Top 20 Global Companies in 2011

COUNTRY	COMPANY	RANK	EMPLOYEES	SALES ($ billions)
US/CHINA	Wal-Mart Stores	1	2,100,000	422
Neth	Royal Dutch Shell	2	97,000	378
US	Exxon Mobil	3	103,700	355
UK	BP	4	79,700	309
CH	Sinopec Group	5	640,535	273
CH	China National Petroleum	6	1,674,541	240
CH	State Grid	7	1,564,000	226
JP	Toyota Motor	8	317,716	222
JP	Japan Post Holdings	9	233,000	204
US	Chevron	10	62,196	196
FR	Total	11	92,855	186
US	ConocoPhillips	12	29,700	185
GR	Volkswagen	13	399,381	168
FR	AXA	14	102,957	162
US	Fannie Mae	15	7,300	154
US	General Electric	16	287,000	152
Neth	ING Group	17	106,139	147
Swiss	Glencore International	18	57,656	145
US	Berkshire Hathaway	19	260,519	136
US	General Motors	20	202,000	136
US	Chrysler	205	51,623	42

Source: CNNMoney.com, Global 500, July 25, 2011.

To call Wal-Mart a U.S. company is debatable. In truth, they operate more like a Chinese retail and distribution channel that is headquartered in the U.S., since their sales are primarily the result of selling low-cost products imported from communist China. It is also well documented that they use their economic power to force U.S. companies to move their manufacturing operations to China. The contrast between GM (ranked first in 1978) and Wal-Mart (ranked first in 2011) could not be any starker. The comparison paints a pretty clear picture of what is driving the decline in U.S. manufacturing and its impact on American families.

	General Motors	Wal-Mart
Business Model	Manufacturer who, in 1978, produced its cars and trucks in the U.S. and Canada.	Retailer selling products that are primarily manufactured in China.
Wages	The average U.S. autoworker makes $29 an hour, or $51,198 per year.	The average Wal-Mart "associate" makes $11.75 an hour, or $20,744 per year.
Health Insurance	Provides affordable health insurance to its workers and their families.	Does not provide affordable health insurance to its employees. In fact, a substantial number of Wal-Mart associates are uninsured and enrolled in publicly-funded Medicaid.
Economic Impact	Purchases high-value goods and services from other U.S. manufacturers, who in turn hire U.S. workers and pay them wages similar to those paid by GM.	Wal-Mart sources the majority of the products it sells from communist China and forces other U.S. companies to do the same—destroying hundreds of thousands of U.S. manufacturing jobs.
Social Impact	GM and its suppliers played a major role in creating middle-class America after World War II.	Wal-Mart and its suppliers are playing a major role in destroying middle-class America by forcing offshoring and outsourcing.

Wal-Mart's De-Industrialization of Ohio

Between 2001 and 2004 Ohio lost 170,000 manufacturing jobs, which was a decline of 17 percent. Wal-Mart played a key role in these job losses by pressuring U.S. manufacturers to close factories in Ohio and relocate to China. Here are the emblematic stories of three Ohio companies as told in a paper entitled *Wal-Mart Imports From China, Exports Ohio Jobs* published by the AFL-CIO in September 2005 *(Cornell University ILR School).*

Rubbermaid

Rubbermaid was formed in Wooster, Ohio, in 1920. In 1993 and 1994, the Rubbermaid company and its products were so highly regarded that Rubbermaid was voted the nation's most-admired company. At about the same time, Rubbermaid went from selling nothing to Wal-Mart one year to having Wal-Mart as one of its largest customers the next. That was until the price of raw materials used to make plastics increased by about 80 percent and Rubbermaid tried to get a price increase for its products to offset the increased cost. Wal-Mart refused their request. A former Rubbermaid executive explained that Wal-Mart's answer was, "Yes, you may be Rubbermaid and you're big Rubbermaid and you got the great name and all that, but you're not going to tell us what to do. We're not going to take your price increase, and we don't care what it does to you." Wal-Mart promptly dropped a number of Rubbermaid products and replaced them with goods molded by their competitors, Sterilite, for example. Rubbermaid's earnings plummeted 30 percent in 1995, and Newell, a major competitor based in Atlanta, scooped up the struggling company in 1999. In 2003, Newell announced the closure of Rubbermaid's flagship factory in Wooster, Ohio, eliminating 850 jobs and moving out another 400 administrative jobs. Rubbermaid had played an integral role in the city of Wooster for over eighty years and the shock was profound and devastating.

Rubbermaid's contributions to the city far exceeded the jobs it created. The company and its workers were among the biggest taxpayers in the city—Wooster's city finance director said Rubbermaid's employees accounted for about 7 percent of the city's annual tax receipts. The school district was hit hard and lost $1 million a year in taxes once the plant closed. Ninety of the 600 employees in the Wooster City School District were laid off and one of its elementary schools was shut down because of lost tax revenues. Wooster is now considering closing more schools due to financial constraints.

Thomson Electronics (RCA)

In late 2003, French-owned Thomson Consumer Electronics closed its RCA television-manufacturing plant in Circleville, Ohio, after losing orders from Sanyo. Sanyo was under enormous pressure from Wal-Mart to bring down its prices. The Circleville factory was one of the last remnants of RCA, the former U.S. company that pioneered and once dominated the television and consumer electronics industries. Ironically, the final death blow to this former RCA factory was being delivered by Sanyo, a Japanese company that helped destroy the U.S. consumer electronics industry, and Wal-Mart, China's direct distribution channel into the U.S. consumer market.

As a result of this factory closure, nearly 1,000 workers in Circleville lost their jobs. Meanwhile, Thomson's imports of big-screen TVs made in Asia grew about 38 percent to four million units in 2003. While it was shutting its RCA plant in Ohio, Thomson was planning strategic partnerships and developing a plan to spin off its business to a Chinese television manufacturer, TCL, which it did in late 2003. RCA-branded televisions are now manufactured in China by TCL. Ironically, Wal-Mart built a Supercenter on a patch of land close to the RCA plant it had pressured Thompson to close. The retail jobs created by this new Wal-Mart store are far fewer and pay much less than the manufacturing jobs that were displaced. They also do not offer families the same health insurance and pension benefits.

Huffy Bikes

Huffy sells its bicycles through high-volume retailers that account for about 85 percent of all wheeled products sold in the U.S. Pressure from Wal-Mart—the largest seller of bicycles in the country—to lower the cost of its bikes forced Huffy to close its plant in Celina, Ohio, and move these jobs to China. John Mariotti, former president of Huffy, said Wal-Mart "is tough as nails. But they give you a chance to compete. If you can't compete, that's your problem." In the end, Huffy could not compete, and U.S. workers suffered. In June 2005, Huffy announced plans to have the federal government take over paying its retirement benefits and reached an agreement on reorganization that would give Huffy's Chinese suppliers controlling interest in the company. The former mayor of Celina, Paul Arnold, explained that Wal-Mart's demand for cheaper bicycles drove Huffy out of Celina and into such sweatshops as the Baoan Bicycle Factory in southern China.

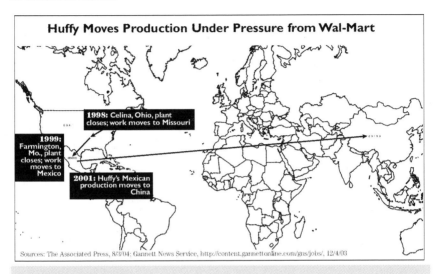

Huffy Moves Production Under Pressure from Wal-Mart

1998: Celina, Ohio, plant closes; work moves to Missouri

1999: Farmington, Mo., plant closes; work moves to Mexico

2001: Huffy's Mexican production moves to China

Sources: The Associated Press, 8/3/04; Gannett News Service, http://content.gannettonline.com/gns/jobs/, 12/4/03

Wal-Mart Pushes Huffy Downhill

1954: Huffy opens the Celina, Ohio, plant. At its peak, the plant produced a million bikes a year.

1998: Pressure from Wal-Mart forces Huffy to close the bicycle plant in Celina, putting 1,100 employees out of work. The jobs were moved to a non-union factory in Missouri.

1999: Huffy, pressured to continue lowering costs, closes its last two U.S. bicycle plants—in Farmington, Missouri, and Southaven, Mississippi. The move eliminates 600 jobs. The company contracts with factories in Mexico and China.

2001: Huffy ends its manufacturing contracts with Mexico and begins relying almost entirely on factories in China, where Chinese workers earn only 33 cents an hour and frequently work seven days a week.

Sources: Associated Press, 8/3/04; Gannett News Service, http://content. gannettonline.com/gns/jobs/

This pattern has been repeated by Wal-Mart countless times across America and has destroyed hundreds of thousands of U.S. manufacturing jobs. Wal-Mart has prospered enormously through its partnership with communist China while doing catastrophic damage to U.S. manufacturing and our overall economy. They have exploited and been the primary beneficiaries of our misguided trade policies. All that being said, Wal-Mart is not the problem—they are merely a very visible and powerful symptom of the problem. The problem is our misguided trade policies and the lack of a cohesive industrial policy and manufacturing strategy that puts U.S. national interests and security above all else.

As GM Goes, So Goes the Nation

Such was the conventional wisdom back in 1978 when GM was the largest company in the world dominating the auto industry along with Ford and Chrysler—the Big Three. In 1978, the Big Three directly employed 1.5 million people and indirectly supported millions more high-paying U.S. manufacturing jobs. Ford was the fourth-largest company in the world, Chrysler was ranked fourteenth, and Toyota was twentieth. GM's sales were about five times those of Toyota, Ford's about three-and-a-half times, and Chrysler's sales were just slightly higher than Toyota's. However, as discussed in chapter two, Japan Inc. had a national strategy for overtaking the U.S. auto industry, similar to their plan to dominate the U.S. consumer electronics industry, and they executed it with deadly precision. In 2011, the Big Three employed 418,000 people—less than one-third of its employee total in 1978. Toyota is now the largest auto manufacturer in the world, with sales that are five times that of Chrysler's and almost double those of both GM and Ford. In the 2011 Global Fortune 500, Toyota is ranked eighth, GM is twentieth, Ford is twenty-fifth, and Chrysler trails far behind at 205th! Toyota has crushed the Big Three and destroyed millions of high-paying U.S. manufacturing jobs in the process.

Japanese Assembly Plants in the U.S.—Trojan Horses

The metaphor of the Trojan horse comes out of a tale from the Trojan War about the strategy that allowed the Greeks to finally enter the heavily protected city of Troy and conquer it. After an unproductive ten-year siege on the city of Troy, the Greeks constructed a huge wooden horse and hid soldiers inside. The Greeks pretended to sail away, and the Trojans pulled the horse into their city as a victory trophy. That night the Greek soldiers crept out of the horse and opened the gates for the rest of their army, which had sailed back under cover of night. The Greeks entered and destroyed the city of Troy, decisively ending the war. The Japanese, being good students of history, have used a similar strategy to invade the U.S. market and take over the consumer electronics and automotive industries. They were also able to divide and conquer by having states compete against each other for Japanese assembly plants. Many of the states also provided huge subsidies and tax incentives to attract the Japanese-sponsored plants. In addition, Japanese companies have used U.S. media and public relations firms to wage a very effective propaganda war that helped turn U.S. consumers against domestic manufacturers by convincing them that it didn't matter if they purchased products from Japanese- or American-owned companies. After all, the Japanese products were now also "Made in the USA"! In fact, the mainstream U.S. media reports that Japanese cars assembled in the U.S. actually have a higher percentage of U.S.-manufactured parts. That sounds great, but like most propaganda, it is a combination of truth, half-truths, and lies that are very hard to decipher unless you look deeper. Let's have a closer look starting with the consumer electronics industry.

Destruction of the U.S. Television Industry

1963: Japanese manufacturers begin exporting televisions to the U.S., based on technology licensed from U.S. companies.

1966: Twenty-eight U.S.-owned manufacturers dominate the television industry. Japanese manufacturers sign secret agreements with Sears, Roebuck & Co. and other U.S. retailers to provide illegal rebates (kickbacks) on every Japanese TV sold in the U.S.

1968: The United States Electronic Industry Association files a complaint with the U.S. government about the illegal "dumping" of televisions. The Japanese stonewall the investigation for three years, enough time to acquire or build factories in the U.S.

1971: The Treasury Department rules that Japanese companies violated U.S. law and owed millions of dollars in antidumping levies. Japan stonewalls for another nine years before a settlement is reached, allowing more time to build or acquire factories in the U.S.

1972: Sony opens the first Japanese-owned television manufacturing facility in the U.S. Other Japanese companies follow shortly thereafter. The Trojan horse is in!

1974: Motorola sells its television business to Panasonic.

1976: Only 6 of 28 U.S.-owned companies manufacturing TVs remain. The other twenty-two were purchased by Japanese or European companies or went out of business.

1977: Japanese manufacturers sign an Orderly Marketing Agreement, limiting exports to the U.S. to 1.5 million TVs annually. Televisions manufactured in the U.S. and other countries such as Mexico are not included, rendering the agreement meaningless.

1979: The Carter administration signs a "secret" agreement with Japan to settle the dumping case filed in 1968 that sells out the remaining U.S. television manufacturers.

1986: GE sells RCA to Thompson, a French company, and exits the television business. Zenith is the only remaining major U.S. manufacturer.

1999: After struggling financially for more than fifteen years, **Zenith files for bankruptcy and is purchased by LG Electronics, a Korean company.**

2008: Sony closes the last TV-manufacturing facility in the U.S.

After the Japanese started aggressively attacking U.S. consumer electronics companies in the 1960s, they anticipated that the U.S. government might try to stop them by limiting how much product they could export into the U.S. market. The Japanese view our legalistic approach to such matters as foolishness and are very clever at using it against us. They were also very much aware that they needed to manage U.S. public opinion to avoid a strong political backlash. Moving some of their production into the U.S. solved both problems. They could now claim to be a U.S. manufacturer and give the appearance of helping the U.S. industry that they were attacking. The transplant factories also made any legal agreements restricting imports of their products meaningless. That's why they stalled the U.S. government for so many years after the anti-dumping complaint was filed in 1968. It allowed them time to firmly establish factories and their own supply and distribution networks in the U.S. It was a brilliant business strategy that obviously worked. As for public opinion, once the Japanese companies set up U.S. factories, they used U.S. PR firms and the media to promote their "investments" in the U.S. and how they were winning business fairly in the free market (which was only free and open in the U.S., not back home in Japan). It worked, since most Americans blamed the failure of U.S.-owned companies on their inability to compete with Japanese-owned companies in the free market and apparently thought "What's the big deal?" now that Japanese companies were manufacturing their products in the U.S. Most people didn't realize these factories were "screwdriver" operations that required fewer and less-skilled workers than the U.S.-owned factories they replaced. The high-value work was still being performed in Japan by Japanese workers. Also, these factories purchased the components used in their products almost exclusively from Japanese suppliers either co-located in the U.S. or based in Japan. When they wiped out a U.S.-owned factory, not only did American workers lose the high-value jobs at those factories, but U.S. component suppliers also lost significant business and had to lay off American workers and close factories because the Japanese would not buy from them.

Now let's take a look at how the same Trojan-horse strategy has been used to attack and destroy the U.S. automotive industry.

Destruction of the U.S. Automotive Industry

1939: GM and Ford kicked out of Japan and never allowed to return. The two companies had dominated the Japanese automobile market.

1957: Japanese manufacturers begin exporting automobiles to the U.S.

1970: Japan has **3.7 percent** of the U.S. auto market. The U.S. has **0 percent** of the Japanese auto market. Japan charges a *50 percent* tariff on imported cars.

1978: GM is ranked first, Ford is fourth, and Chrysler is fourteenth in the Global Fortune 500. Toyota is twentieth.

1980: Japan has **17.6 percent** of the U.S. auto market. The U.S. has **0 percent** of the Japanese auto market. The Big Three close factories and lay off hundreds of thousands of workers. Chrysler, in danger of bankruptcy, asks for and receives a loan guarantee from the U.S. government.

1980s: Individual states offer incentives and open overseas offices to lure Japanese auto investors.

1982: Honda opens the first Japanese-owned automobile manufacturing facility in the U.S. Other Japanese companies follow shortly thereafter. The "Trojan Horse" is in!

1990: Japan has **23.6 percent** of the U.S. auto market. The U.S. has **0.5 percent** of the Japanese auto market. More factories are closed by the Big Three, and they resort to more layoffs.

1992: There are now eight transplant automobile-assembly complexes in the U.S. (three more are in Canada near the U.S. border); more than 250 transplant parts suppliers; sixty-six Japanese-owned or Japanese-U.S. joint venture steel producers, steel coating lines, and steel service centers; and twenty Japanese-owned rubber and tire plants.

1995: Japanese manufacturers sign a Memorandum of Understanding, agreeing to open the Japanese market to U.S. auto imports.

2000: Japan has **25 percent** of the U.S. auto market. The U.S. has **0.4 percent** of the Japanese auto market. There are more factory closings by the Big Three and more layoffs.

2008: Toyota surpasses GM to become the world's largest car manufacturer. GM and Chrysler file for bankruptcy and reorganize with assistance from the U.S. government, averting massive layoffs.

2010: Japan has **38%** of the U.S. auto market. The U.S. has **0.2%** of the Japanese auto market. GM is ranked thirty-eight, Ford is twenty-third, and Chrysler isn't listed in the Global Fortune 500. Toyota is now ranked fifth.

Japanese auto manufacturers used the same Trojan-horse strategy that was used by the Japanese consumer electronics companies, and it was even more effective. They decimated the Big Three auto manufacturers and got the U.S. federal and state governments to help them do it. Using their U.S. subsidiary companies, they bypassed U.S. campaign laws against foreign contributions and funneled millions of dollars in contributions to political campaigns. They also spent tens of millions of dollars on high-powered Washington lobbyists and public relations firms and gained considerable control over U.S. media through advertising expenditures. A recent example is how Toyota used their leverage with the U.S. media and members of Congress to influence the investigation related to the recall of vehicles due to unintended acceleration *(Kindy, Whoriskey, and Lebling) (Valdes-Dapena)*.

Japanese auto manufacturers have also used their influence in the U.S. media and political system to wage an effective propaganda campaign against U.S. auto manufacturers. The campaign has been so effective that most Americans blame the Big Three for the collapse of the U.S. auto industry and assign little or no blame to Japan Inc. Most Americans also now believe it makes absolutely no difference if they buy a car manufactured by a Japanese- or U.S.-owned company. This is quite a shift from public opinion in the 1970s and 1980s. The U.S. media has helped reinforce the Japanese auto industry's propaganda with reports that the American-made parts' content of Japanese cars built in America is actually higher, in some cases, than cars built by GM, Ford, or Chrysler. What they failed to uncover in these reports is that the so-called American-made parts being used by Japanese manufacturers are actually coming from Japanese auto parts manufacturers with U.S. subsidiaries. As in the consumer electronics industry, the Japanese transplant factories are hiring fewer and less-skilled workers and keeping higher-wage jobs in Japan. Certainly there are a few exceptions that these companies and their supporters like to promote to the media—but they are exceptions used for propaganda purposes, not the general rule. There is also a general misperception—promoted by Japanese companies and their supporters—that most of the jobs lost at U.S. auto factories are being replaced by the Japanese transplant factories. This leads the American public to believe that we are not losing jobs in the automotive industry. In reality, these jobs are merely shifting from U.S.- to Japanese-owned companies. This is totally false—here are the facts:

U.S./Japan Automotive Manufacturing Employment Shift

	1978	2011	Change +/-	Change %
GM/Ford/Chrysler	1,503,489	417,623	-1,085,866	-72%
Japanese U.S. Transplants	0	50,927	50,927	N/A
Japanese Domestic	154,498	857,103	702,605	455%

Sources: *Fortune* Magazine, May 15, 1979; CNN Money Global 500, July 25, 2011; and the Japan Automobile Manufacturing Association

As these numbers clearly illustrate, the Big Three U.S. auto manufacturers lost more than a million jobs between 1978 and 2011, while Japanese auto manufacturers gained more than 750,000 jobs during the same period. Japanese U.S. transplant factories employed a little over 50,000 workers, which means that fewer than 5 percent of the jobs lost at U.S. auto manufacturers were replaced with jobs at Japanese transplant factories in the U.S. This is hardly just a shift of U.S. auto manufacturing jobs that many Americans believe is taking place. To make matters worse, Japanese transplant factories in the U.S. purchase their parts and other materials—steel, glass, tires, engines, transmissions, etc.—almost exclusively from Japanese suppliers either co-located in the U.S. or based in Japan. This has had a devastating impact on the formerly thriving U.S. auto parts industry, which lost more than 450,000 high-paying manufacturing jobs between 2000 and 2010 *(U.S. Department of Commerce)*, in addition to the hundreds of thousands of jobs lost between 1978 and 2000. My father, who worked in the steel industry, instructed me to never buy a foreign car since doing so would be putting Americans out of work. He passed away many years ago, but I never forgot his advice and have always purchased vehicles manufactured by Ford, GM, or Chrysler. Over the years, I have been ridiculed by some of my peers, who told me my thinking was outdated and it didn't matter what type of car I purchased. Well, it turns out that my father was right!

Loss of U.S. Computer, Semiconductor, Solar, and Other High-Tech Industries

The decline in manufacturing and loss of high-wage jobs isn't isolated to the automotive and other traditional industries. It is also happening in high-tech industries such as computers, semiconductors, biotechnology, and the emerging green technologies in the solar and wind industries, as told by Andy Grove, co-founder of Intel, in a recent article published by *Business-Week (Grove)*. In 2010 manufacturing employment in the U.S. computer industry was about 166,000—lower than it was before the first PC was introduced in 1975. Meanwhile, thanks to outsourcing and free trade, a huge computer manufacturing industry has emerged in Asia, employing about 1.5 million workers—factory employees, engineers, and managers. The products these factories produce are primarily being exported back to the U.S. and include all the major U.S. brands such as Apple, HP, Dell, and Microsoft. The largest of these manufacturing companies in Asia is Hon Hai Precision Industry, also known as Foxconn Technology Group. The company has grown at an astonishing rate, first in Taiwan and later in China.

> 800,000 MANUFACTURING JOBS IN ASIA HAVE ELIMINATED 12.8 MILLION JOBS IN THE U.S.

Its revenues in 2009 were $64 billion, increasing to $95 billion in 2010. This is larger than Apple, Microsoft, Dell, or Intel. Foxconn employs over 800,000 people, more than the combined worldwide head count of Apple, Dell, Microsoft, Hewlett-Packard, and Intel.

Recall for a moment the Milken Institute study that stated every computer-manufacturing job creates an estimated fifteen jobs outside the factory. That means those 800,000 manufacturing jobs in Asia have eliminated 12.8 million jobs in the U.S. Outsourcing these jobs to Asia has also robbed the U.S. Treasury along with state and local governments of billions of dollars in tax revenues. Many Americans have probably never heard of Foxconn, but most are familiar with the products it makes: iPhones, iPads, and iMacs for Apple, computers for Dell and HP, Nokia cell phones, Microsoft Xbox 360 gaming consoles, and countless other familiar electronic gadgets. There are 250,000 Foxconn employees in southern China alone producing Apple products. This is ten times the 25,000 employees that Apple has in the U.S. So for every Apple worker in the U.S., there are 10 Chinese workers involved in the production of iMacs, iPods, and iPhones. A similar ten-to-one relationship holds true for Dell, HP, and other U.S. high-tech companies *(Grove).*

While the U.S. investment in technology companies has increased dramatically since 1975, the jobs being created by these companies are mostly in Asia, not the U.S. Rather than hiring U.S. workers, companies are contracting their manufacturing and engineering work to off-shore subcontractors like Foxconn.

Will the Green Revolution Create New U.S. Manufacturing Jobs?

In a word, no. What about the promise of the solar industry? There was only one American company (First Solar) among the top ten worldwide in photovoltaic-cell production in 2009. However, the European Commission doesn't even classify First Solar as a U.S. company, instead labeling it "international" because it does most of its production in Asia *(McCormack).* In 2009 the U.S. accounted for only 5.4 percent of the global production of photovoltaics, down from 30 percent in 1999. On the other hand, Chinese production represented only 1 percent of the global output of photovoltaics in 1999, but its output rose to 36 percent of global production by 2009. This is a national disgrace since photovoltaic-cell technology was invented in the U.S. using hundreds of millions of U.S. tax dollars! The technology is being hijacked by the communist Chinese government with the assistance of U.S. companies. Worse yet, the U.S. government is subsidizing companies that are outsourcing the manufacturing of their panels to China. This is a clear example of why the U.S. desperately needs a manufacturing strategy and industrial policy that protects the investments U.S. taxpayers and companies make to develop new technologies. We can no longer afford to allow other countries to steal our technologies along with the industries and high-wage jobs they create.

What about the wind-energy industry? In 2010 only one U.S. company (General Electric) ranked among the ten largest in the world. GE's world-wide market share in 2010 was 10 percent—down from 18.6 percent in 2008—while four Chinese companies were in the top ten, with China's Sinovel coming in at number two with 11 percent market share. Chinese companies have risen from virtually nothing five years ago to become top-five players in global wind energy *(Green World Investor)*. They are heavily subsidized and protected by the Chinese government and use industrial espionage to steal secrets from other companies. Here is an example reported by *Forbes* in September 2011 *(Lappin)*:

American Superconductor Destroyed For A Tiny Bribe

When it Comes To China, Seller Beware If You Want To Get Paid

The story about the problems at American Superconductor and its former customer Sinovel keeps getting more and more bizarre. Most amazing so far is the tiny amount of money paid to the AMSC employee who has reportedly pled guilty to the charges that he was bribed to reveal the source code for core electrical components for Sinovel's wind turbines. The bribe was so small he couldn't even have bought a lowend Mercedes for his troubles.

According to REcharge, "the global source for renewable energy news," it has now become public that the unnamed "perp" is a Serbian who was employed in the Austrian operation of AMSC known as Windtec. This individual was one of a handful of people who had access to the source code to operate Sinovel's wind turbines. The article says the code was passed in the first half of this year for the very meager fee of just 15,000 Euros, or about $20,500, for his actions. AMSC has had to write off hundreds of millions in past and present sales to Sinovel which has really put American Superconductor down for the count and it has wiped out hundreds of millions of dollars in market value for AMSC and its shareholders.

Sinovel (SI) represented about 80% of American Superconductors revenues when the Chinese wind turbine manufacturer stopped paying for past shipments that had already been delivered and locked its gates to stop receipt of any further shipments to its facilities in China. AMSC didn't help itself by continuing to make shipments when it hadn't been paid for a very long time.

American Superconductor is on a March fiscal year and the stopped payments and delivery refusals occurred just prior to the end of that last quarter of its 2011 fiscal year. The initial round of announcements about the nature and severity of the problems were made public, rather promptly, on April 5th. At that time, AMSC still hoped to resolve the issues with a client that had come to represent the lion's share of its revenues and its perceived path to profitability after decades of losses.

The developments forced the founder Greg Yurek to resign as Chairman, 10% staff cuts to be enacted, caused the company to be unable to file timely and accurate financial statements for the 2011 year, and when its anticipated earnings crumbled away to losses, the stock to collapse. That led to the filing of many class action lawsuits by the usual vultures who show up in such circumstances, looking for those who might have held the stock and want to become the lead plaintiff. AMSC has also been shown to have had inadequate financial controls by the SEC's definition. Its proposed acquisition of The Switch Engineering OY has been postponed until September 30th with two more 30 day extensions in the last amended agreement. If the deal doesn't close, The Switch will retain the 14.2 million Euro break up fee.

American Super had been in a self imposed silence for several weeks while it worked through its issues. It broke its silence in September when it announced theft of its property, the cessation of its relationship with Sinovel and other details. After the initial revelations of the problems and their scale and scope, Dan McGahn was promoted to CEO from President on May 24th and named a member of the Board of Directors effective June 1st. McGahn arrived at AMSC in December 2006 with the goal of finding new markets to enter that would accelerate AMSC's growth trajectory. American Super has worked hard for years on products for the power grid and in developing high temperature superconducting wire. They are excellent products and would solve many grid problems in the U.S. but nobody here has cared much to do a thing about deploying them. According to a recent press release, McGahn's "primary initial objective was to establish and operate AMSC China." It would appear that his success in garnering the Sinovel business was a key in his advancement to SVP and then President and COO in December 2009 when things looked very rosy. While he knows the situation inside and out, he also appears to have been a key victim in Sinovel's "Big Bamboozle."

The stock is now down 84% for this year. Yahoo had its stake in Ali Baba diminished in value earlier this year when its Chairman Jack Ma simply decided to move a key asset into another company which he controlled and in which Yahoo had no interest. As everyone rushes headlong into doing business in China, it is clear that you cannot ever be too sophisticated when dealing over there. Sinovel is claiming that the "goods" AMSC was delivering were inferior and didn't meet requirements of the Chinese Government. Even so, AMSC has filed suit against the arrested employee and Sinovel accusing it of stealing the very code it says was inferior.

It has become the Wild West on that other side of the globe. There is little or no respect for Intellectual Property. Copyrights and patents are ignored. Accounting issues have recently also come into question for many Chinese companies that have bought U.S. shell corporations to simplify the process of going public in the West. Rough and tumble attitudes must be expected. Any American company doing business in China must anticipate the worst even as it hopes for the best in expanded marketing opportunities. As in this example, Seller Beware! Letters of Credit and prepayments are a very good idea if you want to be paid for your goods and services. Without them, you are easily toast. Investors must make stock selections with great care, too.

We own no positions in American Superconductor at this time.

—JOAN E. LAPPIN, CFA GRAMERCY CAPITAL MGT. CORP

As Ms. Lappin points out in her article, China has absolutely no regard for U.S. or international law. They simply have done and will continue to do what they deem is in their best interest—regardless of U.S. or international laws. Unless we take quick and decisive action, the U.S. will lose the solar and wind turbine industries—that we invented!—to China. There's no time to waste; it may already be too late.

The Theft of U.S. Intellectual Property

Intellectual property is a term that encompasses copyrights, trademarks, patents, industrial design rights, and trade secrets. Intellectual property is the lifeblood of modern industry. It is no understatement to say that the creation and commercialization of intellectual property is what propelled America to become the most successful and richest nation in history. The list of innovations is endless: the steam engine, cotton gin, light bulb, telephone, airplane, submarine, computer, television, radio, phonograph, cell phone, transistor, semiconductor, microprocessor, nuclear energy, antibiotics, and countless others. These inventions built entire industries that generated wealth in America, and improved all of our lives. This is no longer the case. Instead, American intellectual property is being stolen, and in many cases given away, to foreign governments and corporations. As a result, the U.S. is losing entire industries and the wealth and jobs generated by them. This is true of all the industries I discuss in this book, and many others I haven't discussed.

The theft of innovations is not a recent phenomenon. The Japanese automotive, steel, consumer electronics, computer, nuclear, and semiconductor industries, among others, were developed with technology the U.S. either gave to Japan or they acquired by theft or by leveraging U.S. companies that wanted to do business in Japan as was discussed in chapter three. The same is true for the other East Asian economies, such as Korea and Taiwan. Following this example, China is acquiring technology from the U.S. and other nations at an unprecedented level through theft, leverage, and any other means possible. The rate at which they are doing so is unmatched in human history. Unlike Japan in the 1950s and 1960s, communist China has the Internet and email to assist its process. The communist Chinese government monitors all email and Internet traffic going in and out of China. This includes the email communications of U.S.-based and other foreign corporations. My nine years in the U.S. Navy as a cryptologist tell me that it's very easy for the Chinese government to glean whatever information they deem valuable from electronic communications. In addition, like the Japanese, communist China has very restrictive laws controlling foreign ownership of companies, and they use these laws to force foreign companies into "partnerships" with Chinese-owned companies. This gives Chinese companies easy access to the intellectual property of foreign companies. Once they take what they need, the "partnership" is dissolved, and the foreign-based company finds its trade secrets stolen and no new business in China. Worse yet, the Chinese company that stole its trade secrets can now compete for the company's business outside of China, including its home market. The communist Chinese call this their policy of indigenous innovation, which forces the transfer of technology in exchange for access to its growing market. Japan used this same strategy to acquire the technology it needed to overtake the U.S. consumer electronics, steel, automotive, and other industries, as I've discussed.

A related concern is the loss of research and development (R&D) initiatives—which create new intellectual property—as U.S. companies continue to move manufacturing offshore. A 2004 report from George W. Bush's Council of Advisors on Science and Technology (*Council Report*) warned that the "proximity of research, development, and manufacturing is very important to leading-edge manufacturers." The continuing shift of manufacturing to lower-cost regions, especially China, is pulling high-end design and R&D capabilities out of the U.S. This is further accelerating the decline of U.S. manufacturing.

Undermining Our National Security

The decline in U.S. manufacturing threatens our national security. The U.S. cannot expect to maintain a high-tech, world-leading military by depending on foreign-supplied products and technologies. We also cannot afford to put the defense of the United States of America in the hands of other nations—even if we consider those nations long-time allies or traditionally friendly countries. To do so is dangerous and foolishly jeopardizes our security. Recall the words of Alexander Hamilton:

> "Not only the wealth, but the independence and security of a country, appear to be materially connected with the prosperity of manufactures. Every nation. . . ought to endeavor to possess within itself all the essentials of a national supply. These comprise the means of subsistence, habitation, clothing and defense."

Imagine how World War II would have ended if the U.S. was outsourcing its manufacturing to Asia in 1941 and did not have the ability to produce the planes, tanks, guns, and munitions needed to defeat the Axis powers. Those of us in the post-WWII generations take for granted that the U.S. and our allies won the war, but forget that there was no guarantee of this outcome. In fact, if it hadn't been for the U.S. entering the war in 1941, Great Britain would have most likely fallen to Germany and the world, including the U.S., would be living under a German and Japanese dictatorship.

Instead, our freedom was secured because of the U.S. industrial base that Franklin Roosevelt called "the arsenal of democracy." Ironically, this industrial base has been under assault since the end of WWII, and is almost totally depleted due to our misguided globalization and free-trade policies. This decline is compromising our national defense. For example, when Defense Secretary Robert Gates decided to increase production of armored trucks for the Iraq counter-insurgency campaign in 2007, it was discovered there was only one steel plant in the nation producing steel of sufficient strength to meet military needs. That plant—the old Lukens Steel Company facility in Coatesville, Pennsylvania—had been bought by Indian-owned, European-based steel giant ArcelorMittal, which already had weapons makers waiting in line for the output its limited capacity could support. Other items needed for the Iraq-bound military vehicles also were in short supply, such as oversized tires. The Pentagon had to cobble together an ad hoc network of domestic and foreign suppliers to ramp up production of the vital trucks *(Thompson)*.

The U.S. industrial complex, FDR's "arsenal of democracy," no longer exists. It is rapidly being replaced by the arsenal of communism, with communist China leading the world in the production of everything from steel to computers. What if communist China, Japan, or other countries that we now depend on to supply technologies needed for our defense disagree with our foreign policy and threaten to withhold the supply unless we do as they demand? Or worse yet, what happens if we go to war someday with communist China over Taiwan? Will they continue to ship us the technology that we need then? What about the numerous U.S. companies with the bulk of their manufacturing operations in communist China? Would the Communist Chinese permit them to continue operations in China or ship their products back to the U.S.? Of course not! What if our allies in this region chose not to stand with us because of their fear of communist China?

Some may say these scenarios are highly unlikely. Oh, really? Well then, let's look at how communist China reacted to the recent U.S. sale of F16 fighter jets to Taiwan. As reported in a *Financial Times* article from September 22, 2011, titled "China hits at US over Taiwan arms deal" *(Hille)*, the Chinese military expressed much anger and threatened retaliation in response to the sale. Through the government-controlled media, there were threats of deploying nuclear missiles aimed at Taiwan (and the U.S.), recalling the former Soviet Union's response to the U.S. proposal to deploy a missile defense system in central Europe during the 1980s. In the same article Mark Stokes, a former Pentagon official, states, "We now have a policy in Washington towards Taiwan that sometimes seems too much coordinated with Beijing." So, why is the free and independent government of the United States of America coordinating its policies with the communist Chinese government in Beijing? Are we still a free and independent nation? Or are we slowly becoming a puppet state of communist China? Our recent behavior would suggest the latter.

CHAPTER EIGHT

Corporate Greed & Corruption—Selling Out America

The things that will destroy America are prosperity at any price, peace at any price, safety first instead of duty first, and love of soft living and the get-rich-quick theory of life.

—Theodore Roosevelt

Some Historical Perspective

Corporate greed and corruption are not new. They have been with us, subverting the "Glorious Cause of America" since the founding of our country. Theodore Roosevelt, a Republican and one of the greatest American presidents in our history, delivered a powerful speech to the citizens of Osawatomie, Kansas, on August 31, 1910, called "The New Nationalism" that eloquently discusses this topic. This speech is as relevant today as it was in 1910. You can find the entire speech printed as an addendum to this book. Here are some excerpts:

We come here to-day to commemorate one of the epoch-making events of the long struggle for the rights of man—the long struggle for the uplift of humanity. Our country—this great Republic—means nothing unless it means the triumph of a real democracy, the triumph of popular government, and, in the long run, of an economic system under which each man shall be guaranteed the opportunity to show the best that there is in him . . . .

. . . .I stand for the square deal. But when I say that I am for the square deal, I mean not merely that I stand for fair play under the present rules of the games, but that I stand for having those rules changed so as to work for a more substantial equality of opportunity and of reward for equally good service . . . .

Now, this means that our government, National and State, must be freed from the sinister influence or control of special interests . . . .the great special business interests too often control and corrupt the men and methods of government for their own profit. We must drive the special interests out of politics. That is one of our tasks to-day. Every special interest is entitled to justice—full, fair, and complete . . . but not one is entitled to a vote in Congress, to a voice on the bench, or to representation in any public office. The Constitution guarantees protections to property, and we must make that promise good. But it does not give the right of suffrage to any corporation. The true friend of property, the true conservative, is he who insists that property shall be the servant and not the master of the commonwealth; who insists that the creature of man's making shall be the servant and not the master of the man who made it. **The citizens of the United States must effectively control the mighty commercial forces which they have themselves called into being.**

There can be no effective control of corporations while their political activity remains. To put an end to it will be neither a short nor an easy task, but it can be done.

We must have complete and effective publicity of corporate affairs, so that people may know beyond peradventure whether the corporations obey the law and whether their management entitles them to the confidence of the public. It is necessary that laws should be passed to prohibit the use of corporate funds directly or indirectly for political purposes; it is still more necessary that such laws should be thoroughly enforced. **Corporate expenditures for political purposes, and especially such expenditures by public-service corporations, have supplied one of the principal sources of corruption in our political affairs.**

It has become entirely clear that we must have government supervision of the capitalization, not only of public-service corporations, including, particularly, railways, but of all corporations doing an interstate business. . . .

I believe that the officers, and, especially, the directors, of corporations should be held personally responsible when any corporation breaks the law.

Combinations in industry are the result of an imperative economic law which cannot be repealed by political legislation. The effort at prohibiting all combination has substantially failed. The way out lies not in attempting to prevent such combinations, but in completely controlling them in the interest of the public welfare. For that purpose the Federal Bureau of Corporations (now called the Federal Trade Commission) is an agency of first importance. Its powers, and, therefore, its efficiency, as well as that of the Interstate Commerce Commission, should be largely increased. We have a right to expect from the Bureau of Corporations and from the Interstate Commerce Commission a very high grade of public service. We should be as sure of the proper conduct of the interstate railways and the proper management of interstate business as we are now sure of the conduct and management of the national banks, and we should have as effective supervision in one case as in the other . . . .

The absence of effective State, and, especially, national, restraint upon unfair money-getting has tended to create a small class of enormously wealthy and economically powerful men, whose chief object is to hold and increase their power. The prime need is to change the conditions which enable these men to accumulate power which is not for the general welfare that they should hold or exercise. We grudge no man a fortune which represents his own power and sagacity, when exercised with entire regard to the welfare of his fellows . . . .We grudge no man a fortune in civil life if it is honorably obtained and well used. It is not even enough that it should have gained without doing damage to the community. We should permit it to be gained only so long as the gaining represents benefit to the community. This, I know, implies a policy of a far more active governmental interference with social and economic conditions in this country than we have yet had, but I think we have got to face the fact that such an increase in governmental control is now necessary.

No man should receive a dollar unless that dollar has been fairly earned. Every dollar received should represent a dollar's worth of service rendered—**not gambling in stocks, but service rendered**. The really big fortune, the swollen fortune, by the mere fact of its size acquires qualities which differentiate it in kind as well as in degree from what is possessed by men of relatively small means. Therefore, I believe in a graduated income tax on big fortunes, and in another tax which is far more easily collected and far more effective—a graduated inheritance tax on big fortunes, properly safeguarded against evasion and increasing rapidly in amount with the size of the estate.

. . . The man who wrongly holds that every human right is secondary to his profit must now give way to the advocate of human welfare, who rightly maintains that every man holds his property subject to the general right of the community to regulate its use to whatever degree the public welfare may require it.

But I think we may go still further. **The right to regulate the use of wealth in the public interest is universally admitted. Let us admit also the right to regulate the terms and conditions of labor, which is the chief element of wealth, directly in the interest of the common good.... No man can be a good citizen unless he has a wage more than sufficient to cover the bare cost of living, and hours of labor short enough so that after his day's work is done he will have time and energy to bear his share in the management of the community, to help in carrying the general load.** We keep countless men from being good citizens by the conditions of life with which we surround them. We need comprehensive workmen's compensation acts, both State and national laws to regulate child labor and work for women, and, especially, we need in our common schools not merely education in book learning, but also practical training for daily life and work. We need to enforce better sanitary conditions for our workers and to extend the use of safety appliances for our workers in industry and commerce, both within and between the States. **Also, friends, in the interest of the working man himself we need to set our faces like flint against mob-violence just as against corporate greed; against violence and injustice and lawlessness by wage-workers just as much as against lawless cunning and greed and selfish arrogance of employers.** If I could ask but one thing of my fellow countrymen, my request would be that, whenever they go in for reform, they remember the two sides, and that they always exact justice from one side as much as from the other. I have small use for the public servant who can always see and denounce the corruption of the capitalist, but who cannot persuade himself, especially before elections, to say a word about lawless mob-violence. And I have equally small use for the man, be he a judge on the bench, or editor of a great paper, or wealthy and influential private citizen, who can see clearly enough and denounce the lawlessness of mob-violence, but whose eyes are closed so that he is blind when the question is one of corruption in business on a gigantic scale . . . .

I do not ask for overcentralization; but I do ask that we work in a spirit of broad and far-reaching nationalism when we work for what concerns our people as a whole. We are all Americans . . . . The national government belongs to the whole American people, and where the whole American people are interested, that interest can be guarded effectively only by the national government. The betterment which we seek must be accomplished, I believe, mainly through the national government.

Those who oppose all reform will do well to remember that ruin in its worst form is inevitable if our national life brings us nothing better than swollen fortunes for the few and the triumph in both politics and business of a sordid and selfish materialism.

If our political institutions were perfect, they would absolutely prevent the political domination of money in any part of our affairs. We need to make our political representatives more quickly and sensitively responsive to the people whose servants they are. More direct action by the people in their own affairs under proper safeguards is vitally necessary . . . . **It is particularly important that all moneys received or expended for campaign purposes should be publicly accounted for, not only after election, but before election as well . . . .**

One of the fundamental necessities in a representative government such as ours is to make certain that the men to whom the people delegate their power shall serve the people by whom they are elected, and not the special interests. I believe that every national officer, elected or appointed, should be forbidden to perform any service or receive any compensation, directly or indirectly, from interstate corporations; and a similar provision could not fail to be useful within the States.

The object of government is the welfare of the people. The material progress and prosperity of a nation are desirable chiefly so far as they lead to the moral and material welfare of all good citizens . . . .

No matter how honest and decent we are in our private lives, if we do not have the right kind of law and the right kind of administration of the law, we cannot go forward as a nation. That is imperative; but it must be an addition to, and not a substitution for, the qualities that make us good citizens . . . (emphasis added).

Roosevelt split from the Republican Party in 1912 because they, and the Democratic Party, were controlled by Wall Street and corporations that opposed the reforms he was proposing (sound familiar?). After surviving an assassination attempt in 1912, he created the Progressive Party and ran for reelection as a third-party presidential candidate. The platform of the Progressive Party was "To destroy this invisible Government, to dissolve the unholy alliance between corrupt business and corrupt politics is the first task of the statesmanship of the day." Roosevelt finished in second place behind Democratic candidate Woodrow Wilson, and was the only third-party candidate in U.S. history to finish ahead of a sitting president. As he later wrote in his autobiography,

I quote from the Progressive platform: "Behind the ostensible Government sits enthroned an invisible Government, owing no allegiance and acknowledging no responsibility to the people. To destroy this invisible Government, to dissolve the unholy alliance between corrupt business and corrupt politics, is the first task of the statesmanship of the day. . . . This country belongs to the people. Its resources, its business, its laws, its institutions, should be utilized, maintained, or altered in whatever manner will best promote the general interest." This assertion is explicit. . . . Mr. Wilson must know that every monopoly in the United States opposes the Progressive party. . . . I challenge him . . . to name the monopoly that did support the Progressive party, whether . . . the Sugar Trust, the Steel Trust, the Harvester Trust, the Standard Oil Trust, the Tobacco Trust, or any other. . . . Ours was the only programme to which they objected, and they supported either Mr. Wilson or Mr. Taft . . . .

Roosevelt was a true patriot in same spirit of George Washington and John Adams. He put principle and country above party, and he worked for the common good of all Americans.

President Wilson enacted some of the reforms advocated by Roosevelt. Most of them, though, were not realized until Franklin Delano Roosevelt (fifth cousin to Theodore) enacted the New Deal in the 1930s to pull the country out of the Great Depression. The reforms to banking, corporate, and labor laws brought about by the New Deal ushered in the longest period of economic expansion and shared prosperity in U.S. history. The New Deal reforms also combined with other factors to create the American middle class. From 1945 until 1973 the U.S. economy grew an average of 3.8 percent a year, with real median household incomes surging 55 percent (up 1.6 percent on average per year). This growth came to an end in the mid-1970s due to misguided trade and economic policies. Ironically, it was determined in the late 1970s and 1980s, by both political parties, that the best way to achieve renewed economic growth was to unravel the New Deal policies and regulatory controls that had produced the longest, most stable, and prosperous economic period in U.S. history. During his 1980 campaign, Ronald Reagan said that his economic policy proposals were merely a return to the "free-enterprise principles that had been in favor before the Great Depression." Under the failed leadership of both political parties, we did just that and achieved the same results in 2008 that were achieved in 1929:

- collapse of the stock market, financial, and banking systems

- worst economic crisis since the Great Depression

- endless corporate scandals and corruption with no accountability

- highest concentration of wealth among top 1 percent of affluent citizens since 1929

- a disappearing middle class

- declining labor unions

- a government controlled by Wall Street, corporations, and other wealthy special interests

- disproportionate amount of wealth created from gambling in stock markets instead of from actual work and productivity

However, we added a few of our own modern-day twists:

- changed the U.S. from the world's largest international creditor to the world's leading debtor nation

- largest trade deficits in U.S. history

- largest national debt in U.S. history with almost 50 percent of the total financed by foreign countries

Another creative contemporary twist we've added is the so-called global company, which is an outgrowth of the mythical global free-trade system that exists only in theory. Let's explore this further.

The "Global Company" Myth

The great corporations which we have grown to speak of rather loosely as trusts are the creatures of the State, and the State not only has the right to control them wherever need of such control is shown . . . The immediate necessity in dealing with trusts is to place them under the real, not the nominal, control of some sovereign to which, as its creatures, the trusts owe allegiance, and in whose courts the sovereign's orders may be enforced. In my opinion, this sovereign must be the National Government.

—THEODORE ROOSEVELT

There is no such thing as a *global company*. Nor is there any such thing as a *multinational company*. All companies or corporations exist under a legal charter that is issued and controlled by a national or state government. There is no nation or state on earth designated *global* or *multinational*. In the U.S. corporations are chartered and governed by state laws. Most U.S. Fortune 500 companies are incorporated in Delaware because the state offers the most favorable laws pertaining to incorporation. Corporations are also regulated in the U.S. by federal agencies such as the Federal Trade Commission and the Securities and Exchange Commission. However, since the 1970s, the staffing and the enforcement powers of these regulatory agencies have been significantly reduced. This is what helped create the problems with Enron, WorldCom, and Bernie Madoff, as well as the collapse of Lehman Brothers, Merrill Lynch, AIG, Bear Stearns, Fannie Mae, and Freddie Mac.

Since there is no nation or state called *global* or *multinational*, we must understand that companies are either U.S. or foreign corporations. This is an important distinction that has been frequently and intentionally blurred by clever executives and lawyers of both U.S. and foreign corporations to evade taxes and hide other types of illegal activity. As Roosevelt stated while arguing for more federal control and regulation of corporations:

> The citizens of the United States must effectively control the mighty commercial forces which they have themselves called into being . . . .
>
> The State must be made efficient for the work which concerns only the people of the State; and the nation for that which concerns all the people. **There must remain no neutral ground to serve as a refuge for lawbreakers, and especially for lawbreakers of great wealth, who can hire the vulpine legal cunning which will teach them how to avoid both jurisdictions . . . .**
>
> The immediate necessity in dealing with trusts (corporations) is to place them under the real, not the nominal, **control**

of some sovereign to which, as its creatures, the trusts owe allegiance, and in whose courts the sovereign's orders may be enforced. In my opinion, this sovereign must be the National Government . . . (my emphasis).

Many U.S.-based corporations claim to be global or multinational as justification for showing no loyalty or allegiance to the U.S. They also make this claim to justify their use of legal maneuvering to avoid paying U.S. taxes, to get out of complying with U.S. laws, and to freely outsource U.S. jobs. However, when they need the support of the U.S. government and the taxpayers they reaffirm their status as a "U.S." company. Such was the case with General Motors, who referred to itself as a global company before asking for and receiving a government bailout in 2009. It changed its tune after the 2009 government bailout. On the *Lou Dobbs Show* that aired June 1, 2009, former GM CFO Ray Young was asked if GM was a global company or an American company. He answered emphatically that GM was an American company, not a global company.

In other cases, companies that were initially incorporated in the U.S. and continue to transact the majority of their business here, switch their incorporation to foreign countries to evade U.S. taxes and laws governing their activities. Such is the case with Tyco. The corruption within Tyco captured headlines in 2001 and resulted in the trial and conviction of their CEO and CFO, as well as one of their directors. The corruption at Tyco continues today, as published in their 2010 annual report *(Tyco)*. Here are some excerpts:

Compliance Matters

As previously reported in the Company's periodic filings, the Company has received and responded to various allegations and other information that certain improper payments were made by the Company's subsidiaries and agents in recent years. For example, **two subsidiaries in the Company's Flow Control**

business in Italy have been charged, along with numerous other parties, in connection with the Milan public prosecutor's investigation into allegedly improper payments made to certain Italian entities, and the Company has reported to German authorities potentially improper conduct involving agents retained by the Company's EMEA water business. The Company has since resolved this matter with German authorities while the Italian matter remains outstanding. The Company reported to the U.S. Department of Justice ("DOJ") and the SEC the investigative steps and remedial measures that it has taken in response to these and other allegations and its internal investigations . . . .

As previously disclosed, in early **2007 certain former subsidiaries in the Company's Flow Control business were charged by the German Federal Cartel Office ("FCO") with engaging in anti-competitive practices, in particular with regard to its hydrant, valve, street box and fittings business.** The Company investigated this matter and determined that the conduct may have violated German anti-trust law. The Company is cooperating with the FCO in its ongoing investigation of this violation. The Company cannot estimate the range of potential loss that may result from this violation . . . (*2010 Annual Report*, Tyco International Ltd., 25–26) (my emphasis).

Not only is the company corrupt, it has also been legally cheating the U.S. Treasury out of tens of millions in tax revenues since moving its incorporation offshore. Tyco was first incorporated in Massachusetts in 1962. It changed its incorporation to Bermuda in 1997, and to Switzerland in 2008. By its own admission, these incorporation changes were implemented to avoid paying U.S. corporate income taxes. Here is an excerpt from a financial form the company filed with the U.S. government:

In its current consideration of a potential change of domicile, our board of directors has taken into account both the results of its prior evaluation and the outcome of the 2003 and 2004 shareholder votes. It also has considered legislation introduced in the U.S. Congress to limit tax treaty benefits and legislation that otherwise targets companies that are domiciled in countries like Bermuda—for example, by limiting the ability of such companies to enter contracts with U.S. federal or state governmental authorities. If enacted, such legislation could have a material and adverse impact on Tyco International and its shareholders. In light of these considerations, and to obtain the economic and operational benefits of being a Swiss company that are described above, our board of directors has proposed the Change of Domicile.

Although we expect that the Change of Domicile will provide us with important benefits and help us maintain our worldwide effective corporate tax rate, we cannot assure you that these anticipated results will be realized.

. . . As a major Swiss corporation, we will be able to take advantage of Switzerland's well-established and long-standing network of commercial and tax treaties. We believe that the Change of Domicile will improve our ability to maintain a competitive worldwide effective corporate tax rate.

This is not the first time that our shareholders have been asked to vote on a potential Change of Domicile. In 2003, our board of directors evaluated the potential benefits, costs and disadvantages of remaining a Bermuda company versus reincorporating in another jurisdiction, specifically the United States. Based on its evaluation, our board of directors concluded that moving our jurisdiction of incorporation to the U.S. would have had substantial negative financial consequences for Tyco International and also would have negative consequences for certain of our shareholders. At the time, we estimated that, had Tyco International been a U.S. corporation during fiscal year 2003, the effective tax rate on our income from continuing operations excluding special charges would have increased to more than 35%, resulting in significant declines in our net income and earnings per share. We believe that similar declines would result if Tyco International became a U.S. corporation today. At both the 2003 and 2004 Annual General Meetings, shareholders voted on a proposal to "urge Tyco's board of directors to take the measures necessary to change Tyco's jurisdiction of incorporation" from Bermuda to Delaware (in 2003) and any U.S. state (in 2004). Each year, shareholders overwhelmingly rejected these proposals, which we believe reflected shareholders' desire that we minimize our worldwide effective corporate tax rate (*2009 Special General Meeting Proxy Statement*, Tyco International Ltd., 7).

There is absolutely no justification for Tyco not being incorporated in the U.S. According to Tyco's 2010 Annual Report, 70 percent or $3.4 billion of its physical assets (property, plants, and equipment) are located in the U.S.—not Bermuda or Switzerland. Also, the vast majority of its sales revenues are coming from this country. In 2010 its U.S. sales of $8.3 billion were more than twice its sales in Europe, the Middle East, and Africa combined. The same ratio applies for U.S. sales versus Asia. Here are the numbers:

Net Revenue (Millions): 2010

United States	$8,266
Other Americas	$1,726
Europe, Middle East, and Africa	$3,990
Asia-Pacific	$3,034
Total	**$17,016**

Tyco is just one example of the many companies—both U.S. and foreign—that are corrupt and cheating the U.S. Treasury out of billions of corporate tax dollars. As Roosevelt counseled, "The citizens of the United

States must effectively control the mighty commercial forces which they have themselves called into being." He further counseled us that the way to control these mighty forces is to eliminate "all neutral ground to serve as a refuge for lawbreakers, and especially for lawbreakers of great wealth, who can hire the vulpine legal cunning which will teach them how to avoid both jurisdictions . . . ." The jurisdictions he was referring to are federal and state, but the same principle applies to corporations operating internationally. While we cannot directly control what happens on foreign soil, we can and must re-establish our own economic sovereignty by:

- Passing new laws to require U.S. incorporation of companies such as Tyco.

- Providing special tax rates to companies that incorporate in the U.S., are majority-owned by U.S. citizens, and employ mostly U.S. workers.

- Eliminating tax treaties and trade agreements with countries that are providing tax havens to corporations circumventing U.S. tax laws.

- Increasing substantially the tax rates on foreign-owned corporations.

- Changing our trade policies to support and reward companies that are loyal and show allegiance to the U.S.

I absolutely reject the suggestion made by members of both major political parties that the U.S. should lower its corporate tax rates. That is nonsense! I agree with Roosevelt that we are the masters, not the slaves, of the corporations that we, the American people, have called into being. If corporations want the privilege of doing commerce in our great nation, then they must be willing to contribute to and support the public good. We do not need or welcome blood suckers whose only interest is in feeding on the U.S. economy for their own profits without contributing to the common good.

Endless Scandals with No Justice or Accountability

Our aim is not to do away with corporations; on the contrary, these big aggregations are an inevitable development of modern industrialism, and the effort to destroy them would be futile unless accomplished in ways that would work the utmost mischief to the entire body politic. We can do nothing of good in the way of regulating and supervising these corporations until we fix clearly in our minds that we are not attacking the corporations, but endeavoring to do away with any evil in them. We are not hostile to them; we are merely determined that they shall be so handled as to subserve the public good. We draw the line against misconduct, not against wealth.

—THEODORE ROOSEVELT

This is more wise counsel from President Roosevelt. While we have every right to be outraged by the corruption that is rampant in corporate America and the harm it's doing to our country, we should also realize that corporations in of themselves are neither good nor evil. They do not have flesh, bones, hearts, or souls. They are simply legal structures created to bring people together to conduct business and generate wealth. Their culture or value system is a direct reflection of the people who lead and manage them. Therefore, we should not target our righteous indignation at corporations, but rather at misconduct within corporations perpetrated by those who have no morals, conscience, or ethical standards and will do anything for money and power. We should also remember that there are numerous U.S. and foreign corporations led by good people using their wealth and power to promote and support the common good. I have had the honor and privilege of being associated with a few such companies in my career. That being said, I think we have all had our fill of the corporate corruption and financial scandals that have plagued America over the past thirty years and are destroying our economy and the middle class. I have summarized some of these in the chart below.

Company	Date	Allegations	Investigation Results	Punishment
Adelphia Communications	Apr-02	Founding Rigas family collected $3.1 billion in off-balance-sheet loans backed by Adelphia; overstated results by inflating capital expenses and hiding debt.	Three Rigas family members and two other former executives were arrested for fraud. The company sued the entire Rigas family for $1 billion for breach of fiduciary duties, among other things.	John and Timothy Rigas were convicted and are now serving prison sentences of fifteen and twenty years, respectively.
AIG	Sep-08	AIG sold insurance policies on the toxic debt (CDOs) made from subprime mortgages. When theses mortgages defaulted, the CDOs' value went down and AIG was stuck with billions in liabilities. The policyholders wanted their insurance payments for the failed CDOs.	The U.S. government gave $182 billion to AIG. Company used bailout funds to pay up to $1.2 billion in bonuses in 2009, and to pay for extravagant trips. The week following the bailout, AIG treated employees and distributors to a California retreat costing $444,000 that featured spa treatments, banquets, and golf outings.	AIG had a long history of accounting fraud and other corrupt business practices prior to its 2008 collapse. There have been no prosecutions or recovery of ill-gotten wealth.
AOL Time Warner	Jul-02	As the ad market faltered and AOL's purchase of Time Warner loomed, AOL inflated sales by booking barter deals and ads it sold on behalf of others as revenue to keep its growth rate up and seal the deal. AOL also boosted sales via "round-trip" deals with advertisers and suppliers.	An SEC investigation found that AOL overstated revenues by $690 million from 2000 to 2002. It also inflated the number of subscribers to meet Wall Street expectations.	AOL Time Warner paid a $300 million penalty to the SEC. Six former AOL executives were prosecuted and reached plea agreements with the government. Charles Johnson, former CEO of PurchasePro, was sentenced to eight years in prison.

Company	Date	Allegations	Investigation Results	Punishment
Arthur Andersen	Nov-01	Shredding documents related to audit client Enron after the SEC launched an inquiry into the company.	Andersen was convicted of obstruction of justice in June 2002, and ceased auditing public firms in August 2002. This conviction was overturned by the U.S. Supreme Court, based on technicalities, in May 2005.	As of 2011, Arthur Andersen LLP has not been formally dissolved and hasn't declared bankruptcy. Ownership of the partnership has been ceded to four limited liability corporations.
Bank of Credit and Commerce International (BCCI)	Mar-91	BCCI perpetrated international financial crime on a massive and global scale. It was the bank of choice for money-launderers and terrorists. It defrauded investors of more than $18 billion. It handled money for dictators such as Saddam Hussein, Manuel Noriega, Hussain Mohammad Ershad, and Samuel Doe. Other accountholders included the Medellin Cartel and Abu Nidal.	An investigation spearheaded by Sen. John Kerry and NY District Attorney Robert Morgenthau exposed the massive criminal enterprise of BCCI. The CIA held accounts at BCCI used for illegal covert operations. James Bath, a former business partner of George W. Bush, was a BCCI director. Many corrupt U.S. lawyers and politicians accepted money from and assisted BCCI.	BCCI was shut down and its assets liquidated in 1991. The company paid $10 million in fines and forfeited all $550 million of its American assets—at the time, it was the largest single criminal forfeiture ever obtained by federal prosecutors. James Bath was never indicted or prosecuted for his involvement with BCCI. Only one U.S. lawyer or politician who assisted BCCI was convicted of a crime, but did not serve any prison time. Perhaps this was the largest cover-up in U.S. history?
Bear Stearns	Mar-08	Accused of using fraudulent accounting to mislead investors and shareholders. Investors lose $1.6 billion when hedge funds collapse and shareholders lose $18 billion when the company is sold to J.P. Morgan.	Civil suits have been filed by shareholders and investors. The SEC has not brought any action against the company. It tried unsuccessfully to prosecute two former hedge-fund managers.	In March 2008 Bear Stearns was hastily purchased by J.P. Morgan in a deal brokered and supported by the Bush administration and Federal Reserve. There have been no prosecutions or recovery of ill-gotten wealth.

Company	Date	Allegations	Investigation Results	Punishment
Bernard L. Madoff Investment Securities LLC	Dec-08	Former NASDAQ chairman Bernard Madoff caught running an elaborate Ponzi scheme (paying old clients with newer clients' money).	On March 12, 2009, Madoff pled guilty to eleven federal crimes and admitted to operating the largest Ponzi scheme in history, which defrauded investors of an estimated $64.8 billion. Investigators have determined others were involved in the scheme and believe the fraud may have begun in the 1970s.	Bernard Madoff sentenced to 150 years in prison with restitution of $170 billion. Eight others were arrested, but there have been only three convictions thus far.
Bristol-Myers Squibb	Jul-02	Fraudulent accounting inflated the company's revenue by $1.5 billion in 2001.	Illegally used "channel stuffing," or forcing wholesalers to accept more inventory than they can sell to get it off the manufacturers' books.	Agreed to pay $150 million in fines to the SEC in August 2004. Two former executives were indicted but never convicted. The case was dismissed in June 2010.
CA Technologies	Mar-02	Misstated more than $500 million in revenue in its 1998 and 1999 fiscal years in order to artificially inflate its stock price. Also made $1.1 billion in payouts to CEO Charles Wang and other top executives tied to these false reports.	An investigation by the Securities and Exchange Commission (SEC) resulted in charges against the company and some of its former top executives. The SEC alleged that from 1998 to 2000, CA routinely kept its books open to include quarterly revenue from contracts executed after the quarter ended to meet Wall Street analysts' expectations.	CA agreed to pay $225 million in restitution to shareholders in 2004. Eight CA executives have since pleaded guilty to fraud charges—most notably former CEO and chairman Sanjay Kumar, who received a twelve-year prison sentence for orchestrating the scandal. Charles Wang was never charged.
Cendant Corporation	Apr-98	Fraudulent accounting had inflated the company's revenue by $500 million over a period of three years.	After merging with CUC International, Cendant uncovered massive accounting fraud at CUC, which resulted in one of the largest financial scandals of the 1990s and, at the time, the largest case of accounting fraud in the country's history.	Former Vice Chairman E. Kirk Shelton was later sentenced to ten years in prison and former CEO Walter Forbes was sentenced to twelve years in prison.

Company	Date	Allegations	Investigation Results	Punishment
CMS Energy	May-02	Executing "round-trip" trades to artificially boost energy trading volume by $5 billion.	Appointed Thomas J. Webb, a former Kellogg's CFO, as its new chief financial officer in Aug-02.	SEC filed charges against the company and former executives in 2004. CMS paid fines to the SEC and company shareholders of over $200 million.
Duke Energy	Jul-02	Engaged in twenty-three "round-trip" trades to boost trading volumes and revenue.	The company says an internal investigation concluded that the trades had "no material impact on current or prior" financial periods.	Company fired the executives involved and affirmed to the SEC that such trades are in conflict with the company's policies and procedures.
Dynegy	May-02	Executing "round-trip" trades to artificially boost energy trading volume and cash flow.	The SEC found that Dynegy engaged in securities fraud and negligently included materially misleading information about the round-trip energy trades in two press releases it issued in early 2002.	Dynegy settled with the SEC in 2002 paying a $3 million fine. There were no convictions.
El Paso	May-02	Executing "round-trip" trades to artificially boost energy trading volume.	The SEC charged El Paso Corp. and five former employees with fraud. Revenues were inflated by $1.7 billion for the years 1999 through 2002 and the first nine months of 2003.	Shareholders won a $286 million settlement against El Paso in 2007. The SEC settled with the company and executives in 2008. Over $200,000 in fines were levied but there were no convictions.
Enron	Oct-01	Boosted profits and hid debts totaling more than $1 billion by improperly using off-the-books partnerships; manipulated the Texas power market; bribed foreign governments to win contracts abroad; manipulated California energy market.	Fraudulently reported earnings and made false and misleading statements concerning financial results. Charges also levied for insider trading that generated ill-gotten wealth in the hundreds of millions. This was one of the biggest corporate frauds in American history.	Hundreds of charges were made by the SEC and Department of Justice-nineteen former executives pleaded guilty or were convicted. Only three received prison sentences. Also, only a tiny fraction of the ill-gotten wealth was recovered.

Company	Date	Allegations	Investigation Results	Punishment
Fannie Mae	Sep-04	The combination of earnings manipulation, mismanagement, and unconstrained growth resulted in an estimated $10.6 billion of losses, well over a billion dollars in expenses to fix the problems, and ill-gotten bonuses in the hundreds of millions of dollars.	Office of Federal Housing Enterprise Oversight issued a report to congress in May 2006. It described an arrogant and unethical corporate culture where Fannie Mae employees manipulated accounting and earnings to trigger bonuses for senior executives from 1998 to 2004.	The financial crisis created on Wall Street combined with mismanagement caused the collapse of Fannie Mae. On September 9, 2008, the Bush administration seized control of Fannie Mae and ousted the CEO and board of directors. This significantly increased U.S. national debt by about $1 billion. There have been no prosecutions or recovery of ill-gotten wealth.
Freddie Mac	Jan-03	Overstated earnings by $989 million in 2001 and understated profit by more than $5 billion in 2000 and 2002 to smooth out results and show the steady growth favored on Wall Street. Also made $1.7 million in illegal campaign contributions in 2006.	Office of Federal Housing Enterprise Oversight issued a report to congress in June 2006. According to the report profits were "illusions deliberately and systematically created by the company's senior management." The problems at Freddie Mac worsened as the housing market continued to decline.	The financial crisis created on Wall Street combined with mismanagement caused the collapse of Freddie Mac. On September 9, 2008, the Bush administration seized control of Freddie Mac and ousted the CEO and board of directors. This significantly increased U.S. national debt by about $1 billion. There have been no prosecutions or recovery of ill-gotten wealth.

Company	Date	Allegations	Investigation Results	Punishment
Global Crossing	Feb-02	Engaged in network-capacity "swaps" with other carriers to inflate revenue; shredded documents related to accounting practices.	The SEC charged that Global Crossing deceived investors. Company executives sold billions in stock before some $40 billion in shareholder value evaporated. The company filed for Chapter 11 bankruptcy protection; Singapore Technologies Telemedia later purchased the company for $750 million. In 2011 Level 3 Communications purchased it for $2 billion.	Gary Winnick, the founder and former chairman of Global Crossing, made $734 million selling his shares before it collapsed. No fraud charges were ever filed against Winnick or any other Global Crossing insiders, and none has admitted to any wrongdoing. There have been no prosecutions or recovery of ill-gotten wealth.
Halliburton	Oct-03	Paid bribes to Nigerian officials from 1995 to 2002 totaling $171.5 million to Nigerians to secure contracts worth billions.	Pleaded guilty in Feb-09 to charges related to the Foreign Corrupt Practices Act (FCPA).	Three former executives were charged and pleaded guilty. Sentences received ranged from 1 year probation to 30 months in prison. This is just one of numerous Halliburton scandals.
Healthsouth	Mar-03	CEO Richard Scrushy charged with perpetrating a $2.6 billion accounting fraud by the SEC.	In late 2002, Scrushy sold $75 million in stock several days before the company posted a large loss. An SEC followed, which resulted in charges against the company and some of its former top executives. The SEC alleged that from 1999 to 2002, they committed accounting fraud to meet Wall Street analysts' expectations.	Scrushy paid $81 million to settle a lawsuit brought against him by the SEC and was permanently barred from serving as an officer or director of a public company. He was also later convicted of bribery and is serving six years and ten months in a federal prison. Fifteen other executives pled guilty and most received light sentences and fines.

Company	Date	Allegations	Investigation Results	Punishment
Lehman Brothers	Sep-08	Used accounting "gimmicks" that seem fraudulent, along with offshore banking transactions to inflate profits and hide toxic debts totaling more than $50 billion.	A suit was filed against Ernst & Young by the NY Attorney General in Dec-10 accusing the firm of facilitating a "major accounting fraud" by helping Lehman Brothers Holdings Inc. deceive the public about its financial condition. As of Nov-11, this suit is unresolved and no action has been taken by the U.S. government against either Lehman or Ernst & Young.	In Sep-08 Lehman Brothers collapsed into bankruptcy. There have been no prosecutions or recovery of ill-gotten wealth.
Merrill Lynch	Sep-08	Accused of securities fraud and misleading investors and shareholders prior to collapse in 2008.	Civil suits have been filed by shareholders and investors. The SEC has not brought any action against the company. In Sep-08, Bank of America purchased Merrill in deal brokered and forced by the Federal Reserve and Bush administration. The same weekend, Lehman Brothers went bankrupt.	CEO John Thain gave out up to $4 billion in bonuses before Bank of America took the company over. This happened as Bank of America was getting $20 billion more in federal funds due in part to the takeover. There have been no prosecutions or recovery of ill-gotten wealth.
Nicor Energy, LLC, a joint venture between Nicor and Dynergy	Jul-02	Independent audit uncovered accounting problems that boosted revenue and underestimated expenses.	Nicor restated results to reflect proper accounting in the first half of this year.	Company paid a $10 million fine to the SEC. Three former executives were charged with fraud, but the cases were later dropped. There have been no prosecutions or recovery of ill-gotten wealth.

Company	Date	Allegations	Investigation Results	Punishment
Peregrine Systems	May-02	Overstated $100 million in sales by improperly recognizing revenue from third-party resellers.	In 2004, eight former executives of Peregrine Systems, one former outside auditor, and two outside business partners were indicted for conspiracy to commit a multibillion-dollar securities fraud. The company filed for bankruptcy and was later acquired by HP.	Seven of those charged received prison sentences ranging from six months to eight years. Former Chairman of the Board, John Moores, sold more than $600 million of shares during Peregrine's fraudulent period but was never charged. There has been no recovery of ill-gotten wealth.
Qwest Communications International	Feb-02	Inflated revenue using network capacity "swaps" and improper accounting for long-term deals.	The SEC charged Qwest with securities fraud by inflating revenues by $3.8 billion and excluding $231 million in expenses between 1999 and 2002. Former Chairman and CEO Joseph Nacchio and eight other former employees were charged with fraud.	Nacchio was convicted on nineteen counts of insider trading and sentenced to six years in prison. No others received prison time. Qwest paid a $250 million fine to the SEC and agreed to permanently maintain a chief compliance officer to report to an outside director on the company board. There has been no recovery of ill-gotten wealth.
Sunbeam-Oster	Jun-98	Overstated earnings by $60 million in 1997. Accused by the SEC of accounting fraud.	An internal investigation revealed that Sunbeam was in severe crisis, and that CEO Albert Dunlap had encouraged violations of accepted accounting rules. The company filed for Chapter 11 bankruptcy protection in 2001.	Albert Dunlap paid a $500,000 fine to the SEC and was banned from serving again as an officer or director of a public company. He also paid $15 million in damages to investors. He did not serve any jail time.

Company	Date	Allegations	Investigation Results	Punishment
Tyco	May-02	Charged with inflating operating income by at least $500 million from 1998 to 2002 and failing to disclose executive compensation and loans. Company also accused of bribing Brazilian officials.	SEC charged Tyco with a billion-dollar accounting Fraud. It also filed civil fraud charges against former CEO L. Dennis Kozlowski, alleging that he and others failed to disclose multi-million-dollar low-interest and interest-free loans they took from the company, and in some cases never repaid. Charges also filed against CFO Mark H. Swartz and chief legal officer Mark A. Belnick.	Tyco paid $50 million in fines to the SEC and $3 billion to settle investor lawsuits. Dennis Kozlowski and Mark Swartz were convicted of grand larceny, falsification of business records, and conspiracy, and are now serving up to twenty-five years in prison. A former director, Frank Walsh, who received a secret $20 million payment for helping arrange a merger, pleaded guilty to securities fraud, but was not sentenced to prison.
Waste Management	Jun-98	Falsifying financial reports to boost earnings by $1.7 billion	A review of the company's accounting practices revealed that the company had augmented the depreciation time length for its property, plant, and equipment, making their after-tax profits appear higher.	WM paid $457 million to settle a shareholder class-action suit and the SEC fined WM's independent auditor, Arthur Andersen, $7 million for its role.
WorldCom	Mar-02	Overstated the income it reported in its financial statements by $11 billion. Committed securities fraud. The company also gave founder Bernard Ebbers $400 million in off-the-books loans.	The SEC accused WorldCom of engaging in a scheme directed and approved by its senior management that disguised its true operating performance. This fraud misstated WorldCom's earnings in 2001 and 2002 to keep them in line with estimates by Wall Street analysts.	The company paid a $750 million settlement to the SEC and a $6.1 billion settlement to investors. Bernard Ebbers was convicted of fraud and is serving a twenty-five-year sentence. Five other former WorldCom executives were charged and convicted receiving prison sentences ranging from five months to five years.

Company	Date	Allegations	Investigation Results	Punishment
Xerox	Jun-00	Falsifying financial results from 1997 to 2000, boosting income by $1.5 billion.	Xerox used a variety of what it called "accounting actions" and "accounting opportunities" to meet or exceed Wall Street expectations and disguise its true operating performance from investors.	Xerox agreed to pay the SEC a $10 million fine and to restate its financials from 1997 to 2000.

This is not an all-inclusive list. There have been numerous U.S. corporate scandals over the past thirty years and the damage done is so severe that it is mind boggling. Countless innocent lives have been ruined. The entire life savings of hard-working Americans have been wiped out. Cities and towns across America have been devastated. Sadly, the response from our government and political leaders—of both major political parties—has been pathetic! They make great speeches saying that those who have committed these crimes must be held accountable and brought to justice, but it's just political theater with no real substance as the examples summarized above bear out. With few exceptions, those perpetrating these crimes are either not held accountable or receive punishments that are much less than deserved. Worse yet, most of these corporate criminals also keep the wealth that they acquire from their illegal activities and use it to post bail and hire high-powered lawyers. These lawyers file endless appeals that delay sentencing and often reduce or overturn the convictions of these criminals on technicalities. This injustice is no accident—it is the product of a legal and political system that has been corrupted and hijacked by corporations and Wall Street. There are several glaring examples of this in the above chart. Let's take a closer look at a couple of them.

Enron

This scandal broke in October 2001. It was the largest corporate fraud and bankruptcy case in U.S. history before it was surpassed by WorldCom in 2002. Many Americans believe justice was served, given the publicity surrounding this case at the time. I don't think that's true. Here is a summary:

- Of the nineteen former executives who pleaded guilty or were convicted, only three received prison sentences.

- Andrew Fastow, former CFO and mastermind of the Enron fraud, plea-bargained a ten-year sentence that was reduced to six. He was released on December 16, 2011. He paid $23.8 million as part of his sentence but may still have millions in the bank.

- Jeffrey Skilling, former CEO, is serving a twenty-four-year sentence.

- Kenneth Lay, founder and former chairman, was convicted but died before sentencing.

- George W. Bush received more than $290,000 in contributions from former chairman Kenneth Lay. Enron and its executives contributed $1.7 million to both Democrats and Republicans in the 2000 election alone, according to the Center for Responsive Politics.

- $2 billion was lost by 20,000 employees in their 401Ks, but only $85 million was recovered.

- $40 billion was lost by 1.5 million investors, but only $7 billion was recovered.

- $688 million in fees were paid to the law firm that represented investors, the largest amount ever received in a securities fraud case in the United States.

- Linda Lay, wife of Kenneth Lay, receives approximately $32,643 monthly from Enron-era annuities.

- Linda Lay sold seventeen homes she owned in Aspen, Houston, and Galveston for an undisclosed amount. It is not known where the proceeds from these sales went. Linda Lay still owns a "Highrise Castle Retreat" in Houston, which is listed for $6.99 million. Here are some photos.

Source: Swamplot.com

Ken and Linda Lay's "Highrise Castle Retreat": As of January 2012 the asking price was $6.99 million for the home, which takes up the 33rd floor of The Huntingdon at 2121 Kirby in Houston, Texas. Amenities include four balconies, three fireplaces, six elevators (two of them service), four private bedroom suites, nine bathrooms, and a wine closet tucked easily into 12,827 square feet.

Global Crossing

This scandal broke in January 2002—four months after Enron. It was the largest telecom company bankruptcy in U.S. history before the collapse of WorldCom later that same year. Here are the highlights *(Trigaux)*:

- Company founded in 1997 by Gary Winnick, a close associate of Michael Milken, who was indicted on ninety-eight counts of racketeering and securities fraud in 1989.

- Global Crossing went public in August 1998 and filed for bankruptcy in January 2002.

- Gary Winnick made $734 million selling his shares in Global Crossing before it went bankrupt.

- Other company insiders sold a whopping $4.5 billion in stock in three years.

- Terry McAuliffe, who was chairman of the Democratic National Committee in 2002 and a friend of former President Clinton, turned a $100,000 investment in the company into $18 million.

- Anne Bingaman, chief of the Justice Department antitrust division and the wife of Jeff Bingaman, the Democratic Senator from New Mexico, was paid $2.5 million to lobby for Global Crossings in 1999.

- Former President George H. W. Bush took stock in the company in lieu of an $80,000 speaking fee in 1998. That stock later grew in value to $14 million.

- Arthur Andersen, the company that audited Enron, was the auditor for Global Crossings as well.

- Gary Winnick was based in Los Angeles, but the company said it was based in Hamilton, Bermuda.

- Gary Winnick was called "The Emperor of Greed" by *Fortune* magazine in 2002 *(Creswell and Prins)*. However, no fraud charges were ever filed against Winnick or any other Global Crossing insider. They walked away unscathed with billions!

These scandals were a direct result of deregulation and a lack of adequate government oversight. Had we kept and fully enforced the regulations put in place by FDR after the last Great Depression, neither Enron nor Global Crossings would have happened, and most of the other scandals listed would have been avoided as well. It is said that those who fail to learn from history are bound to repeat it—and that's precisely what has happened.

Given the rampant corporate corruption over the past thirty years and the recent Wall Street scandals that led to the collapse of the U.S. financial markets and economy, I find it unbelievable that some are still preaching deregulation and advocating reducing or eliminating enforcement agencies.

Those who continue to push for such deregulation and reduced enforcement are either ignorant of history, blinded by ideology, or corrupt. Any well-educated, rational, reasonable, and honest person can see that government regulation and oversight are needed to protect the employees and share-holders of America's corporations. We also need to strengthen our laws against corporate crime and ensure we have adequate resources to enforce the laws—including seizure of *all* ill-gotten wealth. It is a national disgrace that:

- many who commit corporate crimes and profit from them receive little or no punishment.

- corporate criminals and those associated with them are able to keep some or all of the wealth that was gained through their illegal activities.

- these criminals are able to use the wealth obtained through their illegal activities to hire lawyers who cleverly manipulate our judicial system in favor of the criminals.

That kind of injustice is un-American and will destroy our great nation if we do not act quickly to correct it. Now let's look closer at Wall Street and the collapse of 2008.

U.S. Taxpayer Bailout of Wall Street

And I sincerely believe, with you, that banking establishments are more dangerous than standing armies; and that the principle of spending money to be paid by posterity, under the name of funding, is but swindling futurity on a large scale.

—THOMAS JEFFERSON, IN AN 1816 LETTER TO JOHN TAYLOR

The greed and corruption that caused the collapse of our financial system and led to the massive taxpayer-funded bailout of Wall Street in 2008 is not a new phenomenon. It is a repeat of history. We all know about the Great Depression, but what many may not realize is that bank scandals, bank failures, and unstable financial markets were a common occurrence in the U.S. prior to 1933. Here is another excerpt from Theodore Roosevelt's "the New Nationalism" speech that was delivered in 1910, but could, and perhaps should, be delivered with the same relevance today.

The absence of effective State, and, especially, national, restraint upon unfair money-getting has tended to create a small class of enormously wealthy and economically powerful men, whose chief object is to hold and increase their power. The prime need is to change the conditions which enable these men to accumulate power which is not for the general welfare that they should hold or exercise. We grudge no man a fortune which represents his own power and sagacity, when exercised with entire regard to the welfare of his fellows. Again, comrades over there, take the lesson from your own experience. Not only did you not grudge, but you gloried in the promotion of the great generals who gained their promotion by leading the army to victory. So it is with us. We grudge no man a fortune in civil life if it is honorably obtained and well used. It is not even enough that it should have gained without doing damage to the community. We should permit it to be gained only so long as the gaining represents benefit to the community. This, I know, implies a policy of a far more active governmental interference with social and economic conditions in this country than we have yet had, but I think we have got to face the fact that such an increase in governmental control is now necessary.

No man should receive a dollar unless that dollar has been fairly earned. Every dollar received should represent a dollar's worth of service rendered—not gambling in stocks, but service rendered. The really big fortune, the swollen fortune, by the mere fact of its size acquires qualities which differentiate it in kind as well as in degree from what is possessed by men of relatively small means.

In 1933, Franklin D. Roosevelt signed the Banking Act of 1933 (commonly referred to as the Glass-Steagall Act) into law, which coupled with the similarly named Glass-Steagall Act of 1932 provided financial system regulatory reforms designed to correct the abuses that caused numerous bank failures and financial crises before and after the stock market crash of 1929 *(Wikipedia)*. The later Glass-Steagall Act prohibited commercial banks from involvement in the securities and insurance businesses. It also strengthened the powers of supervisory authorities, increased controls over the volume and use of credit, and provided for the insurance of bank deposits under the Federal Deposit Insurance Corporation (FDIC). These reforms were followed by the Banking Act of 1935, which strengthened the powers of the Federal Reserve Board of Governors in the field of credit management, tightened existing restrictions on banks engaging in certain activities, and enlarged the supervisory powers of the FDIC *(Wikipedia)*. The result of these reforms was the longest period of banking and financial market stability in U.S. history—from 1933 until the 1986 savings-and-loan crisis.

Starting in the early 1980s, the federal government began reversing the financial market regulatory reforms put into place after the Great Depression and passed a series of new laws to deregulate the savings and loan industry. This deregulation allowed savings and loan associations to engage in risky loans and real estate investments. It also enabled fraud and other forms of corruption to go undetected, which led to massive bank failures and emergency government intervention in 1986. Sound familiar? The total cost of that government bailout was $125 billion, which was 5 percent of our $2.1 trillion national debt in 1986 *(Curry and Shibut)*. It seemed like a lot of money at the time. Little did we know it was small potatoes, merely a warm-up act to the trillions spent addressing the greatest financial and economic crisis since the Great Depression.

Now let's fast forward to 1999, which is when the Gramm-Leach-Bliley Act was passed by Congress and signed into law by President Clinton. This new law repealed or eliminated the financial system and regulatory reforms that were enacted by the passage of the Glass-Steagall Act in the

1930s *(Wikipedia)*. This massive deregulation paved the way for a reenactment of the same reckless behaviors and abuses that caused numerous bank failures and financial crises before and after the stock market crash of 1929. Thanks to the passage of Gramm-Leach-Bliley, in September 2008, it was 1929 all over again! We even had a Republican president who presided over the crash of our financial system and then handed the wreckage to a new Democratic president. Unfortunately, that is where the similarities end.

Unlike 1933, the response from our political leaders to this crisis has been weak and those in our financial system, who brought this calamity upon the rest of us, have not been held accountable. There has been no criminal investigation even though there is evidence of fraud and other misdeeds. There also had been no recovery of ill-gotten financial gains. Instead, those involved in creating and perpetrating this financial fraud have been handsomely rewarded with billions of dollars in bonuses and trillions of taxpayer dollars that have been used to pay for fraudulent investments *(Cuomo)*. Who says crime doesn't pay? Unlike FDR's New Deal in the 1930s, the New Deal of 2008 is the privatization of profits and the socialization of debt. Our nation is in more debt—especially foreign debt—than at any other time in our history. The debt is a direct result of the failed economic and trade policies that have been driven, in large part, by the greed and corruption of Wall Street and both major political parties *(Time)*.

> UNLIKE FDR'S NEW DEAL IN THE 1930S, THE NEW DEAL OF 2008 IS THE PRIVATIZATION OF PROFITS AND THE SOCIALIZATION OF DEBT.

Congress should immediately repeal the Gramm-Leach-Bliley Act and reinstate all provisions of the Glass-Steagall Act. The Dodd-Frank Wall Street Reform and Consumer Protection Act passed in 2010 *(Wikipedia)*, by itself, does not adequately address the protections lost when the Glass-Steagall Act was repealed in 1999. By reinstating the Glass-Steagall Act, we will restore all protections to our financial systems that were lost when Glass-Steagall was repealed. Once this is done, a panel of trusted, nonpartisan economic advisors can review Glass-Steagall to determine, what, if any changes to this law should be made, to account for changes in our financial systems since 1933. Any such changes should strengthen, not weaken, the protections provided by Glass-Steagall to ensure the integrity and stability of our financial systems. This panel should then make recommendations to congress and the executive branch to amend the Glass-Steagall Act, as necessary. Any such amendments should then be publicly debated and voted upon by the electorate. This should be the process moving forward for changing any of our long-standing regulatory policies—especially those such as the Glass-Steagall Act that provided financial market stability for almost sixty years. Such important legislation that impacts all of our lives should be debated and passed in the open—not behind closed doors. The aim of our government should not be more or less regulation, but smart and effective regulation that ensures accountability to serve and protect the common good.

By now perhaps you are wondering why our political leaders changed laws that had been in place for sixty years and were working as intended. The short answer is misguided ideology and political corruption. The longer answer is:

1. Our economy began to falter in the 1970s primarily because of our failed economic and trade policies.

2. Rather than changing our trade and economic policies, our political leaders instead tried to convince Japan they needed to "play fair." We know how that worked out—good for them, bad for us.

3. OPEC was also putting the squeeze on the U.S. economy throughout the 1970s.

4. Our economy continued to decline as we lost more jobs to Japan and others—we kept our markets open and they kept theirs closed—good for them, bad for us.

5. In 1980 Ronald Reagan was elected and blamed our economic problems on government. He and the Republican Party begin implementing deregulation on a broad scale.

6. Deregulation continues through the 1980s and 1990s—all seems well, but nobody seems to notice that the trade surplus that we ran throughout our history is now a trade deficit. We also are incurring the largest peace-time national debt in our nation's history.

7. Outsourcing of manufacturing to communist China starts in the 1970s and accelerates in the 1980s, 1990s, and 2000s. The U.S. runs record trade deficits with China.

8. Manufacturing declines from 25.6 percent of the U.S. economy in 1945 to 10.5 percent in 2010, while financial services increases from 10.5 percent to 21.1 percent over the same period. See the chart below.

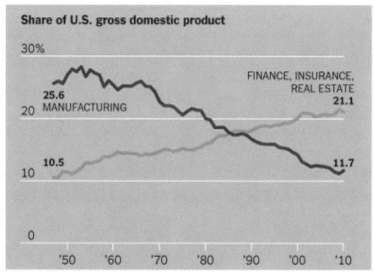

Sources: Bureau of Economic Analysis; the World Bank

9. All of this combined to create the "illusion of prosperity" when, in fact, all we have been doing since the 1970s is running up a huge debt that future generations will have to pay.

We can and must reverse course and put the financial sector back under the control of the U.S. people and our government. This sector should be supporting—not destroying—U.S. manufacturing and the growth of our overall economy. The financial sector must also serve the needs of all Americans and not just the top 1 percent.

In closing, here are some links to government reports if you would like to do some more reading on the causes of the financial and economic collapse of 2008. These are long reports, so settle in for a long read.

The Financial Crisis Inquiry Report—U.S. Financial Crisis Inquiry Commission

http://www.gpoaccess.gov/fcic/fcic.pdf

Wall Street and the Financial Crisis: Anatomy of a Financial Collapse—U.S. Senate

http://hsgac.senate.gov/public/_files/Financial_Crisis/FinancialCrisisReport.pdf

Greedy CEOs and Inflated Executive Compensation Plans

We grudge no man a fortune in civil life if it is honorably obtained and well used. It is not even enough that it should have gained without doing damage to the community. We should permit it to be gained only so long as the gaining represents benefit to the community . . . .

Those who oppose all reform will do well to remember that ruin in its worst form is inevitable if our national life brings us nothing better than swollen fortunes for the few and the triumph in both politics and business of a sordid and selfish materialism.

—THEODORE ROOSEVELT

If Roosevelt were alive today, I have no doubt he would take to his bully pulpit to lead the fight against the greedy CEOs who are destroying America. I think he would be especially appalled at how greedy CEOs in one company after another are moving jobs to communist China and other low-wage countries, while throwing American workers onto the unemployment rolls. Many of these same CEOs dodge taxes and commit accounting fraud to boost short-term profits so they can cash in on bonuses and stock options. It doesn't matter if the company succeeds or fails—either way these greedy CEOs walk away with millions. They have no interest in serving the greater good—only in lining their pockets with gold. The only thing bigger than their compensation packages is their overly inflated egos. Below is a list of the ten highest paid CEOs in America. It was taken from a list of the 500 highest paid CEOs in America published by *Forbes* in early 2011.

America's Highest Paid CEOs

Rank	Name	Company	1-Year Pay ($mil)	5 Year Pay ($mil)	Shares Owned ($mil)
1	Stephen J Hemsley	UnitedHealth Group	101.96	120.47	111.4
2	Edward A Mueller	Qwest Communications	65.8	75	36.3
3	Robert A Iger	Walt Disney	53.32	147.08	43.4
4	George Paz	Express Scripts	51.52	100.21	79.5
5	Lew Frankfort	Coach	49.45	137.87	133.9
6	Ralph Lauren	Polo Ralph Lauren	43	155.25	3,417.80
7	John C Martin	Gilead Sciences	42.72	204.24	76.8
8	James T Hackett	Anadarko Petroleum	38.94	97.38	24.6
9	John T Chambers	Cisco Systems	37.9	170.34	58
10	Ivan G Seidenberg	Verizon Commun	36.75	130.19	76.5

Source: Forbes Magazine --> http://www.forbes.com/lists/2011/12/ceo-compensation-11_rank.html

The number one CEO on this list, Stephen Hemsley of UnitedHealth, made $101.9 million in one year! How can any public company, especially one providing health insurance, justify paying their CEOs such an inflated compensation package? No wonder health-care costs continue to spiral out of control in this country. Not far behind Mr. Hemsley is Edward Mueller of Qwest Communications coming in at $65.8 million! His predecessor, Joseph Nacchio, was convicted of nineteen counts of insider trading and sentenced to six years in prison. The average CEO compensation at S&P 500 companies was $11.3 million in 2010, up 12 percent from 2009, and it breaks down as follows:

2010 Average CEO Pay at S&P 500 Companies	
Salary	$1,093,989
Bonus	$251,413
Stock Awards	$3,833,052
Option Awards	$2,384,871
Nonequity Incentive Plan Compensation	$2,397,152
Pension and Deferred Compensation Earnings	$1,182,057
All Other Compensation	$215,911
TOTAL	$11,358,445

Source: AFL-CIO analysis of pay data from 299 companies, provided by salary.com.

According to the *Forbes* list, 116 CEOs made $12 million or more in total compensation in 2010. In fact, during the past decade, CEOs of the largest American companies received more in compensation than ever before in U.S. history.

Sources: For data through 2005, Carola Frydman, MIT Sloan School of Management, and Dirk Jenter, Stanford Graduate School of Business.[4] For 2009 data, IPS calculations.[5]

Is it possible for any CEO to be worth $100 million, or even $12 million a year? Are their jobs more demanding than, for example, the President of the United States, who makes $400,000 a year? Despite the Great Recession of 2008, CEO pay continues to skyrocket. After adjusting for inflation, CEO compensation in 2009 and 2010 more than doubled the average in the 1990s, more than quadrupled the average in the 1980s, and ran approximately eight times the average for all the decades of the mid-twentieth century.

American workers, by contrast, are taking home less in real weekly wages than they took home in the 1970s. Back then, few top executives made over thirty times what their workers made. According to the AFL-CIO, in 2010 the total compensation for CEOs of major U.S. corporations averaged 343 times the median pay of American workers *(AFL-CIO)*.

CEO Pay Skyrockets Compared with Workers' Wages

In **1980**, CEO pay equaled

42

times the average blue collar worker's pay.

Sources: IBusinessWeek magazine

By **2010**, CEO pay had grown to

343

times workers' median pay — by far the widest gap in the world.

Sources: AFL-CIO calculations, www.paywatch.org

While CEO compensation soars . . .

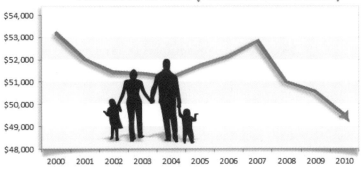

U.S. Median Household Income Fell $3,719 From 2000 to 2010 (Measured 2010 Dollars)

Source: U.S. Census Bureau, Selected Measures of Household Income Dispersion.

. . . median income falls . . .

The Top 1 Percent's Share of National Income Peaked in 1929 and 2007

Source: Emmanuel Saez, U.C. Berkeley Department of Economics

. . . the richest get richer . . . and it starts looking a lot like 1929.

This historical disparity in executive compensation is similar to what occurred in 1929 with the same disastrous effect on our financial system and the overall economy. There is also a direct correlation between this disparity and the misguided free trade, deregulation, and tax policies of the past forty years. Most careful analyses of the 2008 financial meltdown that ushered in the Great Recession have concluded that excessive executive compensation played a major role. So what about Wall Street? Surely the pay of financial executives has gone down since the collapse of 2008 and the massive taxpayer-funded bailout, right? Remember all the speeches from our political leaders about how outraged they were when Wall Street was paying multibillion-dollar bonuses with taxpayer money? Just in case you forgot, here is a quick refresher *(Cuomo)*:

- Merrill Lynch allocated nearly $4 billion in bonuses after being rescued from bankruptcy with a $45 billion taxpayer bailout.
    - The top four bonus recipients received a combined $121 million.
    - The next four bonus recipients received a combined $62 million.
    - The next six bonus recipients received a combined $66 million.
    - Fourteen individuals received bonuses of $10 million or more, and combined they received more than $250 million.
    - Twenty individuals received bonuses of $8 million or more.
    - Fifty-three individuals received bonuses of $5 million or more.
    - 149 individuals received bonuses of $3 million or more, equaling $858 million.
    - 696 individuals received bonuses of $1 million or more.
- Goldman Sachs received a $10 billion taxpayer bailout then allocated $10.9 billion in bonuses to 440 partners worth $3 to $4 million each, and bonuses to assistants, junior analysts, and other employees.

- AIG received $185 billion in taxpayer bailouts, then used the money to pay up to $450 million in bonus payments to employees of its financial services division. This was the division that caused their bankruptcy! Bonuses were estimated at $1.2 billion for the overall company.

When the cameras went away, the political theatrics came to an end and Wall Street continued to go about its business as usual. They paid these much-discussed taxpayer-funded bonuses while millions of Americans lost their jobs, homes, healthcare, and 401Ks. Those who helped create the financial crisis and the Great Recession continue to profit from their destruction of the U.S. economy. Though cash bonuses fell, total compensation for Wall Street firms increased in 2010. According to *Wall Street Journal* estimates *(Lucchetti and Grocer),* the total compensation at large financial services companies rose 5.7 percent in 2010 to a record $135 billion! Instead of contributing to the common good and helping to rebuild America's economy, Wall Street is continuing to destroy it!

Then again, there is a very large American flag hanging out in front of the NYSE. I guess that makes everything okay? Hmmm . . . I can just imagine a dinner meeting in a country club somewhere in Washington, D.C., or New York between some of our political leaders, the Wall Street bankers, and their lobbyists discussing how glad they were to make it through this crisis together and joking about all of the media attention over these bonuses.

In 2010, the Obama administration passed the Dodd–Frank Wall Street Reform and Consumer Protection Act, which has several provisions aimed at curbing excessive executive compensation:

1. Starting in 2011, shareholders of publicly traded companies are required to be given a say-on-pay vote on executive compensation. Although these votes are not binding, they are intended to encourage boards of directors to reform their companies' executive compensation. The theory is that no CEO wants to suffer the embarrassment of shareholders voting against their pay.

2. Board of Directors' compensation committees now must consist entirely of independent directors. Financial companies must ensure that their incentive pay plans do not create excessive risk.

3. Companies will be required to disclose pay-versus-performance information in proxy statements for annual meetings, including the relationship between executive compensation actually paid and the financial performance of the company.

4. CEO Pay Comparison—under this requirement, companies will have to disclose: (a) the median annual total compensation of all employees of the company, excluding the CEO; (b) the annual total compensation of the CEO; and (c) the ratio of the amounts in (a) and (b).

Will these measures rein in excessive executive compensation and begin to significantly narrow the corporate pay gap? It is doubtful since Great Britain has had a say-on-pay provision since 2002, and it hasn't prevented a continuing escalation of executive pay. Despite the recession, British executive compensation has risen significantly above where it was before the pay-on-say requirement was on the books. So what is the solution?

To bring executive pay back down to mid-twentieth-century levels, we must implement more stringent reforms that are clear, direct, and easily enforced by the SEC. Some suggestions are:

1. Establish a maximum total compensation limit for executives of public companies by either using a fixed amount or a multiplier of twenty to thirty times the average worker's pay. In either case, we should target an amount of $1 to $2 million, which would be in line with mid-twentieth-century levels, and closer to what executives are paid in Japan.

2. Use an approach similar to what was enacted in the Netherlands. As of January 2010, executives at any bank based or doing business in the Netherlands may only pocket "variable" pay that adds up to no more than an executive's annual salary. This "variable" pay encompasses all executive pay incentives, not just

bonuses, but also options and other stock awards. This reform does not set a dollar limit on pay, but will likely go much further than many other reforms to bring down CEO pay levels by limiting total compensation to no more than twice the amount of executive salary. It will also help counter the "bonus culture" that encourages high-risk investing.

3. Enact a law limiting total compensation for all employees in a company accepting taxpayer bailout money to no more than the U.S. president's salary, which is currently $400,000. This would act as a deterrent to future fiscal irresponsibility and make the terms of seeking and receiving a taxpayer bailout crystal clear.

Some who read these suggestions will say that they are socialism. They aren't. The same type of regulations were proposed a century ago by Theodore Roosevelt who was a true patriot and a Republican, unlike those who masquerade under that banner today. His rationale was simple, and it's as relevant today as it was in his time. In his 1905 inaugural address, Roosevelt stated that:

> Corporations engaged in interstate commerce should be regulated if they are found to exercise a license working to the public injury. It should be as much the aim of those who seek for social-betterment to rid the business world of crimes of cunning as to rid the entire body politic of crimes of violence. Great corporations exist only because they are created and safeguarded by our institutions; and it is therefore our right and our duty to see that they work in harmony with these institutions.

And again, he later stated that:

> The absence of effective State, and, especially, national, restraint upon unfair money-getting has tended to create a small class of enormously wealthy and economically powerful men, whose chief object is to hold and increase their power. The prime

need is to change the conditions which enable these men to accumulate power which is not for the general welfare that they should hold or exercise. We grudge no man a fortune which represents his own power and sagacity, when exercised with entire regard to the welfare of his fellows. Again, comrades over there, take the lesson from your own experience. Not only did you not grudge, but you gloried in the promotion of the great generals who gained their promotion by leading the army to victory. So it is with us. We grudge no man a fortune in civil life if it is honorably obtained and well used. It is not even enough that it should have gained without doing damage to the community. We should permit it to be gained only so long as the gaining represents benefit to the community. This, I know, implies a policy of a far more active governmental interference with social and economic conditions in this country than we have yet had, but I think we have got to face the fact that such an increase in governmental control is now necessary.

No man should receive a dollar unless that dollar has been fairly earned. Every dollar received should represent a dollar's worth of service rendered—not gambling in stocks, but service rendered. The really big fortune, the swollen fortune, by the mere fact of its size acquires qualities which differentiate it in kind as well as in degree from what is possessed by men of relatively small means. Therefore, I believe in a graduated income tax on big fortunes, and in another tax which is far more easily collected and far more effective—a graduated inheritance tax on big fortunes, properly safeguarded against evasion and increasing rapidly in amount with the size of the estate.

These are not the words of a socialist, but one of the greatest presidents and patriots in American history! Roosevelt was a man of principle and courage who put his country and his fellow countrymen above party politics and misguided ideology. He was not self-serving, as is the case with many of our current politicians, but truly worked for the greater good. It is time we followed his example and took action to once and for all eliminate the injustice of inflated CEO compensation and the harm this practice causes American corporations and workers. For those who say "we will lose many of our best CEOs," I say let them go if they choose to leave. They can be replaced. If they love wealth more than America, we don't need them. As Samuel Adams said in a speech at the Philadelphia State House on August 1, 1776:

> If ye love wealth better than liberty, the tranquility of servitude better than the animating contest of freedom, go home from us in peace. We ask not your counsels or arms. Crouch down and lick the hands which feed you. May your chains set lightly upon you, and may posterity forget that ye were our countrymen.

The China Syndrome

Corruption in communist China is rampant and it threatens the U.S. and world economies. Graft, bribery, embezzlement, kickbacks, theft, extortion, backdoor deals, nepotism, patronage, and fraud are common practices in China. This is a cancer that is spreading to U.S. and European companies and other Western economic and political institutions, such as the NYSE, that operate in communist China. Did you know that Chinese companies are listed on the New York Stock Exchange? This is insane given the corruption that exists within communist China and the lack of transparency or a credible political or justice system. How do we really know these companies are complying with U.S. securities laws? How can we verify their financial reports? What if they break U.S. laws? What power does the U.S. government have to enforce or punish violations and recover damages? This is a real concern given that some 10 percent of investigations of companies for

DID YOU KNOW THAT CHINESE COMPANIES ARE LISTED ON THE NEW YORK STOCK EXCHANGE?

breach of the United States Foreign Corrupt Practices Act (FCPA) in the past five years involve companies doing business in China. Numerous cases concern U.S. companies offering bribes in China. In fact, communist China leads the world in both the number and size of corruption cases prosecuted under the FCPA, as summarized in the chart below (Palazzolo).

U.S. Justice Department and SEC Prosecutions for Corruption in China

Company	Date	Allegations	Investigation Results	Punishment
ITT Corporation	Feb-09	From 2001 to 2005, ITT's wholly owned Chinese subsidiary, Nanjing Goulds Pumps Ltd., paid $200,000 in bribes to Chinese government officials.	The bribes generated more than $4 million in sales for NGP/ITT and more than $1 million in profits. The payments made by NGP were disguised as increased commissions in NGP's books and records.	Agreed to pay $1.7 million in fines to the SEC.
AMAC International	Nov-08	Dr. Shu Quan-Sheng, a native of China, a naturalized U.S. citizen, and physicist was the president, secretary, and treasurer of AMAC International Inc. He Illegally sold sensitive space technology to communist China along with defense information and bribed Chinese officials.	Was awarded a $4 million contract from the Chinese government for a hydrogen liquefier project. AMAC performs research through government grants on behalf of the Department of Energy and the National Aeronautics and Space Administration	Forfeited $386,740 in fines to the DOJ. Sentenced to fifty-one months in prison.
Alliance One International and Universal Corporation	Aug-10	Paid bribes and provided gifts, travel, and entertainment expenses to government officials to secure tobacco sales contracts.	Illegal activity spanned several countries, including China.	Agreed to pay $28.4 million in fines to the SEC and DOJ.

Company	Date	Allegations	Investigation Results	Punishment
Paradigm B.V.	Sep-07	Paid bribes to government officials to secure sales contracts.	Used an agent to make commission payments to representatives of a subsidiary of the China National Offshore Oil Company (CNBOOC) in connection with the sale of software to a CNOOC subsidiary. Illegal activity spanned several countries, including China.	Agreed to pay $1 million in fines to the DOJ.
InVision Technolo-gies	Jun-04	Paid bribes to government officials to secure sales contracts.	Sales agents and distributors made payments or provided gifts to foreign government officials. InVision improperly recorded these payments as legitimate business expenses.	Agreed to pay $1.9 million in fines to the SEC and DOJ.
Veraz Networks	Jun-10	Paid bribes to government officials to secure sales contracts.	Engaged a consultant in China who gave gifts and offered bribes valued at approximately $40,000 to officials at a government-controlled telecom company in China.	Agreed to pay $300,000 in fines to the SEC.
Lucent Technolo-gies	Dec-07	Provided travel and other things of value to Chinese officials and improperly accounted for certain corporate expenditures on behalf of those officials in company books and records.	Provided 315 trips for Chinese officials to the Grand Canyon, Universal Studios, and Disneyland. The company characterized the travel as factory inspections and training.	Agreed to pay $2.5 million in fines to the DOJ and SEC.
Avery Dennison	Jul-09	Paid kickbacks and bankrolled sightseeing trips and gifts for Chinese officials to secure business.	Avery China secured a sale to a state-owned end user by agreeing to pay a Chinese official a kickback of nearly $25,000 through a distributor. Avery China realized $273,213 in profit from this transaction.	Agreed to pay $500,000 in fines to the SEC.
UTStarcom	Dec-09	Paid bribes to government officials to secure sales contracts.	Chinese unit had spent almost $7 million on 225 trips for Chinese government employees.	Agreed to pay $3 million in fines to the DOJ and SEC.

Company	Date	Allegations	Investigation Results	Punishment
Diagnostic Products	May-05	Charged with paying millions in bribes to Chinese hospitals and administrators.	Paid bribes from late 1991 through December 2002 to secure business with these hospitals.	Paid $2.8 million in fines to the SEC.
Faro Technologies	Jun-08	Paid bribes to government officials to secure sales contracts.	Made payments disguised as referral fees to secure contracts worth approximately $4.9 million. Routed these payments to Chinese government officials through a shell company to avoid exposure.	Paid $1.85 million in fines to the SEC.
IBM	Mar-11	Provided improper cash payments, gifts, and travel and entertainment to government officials in South Korea and China.	IBM China subsidiaries engaged in a widespread practice of providing overseas trips, entertainment, and improper gifts to Chinese government officials.	Agreed to pay $10 million in fines to the SEC.
AGA Medical	Jun-08	Paid bribes to doctors and government official.	In exchange for payments, Chinese doctors directed government-owned hospitals to purchase AGA's products. Also made payments to government officials employed by the State Intellectual Property Office to have patents approved.	Paid $2 million in fines to the DOJ.
Control Components	Jul-09	Paid millions of dollars in bribes to government officials to secure $46.5 million in sales contracts.	A decade-long scheme to secure contracts in approximately thirty-six countries, including China, by paying bribes to officials and employees of various state-owned companies, and foreign and domestic private companies.	Two former executives pled guilty and six others have been charged and are awaiting trial. CCI agreed to pay $18.2 million in fines to the DOJ.
RAE Systems	Dec-10	Paid bribes to government officials to secure sales contracts.	China subsidiaries paying improper commissions, kickbacks, and "under table greasing to get deals."	Agreed to pay $2.9 million in fines to the DOJ and SEC.

Company	Date	Allegations	Investigation Results	Punishment
Maxwell Technolo-gies	Jan-11	Paid bribes to government officials to secure sales contracts.	Paid more than $2.5 million to its Chinese agent to secure contracts with Chinese customers, including contracts for sales to state-owned manufacturers. The agent then used money to bribe officials at state-owned entities.	Agreed to pay $13.65 million in fines to the DOJ and SEC.
Schnitzer Steel Industries	Jun-07	Paid $200,000 in bribes to government officials to secure $96 million in sales contracts.	Made illegal payments over almost a 10-year period to officers and employees of nearly all of Schnitzer Steel's government-owned customers in China.	Company paid $15.2 million in fines to the SEC and DOJ. Former executives paid separate fines.
Daimler AG et al	Apr-10	Paid tens of millions of dollars in bribes to government officials in China and 21 other countries to secure contracts for the purchase of Daimler vehicles worth hundreds of millions of dollars.	Within Daimler AG and its subsidiaries, bribe payments were often identified and recorded as *"commissions," "special discounts,"* and/or *"nützliche Aufwendungen"* or *"N.A."* payments, which translates to "useful payment" or "necessary payment," and was understood by certain Daimler employees to mean "official bribe."	Company paid $185 million in fines to the SEC and DOJ. No criminal charges were filed and there were no prosecutions.
Siemens	Dec-08	Made at least 4,283 payments, totaling approximately $1.4 billion, to bribe government officials in return for business around the world, including China.	Used bribes to win contracts for the design and construction of metro transit lines in Venezuela, power plants in Israel, refineries in Mexico, developing mobile telephone networks in Bangladesh, national identity cards in Argentina, and medical devices in Vietnam, China, and Russia.	Agreed to pay $800 million in fines to the DOJ and SEC and $569 million to the Office of the Prosecutor General in Munich. This was the largest FCPA settlement in history. No criminal charges were filed and there were no prosecutions.

This is only the tip of the iceberg! Bribery, fraud, kickbacks, and other forms of corruption are so pervasive and commonplace in China that most of it goes undetected and unpunished. It is common practice for U.S. companies and other foreign firms to enlist the services of local middlemen to interface with corrupt government officials. These third parties help companies cut through red tape by paying the bribes required, and they give U.S. companies deniability in the unlikely event that either the U.S. or Chinese governments investigate the business dealings of their China subsidiaries. In theory, a U.S. company is as liable for the actions of a middleman as it is for its own employees. In actuality, there is a greater chance of being struck by lightning than there is of either the U.S. or communist Chinese governments investigating such activities. In the case of the U.S. government, there just aren't enough resources available to police all of the subsidiaries of U.S. companies operating in China due to both the distance and the lack of communist government transparency. In the case of the Chinese government, they simply have no sincere interest in investigating corruption since they are its perpetrators and primary beneficiaries. The People's Liberation Army (PLA) intelligence officers and their civilian counterparts from the Ministry of Public Security sometimes use evidence of corruption and sexual entrapment to gain cooperation on divulging commercial and industrial secrets from businessmen living or traveling within communist China.

As we discussed earlier in this book, many Americans have been led to believe that communist China is becoming more open and is moving toward democracy. This is nonsense! In fact, the opposite is happening. The U.S. is becoming less democratic and more like communist China, and it's no accident. It's by design. Communist China is not only exporting cheap goods to the U.S., but also corruption that is weakening our economic and political institutions. We are compromising, and in some cases even abandoning, the principles upon which our nation was founded to pursue economic interests in China. There is no better example of this than the assistance U.S. technology and Internet companies have provided to communist China to help suppress free speech and human rights.

U.S. Companies Collaborating with Communist China to Suppress Human Rights

In China there is no bill of rights guaranteeing freedom of speech, press, religion, and the right to assemble and petition the government. For a brief time, the Internet provided the only way for political dissidents in China to freely express their opinions. This came to an end with the help of Cisco, Microsoft, Oracle, EMC, and other major U.S. technology companies. Starting in the early 2000s, Cisco and other major U.S. technology companies began working with the Chinese Communist Party (CCP) to help design, develop, and implement the Golden Shield Project—an Orwellian system used to monitor, track, and censor all Internet traffic into and out of China. The Golden Shield Project, also known as the Great Firewall of China, is used by the government to eliminate references to politically sensitive topics such as Tiananmen Square, Liu Xiaobo, and the Arab Spring Revolutions sweeping through the Middle East. Sites including Facebook, Twitter, YouTube, Radio Free Asia (the BBC's Chinese-language service), and Wikipedia are also blocked *(McMahon and Bennett)*.

Together with the government's controls on traditional media, this Internet surveillance system shut down this briefly open window to the outside world. The Chinese people only hear and read what the CCP allows. Worse yet, this Internet surveillance system is used to detect, identify, track down, and arrest dissidents. In 2011 lawsuits were filed against Cisco in U.S. federal court by Chinese political prisoners and the Falun Gong, a Chinese spiritual movement, founded in 1992. According to the suit, more than 5,000 Falun Gong members were arrested as a result of Golden Shield technology. Many of those arrested were tortured and killed *(Moses)*.

In 2004 Yahoo! China provided Chinese government officials with user data that assisted in the arrest and conviction of at least four people who used email accounts from the Yahoo.com.cn service. The four cases were *(Human Rights Watch)*:

- **Shi Tao:** The Chinese journalist was sentenced in April 2005 to ten years in prison for "divulging state secrets abroad." These alleged state secrets consisted of reporting on the government restrictions on information related to the Tiananmen Square anniversary. In 2007, Jerry Yang, the former CEO of Yahoo!, apologized to the relatives of Shi Tao for giving Chinese authorities information used to track down and convict the reporter.

- **Li Zhi:** The Internet writer was sentenced in December 2003 to eight years in prison for "inciting subversion of the state authority." According to the court verdict originally posted on the Internet by the Chinese law firm that defended him, user account information provided by Yahoo! was used to build the prosecutors' case.

- **Jiang Lijun:** The Internet writer and pro-democracy activist was sentenced in November 2003 to four years in prison for "subversion." According to the court verdict obtained and translated by the Dui Hua Foundation, Yahoo! helped confirm that an anonymous email account used to transmit politically sensitive emails was used by Jiang.

- **Wang Xiaoning:** The Internet writer and dissident was sentenced in September 2003 to ten years in prison for "incitement to subvert state power," on the basis of essays he distributed on the Internet via email and Yahoo! groups. According to the court judgment obtained by the non-governmental organization Human Rights in China, Yahoo! provided information to investigators pertaining to the email address and Yahoo! group used by Wang.

The Beijing-based dissident intellectual Liu Xiaobo wrote a letter to Jerry Yang condemning his company's actions and its justifications for it. Here is an excerpt:

In my view, what Yahoo! has done is exchange power for money, i.e., to win business profit by engaging in political coop-eration with China's police. Regardless of the reason for this action and regardless of what kinds of institutions are involved, once Yahoo! complies with the CCP (Chinese Communist Party) to deprive human rights, what it does is no longer of a business nature, but of a political nature. It cannot be denied that China's Internet control itself is part of its politics, and a despotic politics as well. Therefore, the "power for money" exchange that takes place between Western companies like Yahoo! and the CCP not only damages the interests of customers like Shi Tao, but also damages the principles of equality and transparency, the rules that all enterprises should abide by when engaging in free trade. And it follows that if Yahoo! gains a bigger stake in the Chinese market by betraying the interests of its customers, the money it makes is "immoral money," money made from the abuse of human rights. This is patently unfair to other foreign companies that do abide by business ethics.

Liu Xiaobo, winner of the 2010 Nobel Peace Prize, is serving an eleven-year sentence in China for his political writings.

On July 4, 2011, American Independence Day, Microsoft announced its expansion of censorship and suppression of human rights in communist China through a partnership with Baidu, China's leading search engine that is closely linked to the CCP *(Kwong)*. Baidu has a long history of being the most proactive and restrictive online censor in the search arena. In May 2011 pro-democracy activists sued Baidu for violating the U.S. Constitution with the censorship it conducts in accord with the demands of the Chinese government *(Wikipedia)*. As part of its deal with Baidu, Microsoft will supply censored search results for English-language queries on the Chinese search provider. Like Baidu, Microsoft also has a long history of collaborating with the Chinese government to suppress free speech and human rights within China. In 2005 at the request of the communist Chinese government, Microsoft shut down the site of Chinese blogger Zhao Jung (a.k.a. Michael Anti) who had been addressing sensitive political issues on Microsoft's blog service *(Figliola, Addis, and Lum)*. The service was hosted in the United States—not China! Perhaps Bill Gates should use some of his billions to buy copies of David McCullough's *1776* for himself and his executive management team to remind them of what it means to be an American citizen and an American corporation!

No such reminder is necessary for Google. To its credit, it shut down its operation in mainland China in March 2010, after struggling with the censorship demands of the CCP for five years. It chose principle over profits! In the run-up to the 2008 Olympics, China decided to increase its Internet restrictions. In addition to censoring Google.cn results, the Chinese government demanded that Google purge objectionable links from the Chinese-language version of Google.com. Google refused, since that step would mean that it was acting as an agent of repression for Chinese-speaking people all over the world, including in the U.S. Other search engines, including Microsoft's, agreed to the demands. Tensions over censorship continued to escalate between Google and the Chinese government. Then, just before Christmas 2009, Google's monitoring system detected a break-in of their computer system. Some of the company's most sensitive intellectual property had been stolen and the hackers had dug into the Gmail accounts of Chinese dissidents and human rights activists. Their contacts, their plans, their most private information had fallen into the hands of intruders. The hackers were geographically tied to China—and both the sophistication of the attack and the nature of its targets pointed to the government itself as the instigator of or a party to the attack. Sergey Brin, cofounder of Google, took the incident personally. Insiders observed he was much less perturbed by the theft of Google's intellectual property than the fact that his company had unwittingly been a tool used to identify and silence critics of a repressive government. On January 10, 2010, Google's top executives decided the company would no longer carry out censorship for the Chinese government. Shortly afterward, the company shut down its censored search engine in China and redirected users to its uncensored site in Hong Kong *(Levy)*. For choosing principle over profit and for his passionate defense of freedom, Sergey Brin should be awarded the U.S. Presidential Medal of Freedom!

So where is the U.S. government while all this is going on? Well, our Congress has conducted a few hearings and, of course, there have been the usual political speeches, but it's been nothing more than theatrics. No concrete actions have been taken to force U.S. companies to stop collaborating with the communist Chinese government in their suppression of human rights. Our government also has taken no actions to punish the Chinese government for its attack on Google and other American companies and organizations that support human rights. Instead of being a passive observer, the U.S. government should be taking the lead in managing our trade relationship with communist China—especially when it involves human rights. This should not be left up to U.S. companies to figure out on their own. So why is this not happening? Follow the money . . . .

CHAPTER NINE

Political Scandal and Corruption

Now more than ever before, the people are responsible for the character of their Congress. If that body be ignorant, reckless and corrupt, it is because the people tolerate ignorance, recklessness and corruption. If it be intelligent, brave and pure, it is because the people demand these high qualities to represent them in the national legislature. . . . If the next centennial does not find us a great nation . . . it will be because those who represent the enterprise, the culture, and the morality of the nation do not aid in controlling the political forces.

—JAMES GARFIELD, 20TH PRESIDENT OF THE UNITED STATES

Political scandal and corruption are not new. They have been with us since the founding of our nation and with mankind since the beginning of time. The success or failure of democratic governments is determined, in large measure, by how well the dark forces that bring about political scandal and corruption are controlled. This was well understood by our Founding Fathers—especially John Adams, who was the primary author of the Constitution of the Commonwealth of Massachusetts. This is the oldest functioning written constitution in the world that has been in continuous effect, and it provided the framework for the U.S. Constitution, which was ratified eight years later while John Adams was serving his country as our first ambassador to England.

Our constitution provides us with a government that is based upon the rule of law—not man. However, our laws are created and enforced by men. In the case of our national government, Congress is responsible for creating and abolishing laws, and the judiciary is responsible for interpreting and enforcing those laws. The executive branch can propose and veto laws, but only Congress can create and abolish the laws that govern our country. It's important to remind ourselves of this foundation, since today so much emphasis is placed on the presidency and so little is placed upon the important role of Congress and the judiciary. The power in our federal government is meant to reside primarily within our bicameral Congress—the House of Representatives and the Senate. As Garfield reminded us in 1877, if our congress is ignorant, reckless, and corrupt, then the laws they enact will be ignorant, reckless, and corrupt. On the other hand, if our congress is intelligent, brave, and pure, they will enact laws that reflect those values and character. This is the heart of the matter that this chapter explores.

Abandoning the Glorious Cause

Posterity! You will never know how much it cost the present Generation to preserve your Freedom! I hope you will make good use of it. If you do not, I shall repent in Heaven, that I ever took half the Pains to preserve it.

—John Adams

Over the past forty years, an unprecedented wave of corruption and cronyism has poisoned our politics and crippled our federal, state, and local governments. Our political system has been hijacked and thoroughly corrupted by criminals and traitors to the Glorious Cause of America, who will do anything for money and power. Even more alarming and dangerous has been the acceptance and tolerance of this corruption by the American people. Throughout our history, when a public official was found to have committed a crime or immoral act they would either resign or be removed from office. As a result of violating the public trust, their career in public service would come to an abrupt end and they would be punished appropriately for their misdeeds. This is not the case today. Since the late 1960s public corruption has spiraled out of control and officials who are convicted of crimes rarely go to prison. Some have even won reelection after being convicted of crimes! Those who commit immoral or criminal acts and escape prosecution are also reelected and sometimes even elevated to the status of elder statesman, e.g., Bill Clinton, Newt Gingrich, Barney Frank, and many others. Below is a list, sourced primarily from *Wikipedia*, of those in the U.S. Congress who have been subject to disciplinary action since 1911.

House of Representatives—Expelled

Year	Representative	Party	State	Reason
1980	Michael J. Myers	D	PA	Convicted of bribery in the Abscam scandal.
2002	James Traficant	D	OH	Convicted on ten counts that included bribery, obstruction of justice, and racketeering.

House of Representatives—Censured

Year	Representative	Party	State	Reason
1921	Thomas L. Blanton	D	TX	Unparliamentarily language.
1979	Charles Diggs	D	MI	Payroll fraud, mail fraud.
1980	Charles H. Wilson	D	CA	Improper use of campaign funds.
1983	Daniel B. Crane	R	IL	Sexual misconduct with a House page.
1983	Gerry Studds	D	MA	Sexual misconduct with a House page
2010	Charles B. Rangel	D	NY	Improper solicitation of funds, inaccurate financial disclosure statements, failure to pay taxes.

House of Representatives—Reprimanded

Year	Representative	Party	State	Reason
1976	Robert L. F. Sikes	D	FL	Use of office for personal gain.
1978	Charles H. Wilson	D	CA	Making false statements to a House committee.
1978	John J. McFall	D	CA	Failure to report campaign contributions.
1978	Edward Roybal	D	CA	Making false statements to a House committee, failure to report campaign contributions.
1984	George V. Hansen	R	ID	False statements on financial disclosure form.
1987	Austin J. Murphy	D	PA	Allowed another person to cast his vote; misuse of House funds.
1990	Barney Frank	D	MA	Use of office to fix parking tickets and influence probation officers on friend's behalf.
1997	Newt Gingrich	R	GA	Use of tax-exempt organization for political purposes; provided false information to House Ethics Committee.
2009	Joe Wilson	R	SC	Outburst toward President Barack Obama during a speech to a joint session of Congress.

House of Representatives-elect—Excluded

Year	Representative	Party	State	Reason
1967	Adam Clayton Powell, Jr.	D	NY	Mismanaging his committee's budget in previous Congress, excessive absenteeism, misuse of public funds.

Senate—Resignations as a Result of Expulsion Proceedings

Year	Senator	Party	State	Reason
1922	Truman Handy Newberry	R	MI	Convicted of election fraud, but overturned, for excessive spending in a primary election.
1982	Harrison A. Williams	D	NJ	Convicted for bribery and conspiracy in the Abscam scandal; resigned before a vote by the full Senate.
1995	Robert W. Packwood	R	OR	Charged with sexual misconduct and abuse of power; resigned before a Senate vote.
2011	John Ensign	R	NV	Charged with financial improprieties stemming from an extramarital affair, resigned before vote.

Senate—Censured

Year	Senator	Party	State	Reason
1929	Hiram Bingham	R	CT	Employing as a Senate staff member Charles Eyanson, who was simultaneously employed by the Manufacturers Association of Connecticut.
1954	Joseph McCarthy	R	WI	Abuse and non-cooperation with the Subcommittee on Privileges and Elections during a 1952 investigation of his conduct for abuse of the Select Committee to Study Censure.
1967	Thomas J. Dodd	D	CT	Use of his office to convert campaign funds to his personal benefit. Conduct unbecoming a senator.
1979	Herman Talmadge	D	GA	Improper financial conduct, accepting reimbursements for official expenses not incurred, and improper reporting of campaign receipts and expenditures.
1990	David Durenberger	R	MN	Unethical conduct relating to reimbursement of Senate expenses and acceptance of outside payments and gifts.

As you can see, in the past one hundred years, twenty-seven members of Congress have either been expelled, censured, or reprimanded, or they have resigned—85 percent of these actions have occurred since 1967. These lists do not include numerous members of Congress who resigned or were convicted of crimes without being subject to congressional disciplinary action. But the pattern is the same—with the majority of these incidents also occurring since the late 1960s. It is no coincidence that this political decline correlates with America's economic decline. The two are closely linked. In the House of Representatives, all of the disciplinary actions due to crimes and corruption have occurred since 1967. What is even more disturbing is how few of these members were expelled or sent to prison given the seriousness of their offenses. If an average citizen like the infamous Joe Sixpack committed payroll fraud, mail fraud, tax evasion, or perjury; filed false statements to Congress; or was convicted of sexual misconduct at work, he would lose his job and serve jail time. It's no mystery why the U.S. Congress has the lowest approval rating in history. Now let's take a similar look at the Executive Branch over the same period.

Warren G. Harding Administration, 1921–1923

Name	Office	Party	Details
Albert Fall	Secretary of Interior	R	Bribed by Harry F. Sinclair for control of the Teapot Dome federal oil reserves in Wyoming. He was the first U.S. cabinet member ever to be convicted; he served two years in prison.
Charles Cramer	Veteran Affairs General Counsel	R	Committed suicide.
Charles R. Forbes	Director Veteran Affairs	R	After constructing and modernizing VA hospitals, he was convicted of bribery and corruption and sentenced to two years in jail.
Edwin C. Denby	Secretary of the Navy	R	Abuse and non-cooperation with the Subcommittee on Privileges and Elections during a 1952 investigation of his conduct for abuse of the Select Committee to Study Censure.
Harry M. Daugherty	Attorney General	R	Resigned because of an investigation about a bootlegging kickback scheme by his chief aide Jess Smith. Found not guilty.

Name	Office	Party	Details
Jess Smith	Aide to Attorney General	R	Destroyed incriminating papers and then committed suicide.
Thomas W. Miller	Head Office of Alien Property	R	Convicted of fraud by selling valuable German patents seized after World War I far below market price and bribery. Served eighteen-month sentence.

Richard M. Nixon Administration, 1969–1974

Name	Office	Party	Details
Charles W. Colson	Special Counsel to President	R	Convicted of obstruction of justice related to the Watergate burglary.
Dwight L. Chapin	Deputy Asst. to President	R	Convicted of perjury related to the Watergate burglary.
Egil Krogh Jr.	Aid to Counsel	R	Sentenced to six months.
Frederick C. LaRue	Attorney General Advisor	R	Convicted of obstruction of justice related to the Watergate burglary.
G. Gordon Liddy	Special Investigations Group	R	Convicted of burglary related to the Watergate burglary.
H. R. Haldeman	Chief of Staff	R	Convicted of perjury related to the Watergate burglary.
John Ehrlichman	Counsel to President	R	Convicted of perjury related to the Watergate burglary.
John N. Mitchell	Attorney General	R	Convicted of perjury related to the Watergate burglary.
John W. Dean III	Counsel to President	R	Convicted of obstruction of justice related to the Watergate burglary.
Other Nixon staff and officials	Various	R	A total of 69 government officials were charged and 48 pled guilty to crimes related to the Watergate burglary.
Richard Helms	Director of the CIA	R	Denied his role in the overthrow of Chilean President Salvador Allende and was convicted of perjury.

Name	Office	Party	Details
Richard Kleindienst	Attorney General	R	Found guilty of "refusing to answer questions" related to the Watergate scandal.
Richard M. Nixon	President	R	Due to his role in the Watergate burglary, became the first and only U.S. President to resign.
Spiro T. Agnew	Vice President	R	Convicted of tax fraud stemming from bribery charges in Maryland and forced to resign. Nixon replaced him as V.P. with Gerald R. Ford.

Jimmy Carter Administration, 1977–1980

Name	Office	Party	Details
Bert Lance	Director of OMB	D	Resigned amidst allegations of misuse of funds during the sale of a Georgia bank to BCCI. No charges were ever filed.

Ronald Reagan Administration, 1981–1988

Name	Office	Party	Details
Alan D. Fiers	CIA Chief of Central American Task Force	R	Convicted of withholding evidence, but after a plea bargain was given only one year of probation. Later pardoned by George H. W. Bush.
Caspar Weinberger	Secretary of Defense		Indicted on two counts of perjury and one count of obstruction of justice. Received a pardon from George H. W. Bush before he was tried.
Clair George	CIA Chief of Covert Ops.	R	Convicted on two charges of perjury, but pardoned by George H. W. Bush before sentencing.

Name	Office	Party	Details
Deborah Gore Dean	Executive Assistant to HUD	R	Convicted of twelve counts of perjury, conspiracy, and bribery. Sentenced to twenty-one months in prison.
Duane Clarridge	CIA senior official		Indicted in November 1991 on seven counts of perjury and false statements relating to a November 1985 shipment to Iran. Pardoned before trial by George H. W. Bush.
Edwin Meese	Attorney General	R	Resigned due to alleged involvement in Wedtech Corporation's payment of bribes for Defense Contracts. Never convicted.
Elliott Abrams	Assistant Secretary of State	R	Convicted of withholding evidence, but after a plea bargain was given only two years of probation. Later pardoned by George H. W. Bush.
James G. Watt	Secretary of Interior	R	Charged with twenty-five counts of perjury and obstruction of justice, sentenced to five years of probation, fined $5,000 and 500 hours of community service related to bribery by selected contractors for low-income housing projects.
John Poindexter	National Security Advisor	R	Convicted of five counts of conspiracy, obstruction of justice, perjury, defrauding the government, and the alteration and destruction of evidence. The Supreme Court overturned this ruling.
Joseph A. Strauss	Assistant Secretary of HUD	R	Convicted of accepting payments to favor Puerto Rican land developers in receiving HUD funding.
Joseph F. Fernandez	CIA Station Chief of Costa Rica		Indicted on five counts in 1988 that included obstruction of justice, making false statements, and defrauding the United States. The case was dismissed when Attorney General Dick Thornburgh refused to declassify information needed for his defense in 1990.

Name	Office	Party	Details
Lyn Nofziger	White House Press Secretary	R	Convicted for violating the Ethics in Government Act when he lobbied on behalf of Wedtech Corporation. The conviction was later overturned.
Michael Deaver	White House Deputy Chief of Staff	R	Pled guilty to perjury related to lobbying activities and was sentenced to three years of probation and fined $100,000.
Oliver North	Deputy Director, National Security Council	R	Convicted of accepting an illegal gratuity, obstruction of a congressional inquiry, and destruction of documents, but the ruling was overturned since he had been granted immunity.
Phillip D. Winn	Assistant Secretary of HUD	R	Pled guilty to bribery.
Richard V. Secord	Retired Major General, USAF	R	Organized the Iran arms sales and Contra aid. He pled guilty in November 1989 to making false statements to Congress. Sentenced to two years of probation.
Rita Lavelle	EPA Administrator	R	Misused "superfund" monies and was convicted of perjury. Served six months in prison, was fined $10,000 and given five years of probation.
Robert C. McFarlanes	National Security Advisor	R	Convicted of withholding evidence, but after a plea bargain was given only two years of probation. Later pardoned by George H. W. Bush.
Silvio D. DeBartolomeis	Director of FHA	R	Convicted of perjury and bribery.
Thomas Demery	Assistant Secretary of HUD	R	Pled guilty to bribery and obstruction.
Thomas G. Clines	Former CIA Officer		Became an arms dealer and was convicted in September 1990 on four income tax counts, including underreporting of income to the IRS and lying about not having foreign accounts. Sentenced to sixteen months in prison and fined $40,000.

Name	Office	Party	Details
William Casey	Director of CIA	R	Alleged to have conceived the Iran-Contra plan. Hours before he was scheduled to testify before Congress he was reported to have been rendered incapable of speech, and was later hospitalized.

George H. W. Bush Administration, 1989–1992

Name	Office	Party	Details
Catalina Vasquez Villalpando	Treasurer of the United States	R	Pled guilty to obstruction of justice and tax evasion. The only US Treasurer ever sent to prison.

Bill Clinton Administration, 1993–2000

Name	Office	Party	Details
Bill Clinton	President	D	Impeached for perjury and obstruction of justice. Lied under oath about sexual relations with intern Monica Lewinsky. Acquitted by the Senate and remained in office. Cited for contempt of court and agreed to a five-year suspension of his Arkansas law license. Barred from practicing law before the Supreme Court of the United States.

Name	Office	Party	Details
Bill Clinton	President	D	Granted 140 pardons on his last day in office for a total of 396 throughout his time in office. Those pardoned include: (1) Marc Rich-indicted for evading over $48 million and illegal oil dealings with Iran during the 1970s hostage crisis. Appeared pardon was granted in exchange for financial contributions. (2) Susan Mcdugall-received an eighteen-month jail sentence for contempt of court in the Whitewater trail. Refused to answer questions about whether Clinton lied to a grand jury. (3) Carlos Vignali-was serving a fifteen-year sentence for conspiracy to sell cocaine. His father was a rich and powerful leader in the Los Angeles Hispanic community who made large donations to the Democratic party. (4) Roger Clinton-president's half-brother pardoned for a 1985 cocaine-related offense.
Bill Clinton	President	D	Commuted the sentences of sixteen members of FALN, a violent Puerto Rican terrorist group, who were responsible for six deaths and some 150 injuries during bombings and armed attacks between the late 1970s and 1983. An NYC policeman blinded by a FALN bomb said these sentences were commuted to help Hillary Clinton gain Latino support in her campaign for U.S. Senate.

Name	Office	Party	Details
Chris Wade	Whitewater real estate broker	D	Pled guilty to making a false report to overvalue property and influencing a bank, savings and loan, or a federal agencies-bankruptcy fraud. Sentenced to fifteen months in prison. Received a full presidential pardon in the final hours of Clinton's presidency.
David Hale	Former Arkansas municipal judge and witness in the Whitewater scandal trials	D	Pled guilty to two felonies, testified in U.S. District Court that Clinton pressured him to make a fraudulent $300,000 loan and specifically asked that his name be kept out of the transaction.
Henry Cisneros	Secretary of Housing	D	Resigned and pled guilty to a misdemeanor charge of lying to the FBI about the amount of money he paid Linda Medlar, his former mistress, while he was Mayor of San Antonio, TX. He was fined $10,000. Received a full pardon in the final hours of Clinton's presidency.
James Riady	Deputy Chairman of the Lippo Group, a major Indonesian conglomerate		Pled guilty to violating U.S. campaign finance laws. Ordered to pay an $8.6 million fine for contributing foreign funds to the Democratic Party. James Riady and his father Mochtar Riady had a long-term relationship with China's intelligence agencies.
Jim Guy Tucker	Governor of Arkansas	D	Resigned the governorship and was replaced by Mike Huckabee on July 16, 1996, after his conviction for fraud related to the Whitewater scandal.
Jim McDougal	Business partner of Clinton's	D	Convicted of eighteen felony counts of fraud and conspiracy charges related to the Whitewater scandal. Died in prison.

Name	Office	Party	Details
John Huang	Deputy Assistant Secretary for International Economic Affairs	D	Pled guilty to violating U.S. campaign-finance laws. Funneled money from communist China and other foreign sources to Clinton and the DNC. Also suspected of selling secrets to communist China. His position at the Commerce Department gave him access to classified intelligence on China. While at the department, he met with Chinese embassy officials nine times.
Johnny Chung	Clinton fundraiser	D	Pled guilty to bank fraud, tax evasion, and violation of U.S. campaign finance laws. Funneled money from communist China and other foreign sources to Clinton and the DNC.
Maria Hsia	Fundraiser for DNC/ Clinton-Gore	D	Convicted of laundering foreign donations (from communist China) to the DNC from the Hsi Lai Buddhist Temple during the 1996 presidential election. Sentenced to ninety days' home detention, probation, a fine, and community service. Suspected of operating as an agent of communist China.
Mike Espy	Secretary of Agriculture	D	Resigned amid allegations that he had accepted tickets to sporting events, luggage, and other gifts worth thousands of dollars from people and companies he was supposed to be regulating, such as Tyson Foods, the giant poultry producer based in Arkansas.
Neal Ainley	Perry County Arkansas—Bank President	D	Pled guilty to concealing $180,000 in cash payments to Bill Clinton's 1990 gubernatorial campaign. Embezzled the bank funds for Clinton's campaign and was sentenced to two years of probation.

Name	Office	Party	Details
Robert W. Palmer	Former Madison Guaranty land appraiser	D	Pled guilty to federal conspiracy charges related to the Whitewater scandal. Received a full pardon in the final hours of Clinton's presidency.
Ron Brown	Commerce Secretary	D	Prior to his death in a plane crash in Croatia, was being investigated by a special prosecutor for various offenses, including receipt of bribes and falsification of his financial disclosure report.
Ronald Blackley	Chief of Staff to Secretary of Agriculture	D	Sentenced to twenty-seven months in prison for perjury.
Stephen Smith	Gubernatorial aide to Bill Clinton	D	Pled guilty to conspiracy related to the Whitewater scandal. Received a full pardon in the final hours of Clinton's presidency.
Susan McDougal	Business partner of Clinton's	D	Refused to answer questions for a grand jury about whether President Bill Clinton lied in his testimony during her Whitewater trial. Received a jail sentence of eighteen months for contempt of court. Rewarded for her loyalty to the Clintons with a full presidential pardon in the final hours of Clinton's presidency.
Ted Sioeng	Indonesian businessman with ties to communist China		Illegally donated money to both Democrats and Republicans. Suspected of working, along with his family, on behalf of communist Chinese government interests in the U.S. More than half of the $400,000 that Sioeng's family contributed to the DNC in 1996 was transferred from Hong Kong–based firms.
Webster Hubbell	Associate Attorney General	D	Former law partner of Hillary Rodham Clinton. Pled guilty to mail fraud and tax evasion while in private practice. Sentenced to twenty-one months in prison.

Name	Office	Party	Details
Yah Lin "Charlie" Trie	Commission on United States–Pacific Trade and Investment Policy	D	Convicted for violating U.S. campaign-finance laws. Funneled money from communist China and other foreign sources to Clinton and the DNC.

George W. Bush Administration, 2001–2008

Name	Office	Party	Details
Alberto Gonzales	Attorney General	R	Resigned under threat of impeachment along with eleven other senior Bush staffers who were involved in the politically motivated firing of eleven federal prosecutors. Those involved refused to cooperate with investigators into this matter citing "executive privilege."
Alphonso Jackson	Secretary of Housing and Urban Development	R	Resigned while under investigation by the FBI for revoking the contract of a vendor who told Jackson he did not like George W. Bush.
Bernard Kerik	Nominated as Secretary of Homeland Security	R	Nomination derailed by past employment of an illegal alien as a nanny, and other improprieties. Pled guilty to two counts of tax fraud and five counts of lying to the federal government and was sentenced to four years in prison.
Claude Allen	Advisor to President	R	Resigned after being arrested and convicted for a series of felony thefts in retail stores. Had previously been nominated by the Bush administration as a judge for the U.S. Court of Appeals for the Fourth Circuit.
David Safavian	GSA Chief of Staff	R	Found guilty of blocking justice and lying in connection with Jack Abramoff lobbying scandal. Sentenced to eighteen months in prison.

Name	Office	Party	Details
Dick Cheney	Vice President	R	Charged with corruption by the Nigerian government in connection with his role as the chief executive of Halliburton. A former subsidiary admitted that it bribed Nigerian officials. Halliburton paid Nigeria $250 million to settle this case and, in exchange, Nigeria agreed to drop the corruption charges against Cheney.
Dick Cheney	Vice President	R	Accused of war profiteering by assisting his former company, Halliburton, in securing more than $31 billion in "no bid" contracts to provide logistical support to U.S. troops in Iraq.
Dick Cheney	Vice President	R	As Chairman of the National Energy Development Group, held at least forty secret meetings with representatives of the energy industry and its interest groups to create a new national energy policy. Kenneth L. Lay, then head of Enron Corp., was among the more than twenty oil industry companies and executives who participated in the meetings.
George W. Bush	President	R	The Bush administration used RNC web servers for millions of emails that were later destroyed, lost, or deleted in violation of the Presidential Records Act and the Hatch Act. George W. Bush, Dick Cheney, Karl Rove, Andrew Card, Sara Taylor, and Scott Jennings all used RNC web servers for the majority of their emails. Of eighty-eight officials, no emails were discovered for fifty-one of them. As many as 5 million emails requested by congressional investigators of other Bush administration scandals were therefore unavailable, lost, or deleted.

Name	Office	Party	Details
George W. Bush	President	R	Hundreds of thousands of dollars in illegal payments were made to at least three journalists—Armstrong Williams (R), Maggie Gallagher (R), and Michael McManus (R)—to promote Bush administration policies.
George W. Bush	President	R	Directed the National Security Agency to implement a secret and illegal program to eavesdrop on domestic telephone calls by American citizens without warrants, bypassing the Foreign Intelligence Surveillance Act court that must approve all such actions.
Italia Federici	Secretary of the Interior staff	R	Pled guilty to tax evasion and obstruction of justice in connection with the Jack Abramoff lobbying scandal. Sentenced to four years of probation.
J. Steven Griles	Deputy to the Secretary of the Interior	R	Pled guilty to obstruction of justice in connection with Jack Abramoff lobbying scandal. Sentenced to ten months in prison.
Janet Rehnquist	Inspector General of the Department of Health and Human Services	R	Delayed an audit into an alleged $571 million overpayment to the State of Florida after receiving an urgent call from Governor Jeb Bush's chief of staff Kathleen Shanahan requesting this audit be delayed until after Jeb Bush's election. Rehnquist resigned after Congress began an investigation.
Jared Carpenter	Vice-President of the Council of Republicans for Environmental Advocacy	R	Pled guilty to tax evasion in connection with the Jack Abramoff lobbying scandal. Sentenced to four years of probation.
John Korsmo	Chairman of the Federal Housing Finance Board	R	Pled guilty to lying to Congress. Sentenced to eighteen months of unsupervised probation and fined $5,000.

Name	Office	Party	Details
Julie MacDonald	Deputy Assistant Secretary of the Department of the Interior	R	Resigned in 2007 after giving government documents to land developers.
Karl Rove	Senior Advisor to President	R	Investigated by the Office of Special Counsel for "improper political influence over government decision-making" and for his involvement in several other scandals. Resigned without responding to a Senate Judiciary Committee subpoena claiming, "I just think it's time to leave."
Kenneth Lay	Republican National Committee	R	Financial donor and ally of George W. Bush who was once considered a possible Secretary of the Treasury. Lay was found guilty of ten counts of securities fraud while Chairman and CEO of Enron. Died before sentencing.
Kyle Foggo	Executive Director of the CIA	R	Convicted of honest services fraud in the awarding of a government contract and sentenced to thirty-seven months in federal prison. Steered a CIA contract to the firm of his lifelong friend, Brent R. Wilkes
Lester Crawford	Commissioner of the Food and Drug Administration	R	Resigned after two months. Pled guilty to a conflict of interest and false reporting of information about stocks he owned in companies he was in charge of regulating. Received three years of supervised probation and a fine of $90,000.
Lewis Libby	Chief of Staff to Vice President	R	Convicted of perjury and obstruction of justice. He was sentenced to thirty months in prison and fined $250,000. The sentence was commuted by George W. Bush.

Name	Office	Party	Details
Lurita Alexis Doan	Director of General Services Administration	R	Resigned while being investigated for conflict of interest and violations of the Hatch Act. Among other things she asked GSA employees how they could "help Republican candidates."
Mark Zachares	Department of Labor Staff	R	Bribed by Jack Abramoff, pled guilty to conspiracy to defraud. Sentenced to twelve weekends in jail, four years of probation, two hundred hours of community service, and a $4,000 fine.
Robert E. Coughlin	Deputy Chief of Staff, Criminal Division of the Justice Department	R	Pled guilty to conflict of interest after accepting bribes from Jack Abramoff. Coughlin helped Abramoff get a $16.3 million grant from the Justice Department to build a jail for Abramoff's client, the Mississippi Band of Choctaw Indians. Sentenced to a month in a halfway house, three years of probation, and a $2,000 fine.
Roger Stillwell	Department of Interior staff	R	Pled guilty to falsely certifying that he did not receive reportable gifts from Jack Abramoff. Received a two-year suspended sentence.
Susan B. Ralston	Special Assistant to the President and Senior Advisor to Karl Rove	R	Resigned October 6, 2006, after it became known that she accepted gifts from and passed information to her former boss Jack Abramoff.

The pattern of corruption in the executive branch is similar to that of the Congress with the vast majority of the incidents occurring since the 1970s. While the Republicans win the prize for the highest number of corrupt presidential administrations over the past century, the Democrats aren't much better, as evidenced by the Clinton administration. Both major political parties are extremely corrupt and have abandoned America's Glorious Cause in pursuit of wealth and power. Their corrupt deeds dishonor those who fought and died to secure and preserve our freedom. President Adams must indeed be repenting in Heaven as he looks down upon the rampant and pervasive corruption that is destroying our constitutional government.

The time has come for "we the people" to take back our government from these criminals and traitors. As President Garfield admonished us over a hundred years ago, if Congress is ignorant, reckless, and corrupt, it's because we tolerate their ignorance, recklessness, and corruption. We can no longer afford to do so, however. We must take decisive action to reclaim our government, revitalize our Glorious Cause, and rebuild our nation for future generations. It is our solemn duty to President Adams and his generation, and to all true patriots who have sacrificed so much, including their lives, to secure and protect our liberty since the founding of this great nation.

Failure of the Two-Party System

However [political parties] may now and then answer popular ends, they are likely in the course of time and things, to become potent engines, by which cunning, ambitious, and unprincipled men will be enabled to subvert the power of the people and to usurp for themselves the reins of government, destroying afterward the very engines which have lifted them to unjust dominion.

—George Washington

There is nothing which I dread so much as a division of the republic into two great parties, each arranged under its leader, and concerting measures in opposition to each other. This, in my humble apprehension, is to be dreaded as the greatest political evil under our Constitution.

—John Adams

Our first two presidents were very wise men of impeccable character who saw the danger posed to our nation by political parties. They were also deeply concerned that political parties would subvert the power of the people and take away their constitutional government. Adams expressed concern in his writings about political parties creating divided loyalties. Both he and Washington were concerned that members of such parties would put loyalty to their party above loyalty to their country. He was also deeply concerned that political parties would make it difficult for the best, brightest, and most honorable citizens to obtain public office. Both Washington and Adams predicted that "unprincipled men" would gain control of these parties and use their political power to serve selfish ambitions instead of the common good.

Unfortunately, their predictions came true. While we have wrestled with this issue throughout our history, in the past forty years the two major parties have become so polarized and corrupt that they are destroying our constitutional democracy just as Washington worried they might. Both parties have put their own interests ahead of national interests and have used their political power to enrich themselves and their members instead of serving the greater good. They have rigged our election process to ensure their own survival, and corrupted our laws and judiciary to protect their party members and corporate donors from being held accountable for their misdeeds. Neither party represents the interests of the American people since both are controlled by foreign and domestic corporations and special interest groups that provide the majority of their funding.

The political ideologies of both parties are extreme and out of touch with mainstream America. Both practice dishonest, divisive politics aimed at manipulating and dividing public opinion instead of seeking to build an honest national consensus on important issues confronting our nation. Also, the primary processes used by both parties to select candidates are rigged and make it extremely difficult for our best, brightest, and most honorable citizens to obtain public office. Just look at the 2011 Republican presidential primary process. In my opinion, the best, brightest, and most honorable candidate in this group was former Utah Governor John Huntsman. However, he did not get any support from either the Republican Party or the media. Instead, they focused most of their attention on Herman Cain and Newt Gingrich. If Adams and Washington were alive today, I believe that they would approve of Huntsman's candidacy and would strongly disapprove of Cain and Gingrich. Then there is our current president, Barack Obama, who promised to reform government and deliver "Change We Can Believe In." It was a great campaign slogan, but all we got was more of the same corrupt government that serves corporate and special interests. Immediately after winning election he arranged a meeting with the Clintons and brought Hillary into his administration along with many other former staffers from the corrupt Clinton administration. Given what transpired during the Clinton administration, how do you think Washington and Adams would view this? Let's look at it another way. If they were alive today, do you think either would make it through the primary processes of the Republican or Democratic Parties and be elected president? I would bet not, since neither would be willing to compromise their principles to gain the endorsement of these corrupt political parties.

Actually, for proof of this, we need only look back to 1912 when Theodore Roosevelt was denied the Republican nomination even though he had overwhelming national popular support. Why was he denied the Republican nomination? Because he advocated banking and corporate reform. Just as they are today, the Republican and Democratic Parties back then were controlled by Wall Street and corporations that opposed the reforms he advocated. As I discussed earlier, Roosevelt created another option, the Progressive Party, and ran for reelection as a third-party candidate. Roosevelt was a true patriot in the same spirit as Washington and Adams. He put principle and country above party and worked for the common good of all Americans.

Corporate Influence—Lobbyists and Special Interests

It is necessary that laws should be passed to prohibit the use of corporate funds directly or indirectly for political purposes; it is still more necessary that such laws should be thoroughly enforced. Corporate expenditures for political purposes, and especially such expenditures by public-service corporations, have supplied one of the principal sources of corruption in our political affairs.

—THEODORE ROOSEVELT

This quote is taken from Roosevelt's "The New Nationalism" speech from 1910. In this speech he also states:

Now, this means that our government, national and State, must be freed from the sinister influence or control of special interests. Exactly as the special interests of cotton and slavery threatened our political integrity before the Civil War, so now the great special business interests too often control and corrupt the men and methods of government for their own profit. We must drive the special interests out of politics. That is one of our tasks today . . . .

For every special interest is entitled to justice, but not one is entitled to a vote in Congress, to a voice on the bench, or to representation in any public office. The Constitution guarantees protections to property, and we must make that promise good. But it does not give the right of suffrage to any corporation. The true friend of property, the true conservative, is he who insists that property shall be the servant and not the master of the commonwealth; who insists that the creature of man's making shall be the servant and not the master of the man who made it. The citizens of the United States must effectively control the mighty commercial forces which they have themselves called into being.

There can be no effective control of corporations while their political activity remains. To put an end to it will be neither a short nor an easy task, but it can be done.

We must have complete and effective publicity of corporate affairs, so that people may know beyond peradventure whether the corporations obey the law and whether their management entitles them to the confidence of the public. It is necessary that laws should be passed to prohibit the use of corporate funds directly or indirectly for political purposes; it is still more necessary that such laws should be thoroughly enforced. Corporate expenditures for political purposes, and especially such expenditures by public-service corporations, have supplied one of the principal sources of corruption in our political affairs.

Since the early 1900s the debate over corporate and special interest money in U.S. politics has continued. Laws have been passed to regulate this activity, the most recent being the McCain-Feingold Act of 2002. However, the enforcement of these laws is weak and no action has ever been taken to eliminate all such donations and ban corporations and special interests from participation in all political activity as proposed by Roosevelt. In fact, just the opposite has happened! In 2008 and 2010, the U.S. Supreme Court made rulings in the cases of *Wisconsin Right to Life v. Federal Election Commission* and *Citizens United v. Federal Election Commission* that roll back laws that have limited the role of corporate money in federal elections since Roosevelt was president *(Liptak)*. As a result of these Supreme Court rulings, domestic and foreign corporations and domestic and foreign special interests groups can now contribute and spend unlimited amounts of money to influence the outcomes of U.S. elections. This has resulted in record campaign spending and a dramatic increase in outside and undisclosed "secret" spending to influence U.S. elections as illustrated below.

Totals Spent on U.S. Federal Elections

Cycle	Total Cost of Election	To Dems	To Repubs	Dem %	Repub %
2010	$3,648,232,683	$1,816,201,141	$1,772,688,000	50%	49%
2008*	$5,285,680,883	$3,006,088,428	$2,239,412,570	57%	42%
2006	$2,852,658,140	$1,360,120,917	$1,444,816,900	48%	51%
2004*	$4,147,304,003	$2,146,861,774	$1,963,417,015	52%	47%
2002	$2,181,682,066	$977,041,618	$1,183,255,932	45%	54%
2000*	$3,082,340,937	$1,311,910,043	$1,662,298,674	43%	54%
1998	$1,618,936,265	$731,878,353	$878,130,297	45%	54%

*Presidential election cycle

In 1976 a total of $182 million was spent on all federal elections vs. $5.3 billion in 2008.

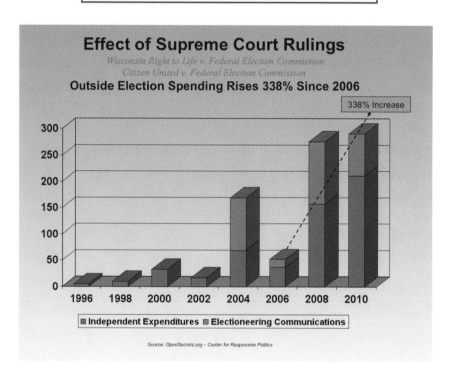

Effect of Supreme Court Rulings
Wisconsin Right to Life v. Federal Election Commission
Citizen United v. Federal Election Commission
Outside Election Spending Rises 338% Since 2006

338% Increase

■ Independent Expenditures ■ Electioneering Communications

Source: OpenSecrets.org – Center for Responsive Politics

230

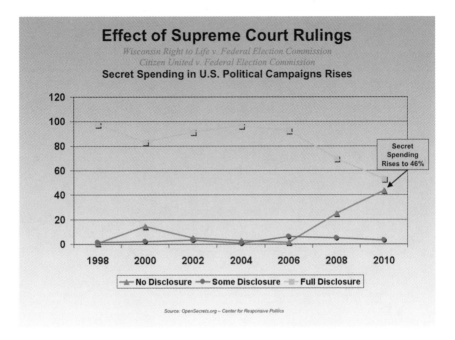

In 1976 a combined total of $171 million was raised by the presidential campaigns and only $67 million was spent. In 2008 a combined total of $1.7 billion was raised by the presidential campaigns and $1.3 billion was spent. This is a tenfold increase in the amount of money raised and twenty times the amount of money spent, and those figures don't even include the additional $300 million-plus raised and spent during the presidential primaries.

Presidential Fundraising and Spending, 1976-2008

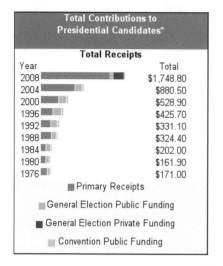

Total Contributions to Presidential Candidates*	
Total Receipts	
Year	Total
2008	$1,748.80
2004	$880.50
2000	$528.90
1996	$425.70
1992	$331.10
1988	$324.40
1984	$202.00
1980	$161.90
1976	$171.00

■ Primary Receipts

■ General Election Public Funding

■ General Election Private Funding

■ Convention Public Funding

Total Spending by Presidential Candidates*	
Total Spent	
Year	Total
2008	$1,324.70
2004	$717.90
2000	$343.10
1996	$239.90
1992	$192.20
1988	$210.70
1984	$103.60
1980	$92.30
1976	$66.90

* In millions
Numbers are not adjusted for inflation.
Source: OpenSecrets.org - Center for Responsive Politics

While these numbers are mind boggling to us average Americans, of even greater concern are the sources of the money being raised and spent. Here are a few charts showing the top contributors to the Obama, Clinton, and McCain campaigns in 2008 and the House and Senate campaigns in 2010.

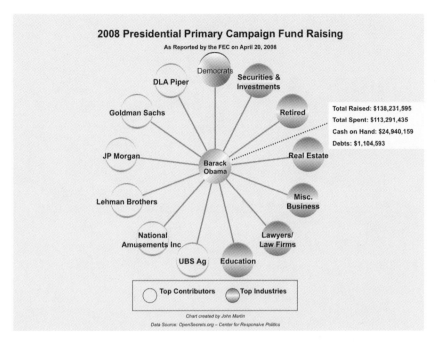

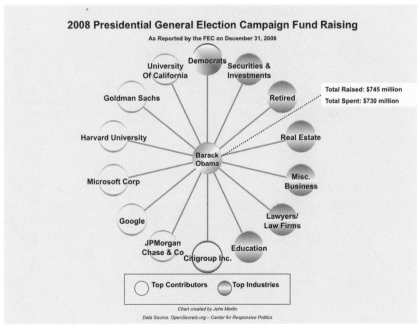

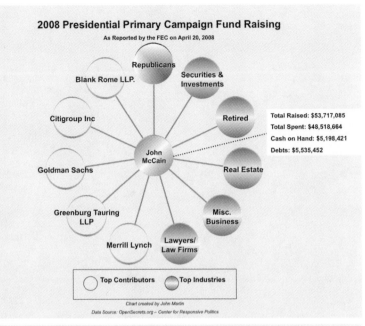

2008 Presidential Primary Campaign Fund Raising
As Reported by the FEC on April 20, 2008

Republicans
Blank Rome LLP.
Securities & Investments
Citigroup Inc
Retired
Goldman Sachs
John McCain
Real Estate
Greenburg Tauring LLP
Misc. Business
Merrill Lynch
Lawyers/ Law Firms

Total Raised: $53,717,085
Total Spent: $48,518,664
Cash on Hand: $5,198,421
Debts: $5,535,452

○ Top Contributors   ● Top Industries

Chart created by John Martin
Data Source: OpenSecrets.org – Center for Responsive Politics

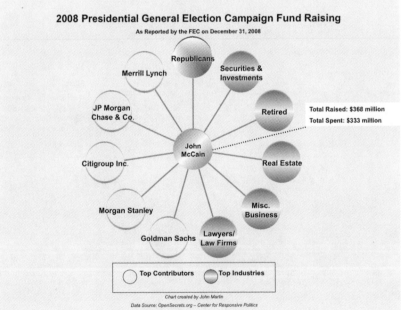

2008 Presidential General Election Campaign Fund Raising
As Reported by the FEC on December 31, 2008

Republicans
Merrill Lynch
Securities & Investments
JP Morgan Chase & Co.
Retired
Citigroup Inc.
John McCain
Real Estate
Morgan Stanley
Misc. Business
Goldman Sachs
Lawyers/ Law Firms

Total Raised: $368 million
Total Spent: $333 million

○ Top Contributors   ● Top Industries

Chart created by John Martin
Data Source: OpenSecrets.org – Center for Responsive Politics

234

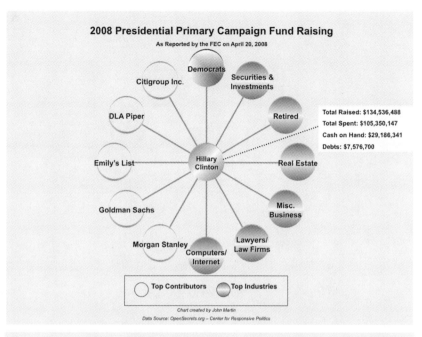

2008 Presidential Primary Campaign Fund Raising

As Reported by the FEC on April 20, 2008

Democrats
Citigroup Inc.
Securities & Investments
DLA Piper
Retired

Total Raised: $134,536,488
Total Spent: $105,350,147
Cash on Hand: $29,186,341
Debts: $7,576,700

Emily's List
Hillary Clinton
Real Estate

Goldman Sachs

Misc. Business

Morgan Stanley
Lawyers/ Law Firms
Computers/ Internet

◯ Top Contributors ◯ Top Industries

Chart created by John Martin
Data Source: OpenSecrets.org – Center for Responsive Politics

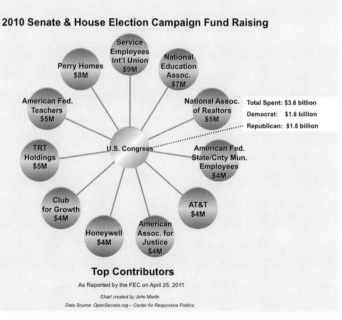

2010 Senate & House Election Campaign Fund Raising

Service Employees Int'l Union $9M
Perry Homes $8M
National Education Assoc. $7M

American Fed. Teachers $5M
National Assoc. of Realtors $5M

Total Spent: $3.6 billion
Democrat: $1.8 billion
Republican: $1.8 billion

TRT Holdings $5M
U.S. Congress
American Fed. State/Cnty Mun. Employees $4M

Club for Growth $4M
AT&T $4M

Honeywell $4M
American Assoc. for Justice $4M

Top Contributors

As Reported by the FEC on April 25, 2011

Chart created by John Martin
Data Source: OpenSecrets.org – Center for Responsive Politics

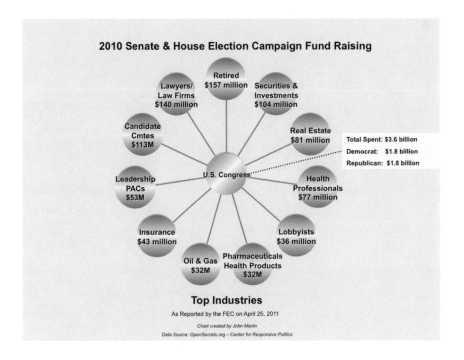

2010 Senate & House Election Campaign Fund Raising

Retired
$157 million

Lawyers/
Law Firms
$140 million

Securities &
Investments
$104 million

Candidate
Cmtes
$113M

Real Estate
$81 million

Total Spent: $3.6 billion
Democrat: $1.8 billion
Republican: $1.8 billion

U.S. Congress

Leadership
PACs
$53M

Health
Professionals
$77 million

Insurance
$43 million

Lobbyists
$36 million

Oil & Gas
$32M

Pharmaceuticals
Health Products
$32M

Top Industries

As Reported by the FEC on April 25, 2011

Chart created by John Martin

Data Source: OpenSecrets.org – Center for Responsive Politics

They say a picture is worth a thousand words, and from these pictures it is clear why Wall Street got a bailout and U.S. taxpayers got the bill. It is also clear why the big banks and Wall Street firms that received these bailouts paid themselves billions of dollars in bonuses with taxpayer money. They knew that they had absolutely nothing to fear from our government since they own the politicians. They also knew that the outrage expressed in speeches delivered by our political leaders, whose campaigns they funded, was nothing more than political theater. Senator Jim Webb (D-VA) was quoted in an interview with Real Clear Politics saying that he couldn't get a vote on a windfall profits tax on bonuses at bailed-out banks due to campaign contributors. "I couldn't even get a vote," Webb explained. "And it wasn't because of the Republicans. I mean they obviously weren't going to vote for it. But I got so much froth from Democrats saying that any vote like that was going to screw up fundraising." The diagrams make clear why not one person has gone to prison for the fraud that caused the worst financial crisis since the Great Depression.

Meanwhile, law enforcement is being ordered to use tear gas, pepper spray, billy clubs, and other means of police force on innocent people who are peacefully protesting this great injustice. I was deeply moved by Scott Olsen, a young fellow veteran who had his skull fractured by the Oakland police while peacefully demonstrating with the Occupy Oakland movement. When asked if he planned on continuing his protest after recovering from his life-threatening injuries, he responded that when he joined the Marine Corps he took an oath to defend the U.S. Constitution from all enemies foreign and domestic, and that is exactly what he planned on continuing to do. Such courage and selfless sacrifice in the face of injustice and adversity represents the best of America. This is the same courage and selflessness shown by those brave young patriots who marched in 1776 with General Washington with no shoes, leaving bloody footprints in the snow. They were dedicated to liberty and the Glorious Cause of America unlike so many of the criminals and traitors in our government today who are selling out America to line their own pockets.

A clear illustration of this is how the financial industry used campaign donations and lobbyists to overturn the Glass-Steagall Act in 1999 leading to the collapse of Wall Street in 2008. In the 1997–98 election cycle, the finance, insurance, and real estate industries (known as the FIRE sector) spent more than $200 million on lobbying and made more than $150 million in political donations to repeal this legislation. Campaign contributions were targeted at members of congressional banking committees and other committees with direct jurisdiction over financial services legislation (PBS). Here is a chronology of the events leading to the repeal of the Glass-Steagall Act.

The Demise of Glass-Steagall.
How Citigroup's Sandy Weill delivered the death blow assisted by his surrogates in the Federal Reserve, Congress, and the White House.

| 1933-56 | Glass-Steagall Act creates new banking landscape |

Following the Great Crash of 1929, one of every five banks in America fails. Market speculation engaged in by banks during the 1920s helped cause the crash.

1933: Senator Carter Glass (D-Va.) and Congressman Henry Steagall (D-Ala.) introduced legislation to eliminate the conflicts of interest created when commercial banks are permitted to underwrite stocks or bonds. The act also establishes the Federal Deposit Insurance Corporation (FDIC), insuring bank deposits and strengthening the Federal Reserve's control over credit.

1956: The Bank Holding Company Act is passed, extending the restrictions on banks, including that bank holding companies owning two or more banks cannot engage in non-banking activity and cannot buy banks in another state.

| 1960s-70s | First efforts to loosen Glass-Steagall restrictions |

1960s: Banks lobby Congress to allow them to enter the municipal bond market, and a lobbying subculture springs up around Glass-Steagall. *Some lobbyists even brag about how the bill put their kids through college.*

1970s: Some brokerage firms begin encroaching on banking territory by offering money-market accounts that pay interest, allow check-writing, and offer credit or debit cards.

| 1986-87 | Fed begins reinterpreting Glass-Steagall; Alan Greenspan becomes Fed chairman |

1986: The Federal Reserve Board, which has regulatory jurisdiction over banking, reinterprets Section 20 of the Glass-Steagall Act, and for the first time since 1933 the Fed allows some previously prohibited activities.

1987: The Federal Reserve Board votes 3-2 in favor of easing regulations under Glass-Steagall Act, overriding the opposition of Chairman Paul Volcker. The vote comes after the Federal Reserve Board hears proposals from Citicorp, J.P. Morgan, and Bankers Trust advocating the loosening of Glass-Steagall restrictions. **Later the same year, Alan Greenspan—formerly a director of J.P. Morgan and a proponent of banking deregulation—becomes chairman of the Federal Reserve Board.**

The Demise of Glass-Steagall.
How Citigroup's Sandy Weill delivered the death blow assisted by his surrogates in the Federal Reserve, Congress, and the White House.

1989-90	Further loosening of Glass-Steagall

1989: The Fed Board approves an application by J.P. Morgan, Chase Manhattan, Bankers Trust, and Citicorp to expand the Glass-Steagall loophole to include dealing in debt and equity securities in addition to municipal securities and commercial paper.

1990: **J.P. Morgan becomes the first bank to receive permission from the Federal Reserve to underwrite securities.**

1980s-90s	Congress repeatedly tries and fails to repeal Glass-Steagall

1984 and 1988: The Senate passes bills that would lift major restrictions under Glass-Steagall, but in each case the House blocks passage.

1991: The Bush administration puts forward a repeal proposal, winning support of both the House and Senate Banking Committees, but the House again defeats the bill in a full vote.

1995: The House and Senate Banking Committees approve separate versions of legislation to get rid of Glass-Steagall, but conference negotiations on a compromise fall apart.

1996	Fed renders Glass-Steagall effectively obsolete

1996: With the support of Greenspan, the Fed Board issues a precedent-shattering decision permitting bank holding companies to own investment bank affiliates. This expansion of the loophole created by the Fed's decision effectively renders Glass-Steagall obsolete. However, the law remains on the books, and along with the Bank Holding Company Act, does impose other restrictions on banks, such as prohibiting them from owning insurance-underwriting companies.

1997	Sandy Weill tries to merge Travelers and J.P. Morgan; acquires Salomon Brothers

1997: Sandy Weill, then head of Travelers insurance company, seeks and nearly succeeds in a merger with J.P. Morgan (before J.P. Morgan merged with Chemical Bank), but the deal collapses at the last minute. In the fall of that year, Travelers acquires the Salomon Brothers investment bank for $9 billion. (Salomon then merges with the Travelers-owned Smith Barney brokerage firm to become Salomon Smith Barney.)

The Demise of Glass-Steagall.
How Citigroup's Sandy Weill delivered the death blow assisted by his surrogates in the Federal Reserve, Congress, and the White House.

1998	**Sandy Weill and John Reed announce Travelers-Citicorp merger—intense new lobbying effort to repeal Glass-Steagall**

April 6, 1998: Sandy Weill of Travelers and John Reed of Citicorp announce a $70 billion merger to create Citigroup Inc., the world's largest financial services company, in what was the biggest corporate merger in history.

The transaction violates regulations in the Glass-Steagall and Bank Holding Company acts governing the industry, which were implemented precisely to prevent this type of company: a combination of insurance underwriting, securities underwriting, and commercial banking. The merger effectively gives regulators and lawmakers three options: change the law to make this merger legal, scuttle the deal, or force the merged company to cut back on its consumer offerings by divesting any business that fails to comply with the existing law.

Citicorp and Travelers quietly lobby banking regulators and government officials for their support. In late March and early April, Weill makes three heads-up calls to Washington, D.C.: to Fed Chairman Greenspan, Treasury Secretary Robert Rubin, and President Clinton. On April 5, the day before the announcement, Weill and Reed make a ceremonial call on Clinton to brief him on the upcoming announcement. The Fed gives its approval to the Citicorp-Travelers merger on September 23, 1998.

Following the merger announcement, Weill immediately plunges into a public-relations and lobbying campaign for the repeal of Glass-Steagall and passage of new financial services legislation (what becomes the Financial Services Modernization Act of 1999). Weill and Reed have to act quickly for both business and political reasons. Fears that the law would not be changed had caused the share prices of both companies to fall.

In May 1998, the House passes legislation by a vote of 214 to 213 that allows for the merging of banks, securities firms, and insurance companies into huge financial conglomerates. In September, the Senate Banking Committee votes 16–2 to approve a compromise bank overhaul bill. Despite this new momentum, Congress is yet again unable to pass final legislation before the end of its session.

As the push for new legislation heats up, lobbyists quip that raising the issue of financial modernization really signals the start of a fresh round of political fundraising. Indeed, in the 1997–98 election cycle, the finance, insurance, and real estate industries (known as the FIRE sector), spend more than $200 million on lobbying and make more than $150 million in political donations. Campaign contributions are targeted to members of congressional banking committees and other committees with direct jurisdiction over financial services legislation.

The Demise of Glass-Steagall.
How Citigroup's Sandy Weill delivered the death blow assisted by his surrogates in the Federal Reserve, Congress, and the White House.

Oct.–Nov. 1999   Congress passes Financial Services Modernization Act

After twelve attempts in twenty-five years, Congress finally repeals Glass-Steagall, rewarding financial companies for more than 20 years and $300 million worth of lobbying efforts. Supporters hail the change as the long-overdue demise of a Depression-era relic.

On October 21, with the House-Senate conference committee deadlocked after marathon negotiations, the main sticking point is partisan bickering over the bill's effect on the Community Reinvestment Act, which sets rules for lending to poor communities. **Sandy Weill calls President Clinton in the evening to try to break the deadlock after Senator Phil Gramm, chairman of the Banking Committee, warned Citigroup lobbyist Roger Levy that Weill has to get the White House moving on the bill or he would shut down the House-Senate conference. Serious negotiations resume, and a deal is announced at 2:45 a.m. on October 22. Whether Weill made any difference in precipitating a deal is unclear.**

On October 22, Weill and John Reed issue a statement congratulating Congress and President Clinton, including nineteen administration officials and lawmakers by name. The House and Senate approve a final version of the bill on November 4, and Clinton signs it into law later that month.

Just days after the administration (including the Treasury Department) agrees to support the repeal, Treasury Secretary Robert Rubin, the former co-chairman of a major Wall Street investment bank, Goldman Sachs, raises eyebrows by accepting a top job at Citigroup as Weill's chief lieutenant. The previous year, Weill had called Secretary Rubin to give him advance notice of the upcoming merger announcement. When Weill told Rubin he had some important news, the secretary reportedly quipped, "You're buying the government?"

Sources: *Frontline* interviews for "The Wall Street Fix," PBS, May 2003, and reports published in the *New York Times, Wall Street Journal, Washington Post, Time, Fortune, BusinessWeek,* and other publications. My emphasis added.

So why would Senator Phil Gramm be making a call to a Citigroup lobbyist advising him of the status of legislation directly related to the pending merger between Citigroup and Travelers? Better yet, why would he be instructing a lobbyist to have Sandy Weill contact the President of the United States to enlist his help in pushing through this legislation? And why would President Clinton take such a call and then do what Sandy Weill requested? Simple, as the below diagrams show—their services were purchased by Citigroup and the other financial corporations lobbying for repeal of the Glass-Steagall Act.

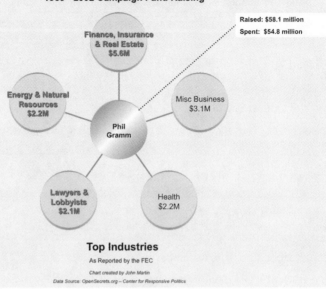

Sen. Phil Gramm, Chairman Banking, Housing, and Urban Affairs Committee
1989 - 2002 Campaign Fund Raising

Raised: $58.1 million

Spent: $54.8 million

Finance, Insurance & Real Estate $5.6M

Energy & Natural Resources $2.2M

Misc Business $3.1M

Phil Gramm

Lawyers & Lobbyists $2.1M

Health $2.2M

Top Industries

As Reported by the FEC

Chart created by John Martin

Data Source: OpenSecrets.org – Center for Responsive Politics

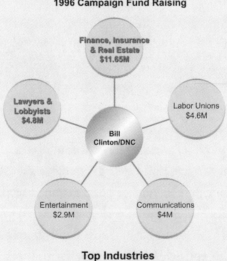

President Bill Clinton/DNC
1996 Campaign Fund Raising

Finance, Insurance & Real Estate $11.65M

Lawyers & Lobbyists $4.8M

Labor Unions $4.6M

Bill Clinton/DNC

Entertainment $2.9M

Communications $4M

Top Industries

As Reported by the FEC

Chart created by John Martin

Data Source: Center for Responsive Politics / Clinton helps Democrats cash in on 'soft money' 09/29/1996 HOUSTON CHRONICLE

And how about the outrageously unethical (if not criminal) actions of Treasury Secretary Robert Rubin, the former co-chairman of Goldman Sachs, in accepting a top job at Citigroup as Weill's chief lieutenant just days after the White House agreed to support the repeal of the Glass-Steagall Act? From his actions it seems painfully obvious that he took the position as Treasury Secretary to serve himself and the financial industry—not the American people. I can imagine a scene in which when Rubin jokingly asks Sandy Weill, "You're buying the government?" Weill replies, "No need to buy it, I already own it." Rubin was handsomely rewarded by Weill for his role in overturning the Glass-Steagall Act and making the illegal merger between Citicorp and Travelers legal. His compensation at Citigroup topped $15 million, not including stock options.

The Clintons and the Gramms have also been very well rewarded by Wall Street and the other corporate interests that they served while in government. When Clinton was elected president, the couple's total net worth was $697,000. Their combined annual income was $145,000 (Bill = $35,000/Hillary = $110,000). In the first eight years after his presidency, the Clintons earned $109 million, which is approximately $13.6 million per year, or 94 times the $145,000 annual income they had in 1992 *(McIntire)*. Talk about cashing in on public service! Hillary was also well rewarded for Bill's support of Citigroup and Wall Street, receiving at total of $328 million in campaign contributions between 2000 and 2008. Citigroup was her number-one donor, followed by Goldman Sachs and J.P. Morgan Chase *(Center for Responsive Politics)*.

Before Phil Gramm was first elected to congress in 1978, both he and his wife, Wendy Gramm, were economics professors at Texas A&M. The average annual salary for this type of position today is between $100,000 and $150,000. The move to Washington began a succession of appointed federal jobs for Wendy Gramm. She headed the economics bureau of the Federal Trade Commission's Division of Consumer Protection, and served as administrator of information and deregulatory affairs in the Office of Management and Budget. In 1988, she was named chairman of the Commodity Futures Trading Commission (CFTC), the powerful regulatory agency that oversees the nation's commodities and futures exchanges. After leaving the CFTC in early 1992, Wendy Gramm accepted lucrative directorships on the boards of several corporations she had regulated—many of which were also financial supporters of Senator Gramm. One of these corporations was Enron. In her final days with the CFTC she helped push through a ruling that exempted many energy futures contracts from regulation, a move that had been sought by Enron. Five weeks later, after resigning from the commission, Wendy Gramm was appointed to Enron's board of directors and served on its internal audit committee *(Herbert)*. As a member of Enron's audit and compliance committee, she helped approve financial statements and acted as a liaison to auditors with accounting firm Arthur Andersen. According to a report by Public Citizen *(Slocum)*, a watchdog group in Washington, "Enron paid her between $915,000 and $1.85 million in salary, attendance fees, stock options and dividends from 1993 to 2001."

Below is an illustration showing Enron's web of influence and corruption. Phil Gramm was one of the top recipients of Enron campaign contributions, and he engineered legislation that exempted energy commodity trading from government regulation and public disclosure. It was a gift tied with a bow for Enron and played a central role in the financial fraud that led to its collapse *(Herbert)*. When the company collapsed, Wendy and Phil Gramm walked away with their ill-gotten financial gains unscathed. Nobel Prize–winning economist Paul Krugman has called former Senator Gramm "the father of the financial crisis" due to his sponsorship of the Gramm-Leach-Bliley Act which repealed the Glass-Steagall Act *(Wikipedia)*. He retired from the Senate in 2002 and immediately took a lucrative lobbyist position as vice chairman of UBS, a Swiss-based banking conglomerate *(Lerer)*. So what is a former U.S. senator doing lobbying the U.S. government on behalf of a foreign-owned bank that has been accused of money laundering? In my opinion, selling out America and watching his bank balance grow.

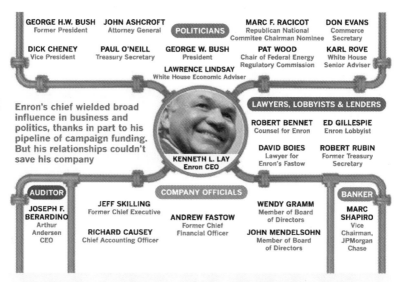

POLITICIANS

GEORGE H.W. BUSH — Former President
JOHN ASHCROFT — Attorney General
MARC F. RACICOT — Republican National Commitee Chairman Nominee
DON EVANS — Commerce Secretary
DICK CHENEY — Vice President
PAUL O'NEILL — Treasury Secretary
GEORGE W. BUSH — President
PAT WOOD — Chair of Federal Energy Regulatory Commission
KARL ROVE — White House Senior Adviser
LAWRENCE LINDSAY — White House Economic Adviser

Enron's chief wielded broad influence in business and politics, thanks in part to his pipeline of campaign funding. But his relationships couldn't save his company

KENNETH L. LAY — Enron CEO

LAWYERS, LOBBYISTS & LENDERS

ROBERT BENNET — Counsel for Enron
ED GILLESPIE — Enron Lobbyist
DAVID BOIES — Lawyer for Enron's Fastow
ROBERT RUBIN — Former Treasury Secretary

AUDITOR

COMPANY OFFICIALS

BANKER

JOSEPH F. BERARDINO — Arthur Andersen CEO
JEFF SKILLING — Former Chief Executive
RICHARD CAUSEY — Chief Accounting Officer
ANDREW FASTOW — Former Chief Financial Officer
WENDY GRAMM — Member of Board of Directors
JOHN MENDELSOHN — Member of Board of Directors
MARC SHAPIRO — Vice Chairman, JPMorgan Chase

George H.W. Bush — Ken Lay was a long-time friend and helped finance his presidential campaign. He was also an overnight guest at the White House during his presidency.

George W. Bush — Enron and its employees gave $312,500 to his gubernatorial campaigns and $413,800 to his presidential war chest and inaugural fund.

Dick Cheney — Met secretly with Enron officials six times in crafting a new national energy policy and refused to show the minutes to Congress.

John Ashcroft — Recused himself from the Justice Department's criminal probe into Enron because the company and its employees gave him $57,499 when he ran for Senate in 2000.

Paul O'Neill — Received a phone call from Lay in October 2001 exploring the possibility of a government bailout the day before Enron's credit rating was downgraded.

Lawrence Lindsay — Made $50,000 as a consultant for Enron in 2000 before moving to the White House.

Marc F. Racicot — Handpicked by Bush, the lawyer retained his salary at a firm that lobbied for Enron.

Pat Wood — A friend of Bush's and Lay's, he was appointed after the Enron chief allegedly soured on his predecessor, Curtis Hebert Jr.

Don Evans — Bush's chief fundraiser accepted Lay's campaign donations and returned his call in October 2001 but declined to intervene.

Karl Rove — Waited five months after taking office to sell more than $100,000 of Enron stock.

Robert Bennet — Represented Bill Clinton in the Paula Jones sexual-harassment suit that led to the Lewinski scandal and impeachment proceedings.

David Boies — Represented Al Gore before the Supreme Court during the 2000 election dispute.

Ed Gillespie — Served as one of Bush's top campaign advisors in 2000 before he started working as a lobbyist for Enron.

Robert Rubin — A top executive at Citigroup in 2001, which had more than $800 million in exposure to Enron, he called a Treasury official in November 2001 to ask about bolstering Enron's credit rating.

Wendy Gramm — Wife of former Texas Senator Phil Gramm and chair of the U.S. Commodities and Futures Trading Commission from 1988-93, where she issued regulations that exempted many energy futures contracts from regulation

Source:."Behind the Enron Scandal – Enron's Pipeline of Influence," *Time*

The corruption that gave us the financial crisis continues unabated. Between 2008 and 2010, when new financial regulations were being written following the financial crisis, the finance, insurance, and real estate industries spent $317 million in federal campaign contributions, with $73 million of that total coming from political action committees *(Jilani)*. Much of the PAC money went to Senator Chris Dodd and Congressman Barney Frank, who were sponsoring this legislation as these charts show.

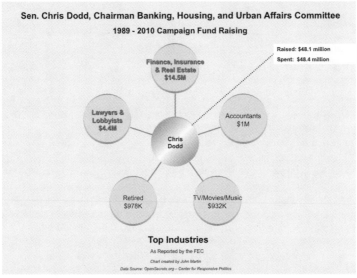

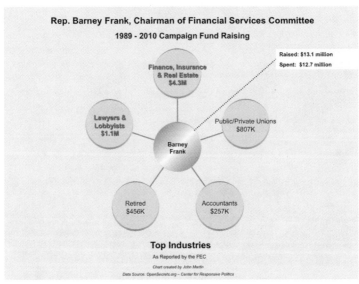

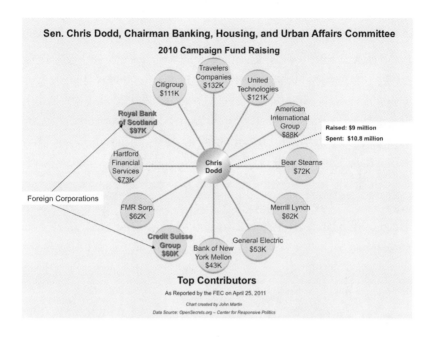

Sen. Chris Dodd, Chairman Banking, Housing, and Urban Affairs Committee

2010 Campaign Fund Raising

Raised: $9 million
Spent: $10.8 million

Foreign Corporations

Top Contributors

As Reported by the FEC on April 25, 2011

Chart created by John Martin

Data Source: OpenSecrets.org – Center for Responsive Politics

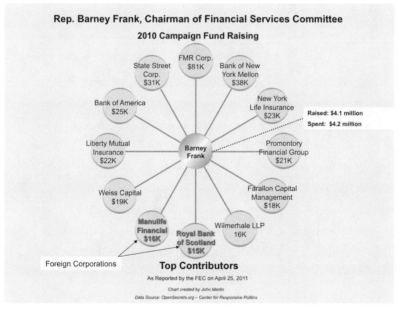

Rep. Barney Frank, Chairman of Financial Services Committee

2010 Campaign Fund Raising

Raised: $4.1 million
Spent: $4.2 million

Foreign Corporations

Top Contributors

As Reported by the FEC on April 25, 2011

Chart created by John Martin

Data Source: OpenSecrets.org – Center for Responsive Politics

When we follow the money it is painfully clear why the Dodd-Frank Wall Street Reform and Consumer Protection Act passed in 2010 does so little to restore the protections and integrity of our financial system that were lost by enactment of the Gramm-Leach-Bliley Act and the repeal of the Glass-Steagall Act in 1999. It also explains why Senator Dodd secretly helped make it possible for billions of dollars in bonuses to be paid to employees in failed Wall Street financial firms with taxpayer money. When it became public, he lied about his involvement and tried to cover for the actions of the Obama administration, who hypocritically expressed outrage while secretly asking Dodd to support payment of these bonuses *(Haber-korn and Seper)*. Dodd retired from the Senate in 2010. Despite repeatedly and categorically insisting that he would not work as a lobbyist, he took a position as chairman and chief lobbyist for the Motion Picture Association of America in March 2011 *(The Washington Post)*. The move should come as no surprise, since the entertainment industry contributed heavily to his campaigns during his thirty-seven years in office. Barney Frank will retire at the end of his term in 2012.

This is precisely the type of corporate and special interest corruption that Theodore Roosevelt warned against in his 1910 speech. While the financial crisis of 2008 is the most recent and visible manifestation of this corruption, it is not isolated to this event or any one branch of our government. The corruption is systemic and has infected our federal, state, and local governments. Both major political parties are benefiting from and actively participating in this corruption. The parties are so corrupt that they have made it virtually impossible for men and women of integrity and principle to obtain and hold public office in the U.S. The money they receive from corporations and special interests helps them keep a virtual monopoly on political power. It is ironic that many within these parties speak about supporting free trade and free markets, yet they use their corrupt political machinery to monopolize political power and suppress political freedom in America. This corrupt monopolization of political power by the two major parties is destroying "the very engines which have lifted them to unjust dominion," just as Washington predicted.

Foreign Influence in U.S. Elections

Foreign influence in U.S. elections is compromising our economic and national security. Since the 1970s foreign governments and foreign-owned corporations have been spending tens of millions of dollars a year buying influence in Washington by hiring well-connected lobbyists. The number of registered foreign agents lobbying or otherwise working on behalf of foreign governments and foreign-owned corporations has grown from 160 in 1944 to more than 1,800 in 2010. What is even more troubling is the number of former high-ranking executive branch officials and members of Congress, including former secretaries of state and chairs of the Senate Foreign Relations Committee, registered as agents for foreign governments. Since the late 1970s, nearly half of all former senior White House trade officials went to work for the people they had negotiated against, namely foreign companies and governments *(Lewis, Benes, and O'Brien, The Buying of the President)*. Many foreign governments maintain advocacy offices in Washington that are independent of their embassies. These offices foster commerce by lobbying Congress directly or through sympathetic American business groups—such as the U.S. Chamber of Commerce. I'll discuss this practice in more detail later.

Foreign governments also fund fellowships and scholarly centers, which indirectly ensure that the government's interests and concerns reach Congress through the advice and testimony of American scholars. Through these organizations, lobbyists, and their U.S. subsidiaries, foreign governments and corporations funnel millions of dollars in campaign contributions to both major political parties, bypassing U.S. laws prohibiting such donations. These donations buy political access and reward those in Congress and the White House who support their interests. In short, foreign interests are laundering political donations through their subsidiaries and lobbyists to do what a lot of other groups in Washington are doing—buying influence. Jon Pevehouse, a political science professor at the University of Wisconsin–Madison, estimates that foreign interests spent about $700 million on lobbying in 2008, with $200 million spent to influence trade policy *(Froomkin)*. This amount does not include the tens of millions of dollars subsequently donated to U.S. political campaigns by lobbyists on behalf of the foreign interests they represent.

Money spent by foreign agents for U.S. lobbyists, $M

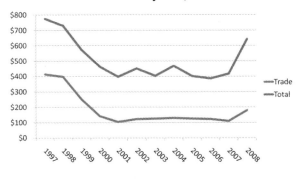

Source: Professor Jon Pevehouse, University of Wisconsin-Madison

Even though federal election law forbids political candidates from knowingly soliciting, accepting, or receiving donations from foreign nationals or foreign entities under any circumstances, these laws are seldom enforced. The reason is simple: money is the fuel that feeds the corrupt machinery of both major political parties. These parties will do whatever it takes to secure the funds necessary to maintain their monopoly on political power. Foreign interests understand this dynamic very well and are exploiting it to their advantage. Not surprisingly, trade policy is the main issue focused on by foreign lobbying. Here is a breakdown from 1997 to 2008.

Trade represents the largest issue area for foreign agent lobbying, $M

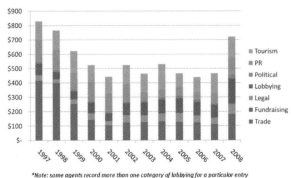

*Note: some agents record more than one category of lobbying for a particular entry

Source: Professor Jon Pevehouse, University of Wisconsin-Madison

Total lobbying expenditures by top 15 countries, 1997-2008

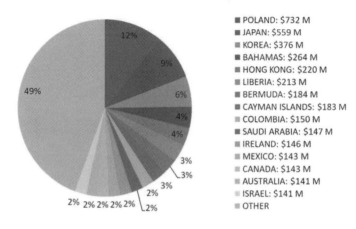

- POLAND: $732 M
- JAPAN: $559 M
- KOREA: $376 M
- BAHAMAS: $264 M
- HONG KONG: $220 M
- LIBERIA: $213 M
- BERMUDA: $184 M
- CAYMAN ISLANDS: $183 M
- COLOMBIA: $150 M
- SAUDI ARABIA: $147 M
- IRELAND: $146 M
- MEXICO: $143 M
- CANADA: $143 M
- AUSTRALIA: $141 M
- ISRAEL: $141 M
- OTHER

Source: Professor Jon Pevehouse, University of Wisconsin-Madison

Notice that Japan, Korea, and China (Hong Kong) are in the top five, spending more than $1 billion on U.S. lobbyists. This provides a clear illustration of why neither major political party is doing much to address the predatory trade practices of the Asian countries that are driving record trade deficits and destroying U.S. manufacturing, the U.S. economy, and the middle class.

A case in point is the money spent by South Korea, Panama, and Columbia to influence the negotiations and passage of U.S. free-trade agreements. All three countries lobbied ferociously to get these agreements ratified by Congress. Among the Washington lobbyists hired by South Korea, for example, was Kirsten Chadwick, a partner at the Republican lobbying firm of Fierce, Isakowitz & Blalock. The Korean government paid her $300,000 in the four months between November 2010 and March 2011. In 2011, *Bloomberg BusinessWeek (Fitzgerald)* named Chadwick one of its fifteen Washington "power brokers." She is the classic Washington insider—rotating between positions as a White House staffer and a lobbyist during both Bush administrations—cashing in on her government service.

Chadwick had dozens of meetings with members of Congress and their staffs advocating on her client's behalf for passage of the U.S.-Korea Free Trade Agreement. She also made numerous campaign contributions to those legislators she met with, as listed in required government disclosure reports *(Froomkin)*.

Another case in point is the passage of the U.S.-Canadian Free Trade Agreement and the North American Free Trade Agreement (NAFTA). A total of $80 million was spent by the Canadian and Mexican governments in lobbying the U.S. government and seeking political support for these agreements. Mexican interests spent more than $40 million to promote the development and enactment of NAFTA, hiring forty-four law firms, lobbyists, public relations companies, and consultants, including thirty-three former U.S. officials *(Lewis, Hogan, and Ebrahim)*.

Then there is the scandal that made headlines in 1997, when allegations emerged that the Chinese government had funneled money to the Democratic National Committee during the 1996 election. Below is a photo of Johnny Chung, one of the key participants in this scandal, during one of his many visits to the White House.

Between 1994 and 1996 Chung made forty-nine separate visits to the White House and donated $366,000 to the Democratic National Committee on behalf of China. Chung told federal investigators that some of the money he donated came from China's military intelligence. Specifically, Chung testified under oath to the House committee investigating the issue in May 1999 that he was introduced to Chinese General Ji Shengde, then the head of Chinese military intelligence. Chung said that Ji told him: "We like your president very much. We would like to see him reelect(ed). I will give you 300,000 U.S. dollars. You can give it to the president and the Democrat Party." The other key players in this scandal were *(Wikipedia)*:

- **Charlie Trie and Ng Lap** collaborated in a scheme to launder money from sources in communist China and other Asian countries and illegally contributed hundreds of thousands of dollars in foreign funds to the DNC and Clinton legal defense fund. Communist China–based businessman Ng Lap Seng wired more than $1 million from accounts he maintains in Macau and Hong Kong to accounts maintained by or accessible to Trie in Little Rock and Washington, D.C. Trie was co-owner of a restaurant in Little Rock, where he befriended Clinton, then governor of Arkansas. After Congressional investigations turned to Trie in late 1996, he left the country for China. Trie returned to the U.S. in 1998, and was convicted and sentenced to three years of probation and four months of home detention for violating federal campaign finance laws by making political contributions in someone else's name and for causing a false statement to be made to the Federal Election Commission. Ng Lap was never charged or convicted—he walked away unscathed.

- **John Huang and James Riady:** Huang was a former employee of the Indonesian company Lippo Group's Lippo Bank and its owners Mochtar Riady and his son James (whom he first met along with Bill Clinton at a financial seminar in Little Rock in 1980). Huang became a key fundraiser within the DNC in 1995; he raised $3.4 million for the party. Huang visited the White House seventy-eight times while working as a DNC fundraiser. James Riady visited the White House twenty times (including six personal visits to President Clinton). In December 1993 Clinton appointed Huang to work in the Commerce Department as deputy assistant secretary for international economic affairs, the job he held immediately before his job with the DNC. His Commerce Department position made him responsible for Asia-U.S. trade matters. He had access to classified intelligence on China. While at the department, it was later learned, Huang met nine times with Chinese embassy officials.

Huang eventually pleaded guilty to conspiring to reimburse Lippo Group employees' campaign contributions with corporate or foreign funds. James Riady was later convicted of campaign finance violations relating to the same scheme. Shortly after Riady pledged $1 million in support of then-Governor Clinton's campaign for the presidency, contributions made by Huang were reimbursed with funds wired from a foreign Lippo Group entity into an account Riady maintained at Lippo Bank and then distributed to Huang in cash. Also, contributions made by Lippo Group entities operating in the U.S. were reimbursed with wire transfers from foreign Lippo Group entities.

An unclassified U.S. Senate Committee on Governmental Affairs report issued in 1998 stated that both James Riady and his father Mochtar "had a long-term relationship with a Communist Chinese intelligence agency." According to journalist Bob Woodward, details of the relationship came from highly classified intelligence information supplied to the committee by both the CIA and the FBI.

The best known of John Huang's fundraising events involved Vice President Al Gore, Maria Hsia, and the Hsi Lai Buddhist Temple in California.

• **Maria Hsia**, a California immigration consultant, was a long-time fundraiser for Al Gore and a business associate of John Huang and James Riady since 1988. She facilitated $100,000 in illegal campaign contributions through her efforts at Hsi Lai Temple, a Chinese Buddhist temple associated with Taiwan in Hacienda Heights, California. The money went to the DNC, to the Clinton-Gore campaign, and to Patrick Kennedy.

Twelve nuns and employees of the temple, including the temple's abbess, refused to answer questions by pleading the

Fifth Amendment when they were subpoenaed to testify before Congress. Two other Buddhist nuns admitted destroying lists of donors and other documents related to the controversy because they felt the information would embarrass the Temple. A Temple-commissioned videotape of the fundraiser also went missing and the nuns' attorney claimed it may have been shipped off to Taiwan. The Temple event became particularly controversial, because it was attended by the Vice President Gore. At first he denied any knowledge that it was a fundraising event, but later acknowledged he had known the visit was "finance-related." Al Gore was trying to insulate himself from this scandal as much as possible since it appeared that this temple was involved in laundering illegal foreign donations to the Clinton-Gore re-election campaign.

- **Ted Sioeng** is an Indonesian entrepreneur who illegally donated money to both Democrats and Republicans. Suspect contributions associated with Sioeng include $250,000 to the DNC, $100,000 to Republican California State Treasurer Matt Fong, and $50,000 to a Republican think tank.

  Sioeng sat with Bill Clinton or Al Gore at three fundraising events and also joined Fong at a meeting in mid-1995 with Newt Gingrich, who at the time was Speaker of the House. Gingrich called the meeting a photo-op. Gingrich was the guest of honor at a luncheon Sioeng organized the day after a Sioeng family company gave the $50,000 think-tank donation, which had been solicited by one of Gingrich's advisors.

  Attorney General Janet Reno and the directors of the FBI, CIA, and the National Security Agency (NSA) told members of the Senate committee they had credible intelligence information indicating Sioeng acted on behalf of communist China.

According to the Senate report *Investigation of Illegal or Improper Activities in Connection with 1996 Federal Election Campaigns (COMMITTEE ON GOVERNMENTAL AFFAIRS)*, prior to 1995 China's approach to promoting its interests in the U.S. was focused almost exclusively on diplomacy, including summits and meetings with high-level White House officials. In these meetings, Chinese officials often negotiated with the U.S. government by using the appeal of their huge commercial market. Around 1995 Chinese officials developed a new approach to promote their interests with the U.S. government and improve China's image with the American people. The proposals, dubbed the "China Plan," instructed Chinese officials in the U.S. to improve their knowledge of members of Congress and increase contacts with its members, the public, and the media. The plan also suggested ways to lobby U.S. officials.

In late 1996 the Justice Department opened a task force to investigate allegations of illegal donations to the Clinton-Gore reelection campaign and Clinton's legal defense fund. Both FBI Director Louis Freeh and Charles La Bella, head of the investigating task force, unsuccessfully argued for the appointment of an independent counsel. For those who aren't familiar with this term, an independent counsel is an attorney appointed by the federal government to investigate and prosecute federal government officials. Given the seriousness of these allegations, why would such a request have been denied? Was this a cover-up? While Justice Department prosecutors did secure the conviction of several fundraisers for various offenses, the big fish walked away unscathed and the punishments meted out to those who were convicted amounted to a slap on the wrist. Why weren't the U.S. citizens involved convicted of treason or espionage (which was clearly called for in the case of Huang), and sentenced accordingly? During my nine years in the U.S. Navy I had access to highly classified information. I can assure you that if I, or any of my colleagues, compromised classified information, it would not have been treated so lightly. And that's how it should be. Why weren't the foreign citizens involved deported and barred from ever entering the U.S. again? If something similar had happened in China, you can bet that everyone involved would have faced a firing squad.

It's disappointing that the full scope and truth about this scandal was never uncovered because the investigations were hamstrung by uncooperative witnesses. Ninety-four people either refused to be questioned, pled the Fifth Amendment against self-incrimination, or left the country altogether.

This appears to have been a successful cover-up by the Chinese government of their "China Plan," which was aided and abetted by culpable and corrupt U.S. politicians.

Let's jump ahead to 2010, the most expensive midterm election in U.S. history. The U.S. Chamber of Commerce, a trade association organized as a 501(c)(6), was accused of spending both domestic and foreign money in a $33-million, anti-Democratic ad-buying spree. Thanks to the U.S. Supreme Court ruling in *Citizens United v. Federal Election Commission*, the U.S. Chamber of Commerce can now raise and spend unlimited funds on political ads without ever disclosing any of its donors. Now why would the "U.S." Chamber of Commerce be funding and running ads for or against candidates of either party? As a 501(c)(6) organization, they are supposed to be a nonprofit, nonpartisan trade association organized to promote the interests of U.S. business. They are not supposed to act as a political arm of either party. Nor are they supposed to be promoting foreign business interests that are undermining the U.S. economy and destroying U.S. manufacturing and jobs. However, this is precisely what they are doing. Here are some excerpts from a 2010 report by Lee Fang of ThinkProgress *(Fang)*.

In recent years, the Chamber has become very aggressive with its fundraising, opening offices abroad and helping to found foreign chapters (known as Business Councils or "AmChams"). While many of these foreign operations include American businesses with interests overseas, the Chamber has also spearheaded an effort to raise money from foreign corporations, including ones controlled by foreign governments. These foreign members of the Chamber send money either directly to the U.S. Chamber of Commerce, or the foreign members fund their local Chamber, which in turn, transfers dues payments back to the Chamber's H Street office in Washington DC. These funds are commingled to the Chamber's 501(c)(6) account, which is the vehicle for the attack ads:

- The U.S. Chamber of Commerce has created a large presence in the small, oil-rich country of Bahrain. In 2006, the Chamber created an internal fundraising department called the "U.S.-Bahrain Business Council" (USBBC), an organization to help businesses in Bahrain take advantage of the Chamber's "network of government and business relationships in the US and worldwide." . . . the U.S. Chamber of Commerce raises well over $100,000 a year in money from foreign businesses through its operation in Bahrain. Notably, the membership form provided by the USBBC directs applicants to send or wire their money directly to the U.S. Chamber of Commerce. The membership form also explicitly states that the foreign-owned firms are welcomed.

- . . . the U.S. Chamber of Commerce operates in India through a fundraising department called the "U.S.-India Business Council" (USIBC), which has offices around the world but is headquartered in the U.S. Chamber of Commerce. Dozens of Indian businesses, including some of India's largest corporations like the State Bank of India (state-run) and ICICI Bank, are members of the U.S. Chamber of Commerce through the USIBC. . . . the USIBC generates well over $200,000 a year in dues for the U.S. Chamber of Commerce from foreign businesses. **On the USIBC website, many of the groups lobbying goals advocate changing American policy to help businesses in India. Under the manufacturing policy goal, USIBC boasts that it "can play a helpful role in guiding U.S. companies to India, while supporting various policy initiatives that will enhance India's reputation as a major manufacturing and investment hub."**

- . . . many foreign "AmChams" operate outside the direct sphere of the U.S. Chamber of Commerce but nonetheless send dues money back to the U.S. Chamber of Commerce. For instance, the American Chamber of Commerce in

Egypt is a separate entity based in Cairo that raises hundreds of thousands of dollars from both Egyptian firms and American businesses . . . it calls itself "the most active affiliates of the U.S. Chamber of Commerce in the" Middle East . . . the Abu Dhabi AmCham, which includes American firms and Esnaad, a subsidiary of the state-run Abu Dhabi National Oil Company, claims that it is a "dues paying member of the U.S. Chamber of Commerce and part of the global network of American Chambers of Commerce." In Russia, the relationship between the American Chamber of Commerce there and the U.S. Chamber of Commerce here is opaque. This might be because many of the dues-paying members of the American Chamber of Commerce in Russia are Russian state-run companies . . . controlled by the Russian government . . . .

Previously, it has been reported that foreign firms like BP, Shell Oil, and Siemens are active members of the Chamber. But on a larger scale, the U.S. Chamber of Commerce appears to rely heavily on fundraising from firms all over the world, including *(Communist)* China, India, Egypt, Saudi Arabia, Brazil, Russia, and many other places. Of course, because the Chamber successfully lobbied to kill campaign finance reforms aimed at establishing transparency, the Chamber does not have to reveal any of the funding for its ad campaigns . . . .

There are many reasons foreign corporations are seeking to defeat Democratic candidates this November. **The Chamber has repeatedly sent out issue alerts attacking Democratic efforts to encourage businesses to hire locally rather than outsource to foreign countries. The Chamber has also bitterly fought Democrats for opposing unfettered free trade deals.** To galvanize foreign businesses, the Chamber has commissioned former Ambassador Frank Lavin—who served as the McCain-Palin Asia campaign director and has appeared on television multiple times recently saying a Democratic Congress is bad for business—to speak before various foreign Chamber affiliates to talk about the stakes for the 2010 midterm elections (emphasis added).

When it comes to lobbying and buying influence in Washington, the U.S. Chamber of Commerce is the 800-pound gorilla of special interest groups, spending $414 million from 1998 through 2011. They are followed by GE who spent $105 million over the same period. What do the two have in common? Both are acting on behalf of foreign interests and against the interests of the U.S. by promoting outsourcing and liberal trade policies. Their motivation is simple: greed!

> WHEN IT COMES TO LOBBYING AND BUYING INFLUENCE IN WASHINGTON, THE U.S. CHAMBER OF COMMERCE IS THE 800-POUND GORILLA OF SPECIAL INTEREST GROUPS

Moving Beyond the Corrupt Two-Party System

For many years the American public has been told that the two-party political system provides an excellent balance between the dictatorship of a one-party system and the instability of a multiparty system. This myth has been propagated by the two major political parties to thwart any challenge to their power duopoly. In fact, the two-party system is extremely corrupt and has done more harm than good to America—especially over the past forty years. This two-party system is hostile to anyone who puts patriotism over partisanship, or our national interest over special interests. The Republican and Democratic Parties manipulate and divide the American people over social and moral issues to deflect attention away from the failed economic and trade policies that are enriching the top 1 percent of Americans, while bankrupting and destroying our country. The top 1 percent of Americans along with corporate, foreign, and special interests are funding the political machinery of the two major parties. In exchange, these parties ensure that the economic and trade policies they enact benefit those who are funding them. It is that simple. Most of the Republican and Democratic candidates allege certain principles and make attractive promises during their campaigns that appeal to the "common people," but upon entering office, they serve the corporate and special interests that fund their parties and campaigns. They disregard the promises they made during their campaigns that do not align with these interests.

While many believe that political parties are essential in a democracy, this view was not shared by our nation's founders. Alexander Hamilton, James Madison, and John Jay warned against the evils to the general public that a "spirit of faction" would cause. George Washington refused allegiance to any political party during his eight-year service as first president of the United States. And John Adams dreaded the possibility of the country being divided into two powerful parties. In a 1780 letter to Jonathan Jackson, Adams addressed his concerns: "This, in my humble apprehension, is to be dreaded as the greatest political evil under our Constitution."

Over the past twenty years, a growing number of Americans have come to similar conclusions and have been leaving both major political parties declaring themselves Independent voters. The percentage of Independent voters is rapidly rising as membership in both major political parties is declining. In fact, Independents are now the largest and fastest-growing segment of the American electorate! According to a 2011 Gallup poll released on January 9, 2012, 40 percent of Americans identified themselves as Independents, which is the highest number to declare themselves in the category since the poll was started back in 1988 *(Seiger)*. Back in 1954, only 22 percent of voters identified themselves as independents, according to the American National Election Survey. This is the new mainstream in American politics, and it's growing among younger voters. More than 40 percent of college undergraduates identify themselves as independents, according to a 2008 survey by Harvard University's Institute of Politics *(Avlon)*. Given the corruption of both major parties and their unwillingness to put country first, 2012 may be the year of a major U.S. political realignment. There is an up-and-coming political movement taking shape that could play a major role in driving such realignment: the Modern Whig Party (ModernWhig. org). I discovered this "centrist" movement while researching this chapter. Here is a brief overview.

Modern Whig Party

Government is a trust, and the officers of the government are trustees.

And both the trust and the trustees are created for the benefit of the people.

—HENRY CLAY, SECRETARY OF STATE, U.S. SENATOR,
SPEAKER OF THE HOUSE, AND WHIG PARTY FOUNDER

- When the American Revolution started, the term *Whig* was first used to refer to any American patriot who supported independence. These patriot Whigs were the leading figures who, in July 1776, declared the United States of America an independent nation. They are also known as the Founding Fathers: John Adams, John Dickinson, Benjamin Franklin, Samuel Adams, Alexander Hamilton, Thomas Paine, Paul Revere, Nathanael Greene, Nathan Hale, Thomas Jefferson, and George Washington.

- Established in 1833, the Whig party is one of America's oldest mainstream political parties. Whigs were the original party of

Abraham Lincoln and four other U.S. presidents, including New York–born Millard Fillmore. The Whig Party had some very well-known members, including Henry Clay, John Quincy Adams, Daniel Webster, Willie Person Mangum, Winfield Scott, William Henry Harrison, Zachary Taylor, Millard Fillmore, and Abraham Lincoln.

- The Modern Whig Party was organized as a national party in late 2007 as a successor to the historical Whig Party. Among its founding members were Afghanistan and Iraq War veterans dissatisfied with the deep ideological divide between the Republican and Democratic parties.

- The Modern Whigs are a pragmatic, common-sense, centrist-oriented party where rational solutions trump ideology and integrity trumps impunity. They are neither conservative nor liberal and do not wish to be confined to the traditional left-right political spectrum. The core philosophy is comprised of:

  1. **INDEPENDENT THINKING**, challenging all assumptions, and mapping and analyzing all possible solutions based on facts and potential outcomes, not on party ideology.

  2. **MERITOCRACY**, we believe that society should reward merit, which is a combination of intelligence, talent, competence, and hard work. Solutions to problems should be formed and judged in a rational manner based on a process of discovery, analysis, and proposed solutions based on their merits, not on prior prejudice, pure self interest, or false beliefs.

  3. **INTEGRITY**, honesty, and a commitment to an ethical approach to politics. Whigs practice what they preach, live up to their promises, and do not make promises they cannot keep. Integrity also means accountability: no one is above the law and everyone lives by the same rules. You'll find modern Whigs near mum on issues of social morality, as these are personal. On issues of ethics or integrity, however, we will

hold our officers, leaders, and candidates to the highest of ethical standards, above today's actual legal requirements.

- Beyond philosophical tenets, modern Whigs also promote a concrete platform of political ideals and policies, which we believe are the most critical issues to the welfare of our country. These principles bind us as moderates, unify us as Americans, and come from a place of inclusiveness, not division.

  1. **Fiscal Responsibility**—Any action of the government must respect principles of fiscal responsibility and public accountability.

  2. **Energy Independence**—Develop practical domestic energy sources and economically viable alternative energy to reduce dependence on foreign energy sources and strive toward energy independence. This is also a component of our inward-looking economic focus.

  3. **Inward-looking economic focus**—We must implement a modern-day version of Henry Clay's "American System" and focus our energies on revitalizing America's manufacturing base as well as domestic demand for American-manufactured products. We must implement trade and economic policies that put America first and foster the creation of jobs that will support American families within the context of a globally interdependent world. We support fair and balanced trade with our nation's trading partners that is mutually beneficial.

  4. **States' Responsibilities**—Each state can generally determine its course of action based on local values and unique needs. Whigs believe in a strong government at every level and separation of powers. Yet, strong and competent local and state governments are important, as they are the level of government where the people can get most involved. All citizens need to ensure the Federal government doesn't usurp its constitutional authority.

5. **Social Acceptance**—When the government is compelled to legislate morality (laws), every citizen should be considered equal.

6. **Education and Scientific Advancement**—Increase public and private emphasis on math and science to promote American innovation to compete in the global economy.

7. **Veterans Affairs**—Vigilant advocacy relating to the medical, financial, and overall well-being of our military families and veterans.

8. **Electoral and Government Reform**—Support efforts and work for governmental reform that makes the American government efficient, fair, and responsive at all levels. Support efforts and work for electoral reform to allow all Americans to have their voices heard and make it rational for citizens to participate in the government and electoral processes.

• Whigs believe it is time to change the antiquated two-party system with a more open and citizen-centric solution.

• Whigs believe that focusing on the processes of governance and refocusing political participation in America, is the ONLY proper long-term solution to enable truly effective public policy and better governance. To engage citizens in the process we have our Whig Roundtables where citizens and members participate with experts and candidates to formulate policy solutions based on ideas from the Whigs and from themselves.

• Offer training through the Whig Academy, which is free and trains citizens for leadership within the party and also to run for office. Courses include Whig-oriented courses, leadership, fiscal administration, public policy, debate, and campaign strategy and efforts.

I encourage those reading this book to investigate the Modern Whig Party, and if you like what you see, give them your full support. If you do not wish to join this movement, please find some other way to support positive change in our political process that strengthens and preserves our democracy for future generations.

One thing is clear: our political process is corrupt and needs major reform. It is also clear that neither of the two major political parties has any real desire to enact meaningful reform, which would diminish their current dominance of political power in America. Real change can only come about through direct political action controlled and funded by the American people. Real change also requires a sustained effort, and the election of candidates at all levels of government—federal, state, and local—who are uncorrupted and dedicated to serving the common good. That's what the Modern Whig Party is working toward. Honestly, I have no idea what impact this movement will have. However, if we choose to do nothing we are guaranteed that nothing will change. If nothing changes, all will be lost. Please join me and millions of other Americans in our efforts to clean up and open up our political process! You can start in the upcoming general election and every election thereafter, by simply casting your vote for 3rd party candidates. This would send a clear signal to the two major parties that we Americans are serious about ending politics as usual and taking back our government! For more information on voting for 3rd party candidates please visit the take action page at Selling-US-Out.com .

CHAPTER TEN

America's Best Days Lie Ahead

Creating an America as Good as Its Promise

This was a powerful phrase used by President Barack Obama during his campaign speeches that resonated with me. It was similar to a phrase used by Ronald Reagan in his third State of the Union Address: "America's best days and democracy's best days lie ahead." During his address Reagan also reminded us that we are a powerful force for good, and that with faith and courage we can perform great things and take freedom's next step. The hope and optimism expressed in his words are the essence of what has made, and will continue to make, this a great nation.

Drawing Strength from Our Past and Building a Better Tomorrow

The challenges we face today are difficult, but in many ways they are no different than those faced by earlier generations of Americans. Take for instance the struggles and sacrifices of those who participated in the American Revolution. Many lost loved ones, wealth, health, and their own lives fighting for the Glorious Cause of America against the wealthiest and most powerful empire on earth at the time. The American Revolution was a struggle filled with hardship, pain, and suffering. One percent of our population perished during the fight for our independence. That equates to three million of our current population. There were countless setbacks and for a while it looked as if all would be lost. However, in spite of it all, those early Americans persevered driven by their common belief in the necessity and rightness of their Glorious Cause. It's difficult to conceive of and begin to understand the sacrifices made to secure the freedoms we take for granted today. In one of her many letters to her husband, who was off in Philadelphia working on the Declaration of Independence, Abigail Adams saliently put the challenges into perspective: "Posterity who are to reap the blessings, will scarcely be able to conceive the hardships and sufferings of their ancestors." If you haven't already done so, I encourage you to read *1776* and *John Adams* by David McCullough to gain a better understanding and appreciation for the tremendous hardships these early Americans endured on our behalf.

While the current crises we face are serious, this isn't the first time we have faced and overcome such adversity. Since its founding, our nation has endured fourteen banking crises, thirty-eight economic recessions, five depressions, a civil war, two world wars, and countless other wars and disasters. There are still many alive today who endured the Great Depression and World War II. Such crises, while hard, often bring out the best in our character, both as individuals and as a nation. We can and should draw strength and hope from knowing that those who went before us persevered and pulled together as one nation to face and overcome past adversities and through their hard work, determination, and sacrifice, passed the Glorious Cause on to the next generation. Like them, we must stand firm and rise up together to confront the challenges of our time for the sake of our children and future generations. To those who say our country is in decline, I say nonsense! America's best days lie ahead!

Recommitting to the Glorious Cause of America

I believe that as individuals and as a nation we need to reconnect with our past and the core principles that define the Glorious Cause of America. Doing so will give us the collective vision and strength to confront and overcome the challenges we face. A good place to start is reading, with fresh eyes, our Declaration of Independence and reflecting upon its meaning. It is as relevant today as it was in 1776.

IN CONGRESS, July 4, 1776.

The unanimous Declaration of the thirteen united States of America,

When in the Course of human events, it becomes necessary for one people to dissolve the political bands which have connected them with another, and to assume among the powers of the earth, the separate and equal station to which the Laws of Nature and of Nature's God entitle them, a decent respect to the opinions of mankind requires that they should declare the causes which impel them to the separation.

We hold these truths to be self-evident, that all men are created equal, that they are endowed by their Creator with certain unalienable Rights, that among these are Life, Liberty and the pursuit of Happiness.—That to secure these rights, Governments are instituted among Men, deriving their just powers from the consent of the governed,—That whenever any Form of Government becomes destructive of these ends, it is the Right of the People to alter or to abolish it, and to institute new Government, laying its foundation on such principles and organizing its powers in such form, as to them shall seem most likely to effect their Safety and Happiness. Prudence, indeed, will dictate that Governments long established should not be changed for light and transient causes; and accordingly all experience hath shewn, that mankind are more disposed to suffer, while evils are sufferable, than to right themselves by abolishing the forms to which they are accustomed. But when a long train of abuses and usurpations, pursuing invariably the same Object evinces a design to reduce them under absolute Despotism, it is their right, it is their

duty, to throw off such Government, and to provide new Guards
for their future security.—Such has been the patient sufferance of
these Colonies; and such is now the necessity which constrains
them to alter their former Systems of Government. The history of
the present King of Great Britain is a history of repeated injuries
and usurpations, all having in direct object the establishment of
an absolute Tyranny over these States. To prove this, let Facts be
submitted to a candid world.

> He has refused his Assent to Laws, the most wholesome and
> necessary for the public good.
>
> He has forbidden his Governors to pass Laws of immediate and
> pressing importance, unless suspended in their operation till
> his Assent should be obtained; and when so suspended, he
> has utterly neglected to attend to them.
>
> He has refused to pass other Laws for the accommodation of
> large districts of people, unless those people would
> relinquish the right of Representation in the Legislature, a
> right inestimable to them and formidable to tyrants only.
>
> He has called together legislative bodies at places unusual,
> uncomfortable, and distant from the depository of their
> public Records, for the sole purpose of fatiguing them into
> compliance with his measures.
>
> He has dissolved Representative Houses repeatedly, for
> opposing with manly firmness his invasions on the rights of
> the people.
>
> He has refused for a long time, after such dissolutions, to cause
> others to be elected; whereby the Legislative powers,
> incapable of Annihilation, have returned to the People at
> large for their exercise; the State remaining in the mean
> time exposed to all the dangers of invasion from without,
> and convulsions within.
>
> He has endeavoured to prevent the population of these States;
> for that purpose obstructing the Laws for Naturalization of

Foreigners; refusing to pass others to encourage their migrations hither, and raising the conditions of new Appropriations of Lands.

He has obstructed the Administration of Justice, by refusing his Assent to Laws for establishing Judiciary powers.

He has made Judges dependent on his Will alone, for the tenure of their offices, and the amount and payment of their salaries.

He has erected a multitude of New Offices, and sent hither swarms of Officers to harrass our people, and eat out their substance.

He has kept among us, in times of peace, Standing Armies without the Consent of our legislatures.

He has affected to render the Military independent of and superior to the Civil power.

He has combined with others to subject us to a jurisdiction foreign to our constitution, and unacknowledged by our laws; giving his Assent to their Acts of pretended Legislation:

For Quartering large bodies of armed troops among us:

For protecting them, by a mock Trial, from punishment for any Murders which they should commit on the Inhabitants of these States:

For cutting off our Trade with all parts of the world:

For imposing Taxes on us without our Consent:

For depriving us in many cases, of the benefits of Trial by Jury:

For transporting us beyond Seas to be tried for pretended offences:

For abolishing the free System of English Laws in a neighbouring Province, establishing therein an Arbitrary government, and enlarging its Boundaries so as to render it at once an example and fit instrument for introducing the same absolute rule into these Colonies:

For taking away our Charters, abolishing our most valuable Laws, and altering fundamentally the Forms of our Governments:

For suspending our own Legislatures, and declaring themselves invested with power to legislate for us in all cases whatsoever.

He has abdicated Government here, by declaring us out of his Protection and waging War against us.

He has plundered our seas, ravaged our Coasts, burnt our towns, and destroyed the lives of our people.

He is at this time transporting large Armies of foreign Mercenaries to compleat the works of death, desolation and tyranny, already begun with circumstances of Cruelty & perfidy scarcely paralleled in the most barbarous ages, and totally unworthy the Head of a civilized nation.

He has constrained our fellow Citizens taken Captive on the high Seas to bear Arms against their Country, to become the executioners of their friends and Brethren, or to fall themselves by their Hands.

He has excited domestic insurrections amongst us, and has endeavoured to bring on the inhabitants of our frontiers, the merciless Indian Savages, whose known rule of warfare, is an undistinguished destruction of all ages, sexes and conditions.

In every stage of these Oppressions We have Petitioned for Redress in the most humble terms: Our repeated Petitions have been answered only by repeated injury. A Prince whose character is thus marked by every act which may define a Tyrant, is unfit to be the ruler of a free people.

Nor have We been wanting in attentions to our British brethren. We have warned them from time to time of attempts by their legislature to extend an unwarrantable jurisdiction over us. We have reminded them of the circumstances of our emigration and settlement here. We have appealed to their native justice and magnanimity, and we have conjured them by the ties of our common kindred to disavow these usurpations, which, would inevitably interrupt our connections and correspondence. They too have been deaf to the voice of justice and of consanguinity. We must, therefore, acquiesce in the necessity, which denounces our Separation, and hold them, as we hold the rest of mankind, Enemies in War, in Peace Friends.

We, therefore, the Representatives of the united States of America, in General Congress, Assembled, appealing to the Supreme Judge of the world for the rectitude of our intentions, do, in the Name, and by Authority of the good People of these Colonies, solemnly publish and declare, That these United Colonies are, and of Right ought to be Free and Independent States; that they are Absolved from all Allegiance to the British Crown, and that all political connection between them and the State of Great Britain, is and ought to be totally dissolved; and that as Free and Independent States, they have full Power to levy War, conclude Peace, contract Alliances, establish Commerce, and to do all other Acts and Things which Independent States may of right do. And for the support of this Declaration, with a firm reliance on the protection of divine Providence, we mutually pledge to each other our Lives, our Fortunes and our sacred Honor.

I believe this document, more than any other, defines who we are as Americans. The signers' pledge of their "Lives, Fortunes, and sacred Honor" to the cause of freedom and independence stands in stark contrast to the rampant greed and materialism of today, which is driving our nation deeper and deeper into debt and jeopardizing our independence and freedom. There are those who would like to maintain the current status quo because they are afraid that to do otherwise might adversely impact their personal wealth or force them to make other sacrifices. I repeat and invite them to consider these words from Samuel Adams, which are as true today as they were in 1776:

> If ye love wealth better than liberty, the tranquility of servitude better than the animating contest of freedom, go home from us in peace. We ask not your counsels or arms. Crouch down and lick the hands which feed you. May your chains set lightly upon you, and may posterity forget that ye were our countrymen.

Adams was making a call for true patriots, those who love liberty more than wealth and are willing to pledge their "Lives, Fortunes, and sacred Honor" to preserve and defend our nation. How do you think he would view those in our country today that are accumulating vast wealth and destroying America from within, by shipping our factories and jobs to China—a communist country? Do they truly love liberty more than wealth? Or what about those U.S. corporations or wealthy Americans who refuse to pay their fair allotment of taxes while our national debt skyrockets and we borrow more and more money from foreign governments?

Adams's words challenge all of us to be selfless in serving our country and the cause of liberty. I believe to do that we must rededicate ourselves to the universal principles that are the foundation of our democracy and transcend politics such as:

1. **Self-reliance:** There is a famous quote by Lao Tzu, an ancient Chinese philosopher: "Give a man a fish; feed him for a day. Teach a man to fish; feed him for a lifetime." We must take control and responsibility for our own lives, both as individuals and as a nation. Our government should not be in the business of handing out fish. We should be teaching those in need how to fish, so they become self-reliant. We should also learn to live

within our means again and eliminate our national and personal debts.

2. **Honesty, integrity, hard work, courage, optimism, fair play, tolerance, loyalty, and patriotism:** These are the core values that define the best of American society. Many of us have strayed from these values in our daily lives, which has resulted in an increasing number of corporate and political scandals. Our democracy is predicated upon these values, and will fail if we don't rededicate ourselves to living up to our values and holding each other accountable. As John Adams put so well, "Avarice, ambition, revenge, or gallantry, would break the strongest cords of our Constitution as a whale goes through a net. Our Constitution was made only for a religious and moral people. It is wholly inadequate for the government of any other."

3. **God, family, country—duty, honor, sacrifice:** We are a nation founded on Christian principles and tradition, a truth that is self-evident in our Declaration of Independence and Constitution. To deny it would be denying our history and heritage. While we should celebrate and honor the Christian principles our nation was founded on, we should also be careful not to violate the letter and spirit of the First Amendment by branding any religion or belief system as more "American" than any other. The blending of Christian fundamentalism and politics in America over the past three decades has caused friction and division. Taken to extremes, it could threaten our democracy. Similarly, the atheist movement to remove God or any reference to God or religion from public documents and public life is equally dangerous, as it seeks to deny our Christian heritage and undermine the moral principles that are essential to preserving our democracy. We must rededicate ourselves to caring for our families and teach our children what it means to be an American and a responsible citizen that contributes and works for the common good of our country. This should be part of the curriculum taught in our schools. We must make duty, honor, and sacrifice mainstream values again—not just campaign slogans.

The Rebirth of "True" Patriotism—Putting America and Americans First!

What is "true" patriotism? It's putting service to your country and fellow countrymen ahead of self-interests to ensure that our shared Glorious Cause continues and is passed on to future generations. We should follow the example of our first two presidents.

As told in David McCullough's book *1776*, George Washington was forty-three years old and a wealthy, successful plantation owner when he was called upon to lead the ragged, ill-equipped, undisciplined, and untrained group of rebels the British called the "rabble" in arms. Although he had prior military experience, Washington had never commanded an army in battle before. He was a man of unquestionable character and integrity, which is why John Adams and the Continental Congress extended this call to him. Washington could have easily refused to accept this commission. However, he chose to accept the heavy burden, as he sometimes called it, because he believed in the Glorious Cause of America. Subsequently, Washington and his army suffered tremendously during the eight-and-a-half years of the Revolutionary War. At the beginning of the war they endured one defeat after another and almost lost entirely to the British at the Battle of White Plains, New York, in October 1776.

After several more lost battles and long marches, Washington led his ill-clothed, starving, and demoralized army of men and boys across the Delaware River on the evening of December 25, 1776. After the crossing, they marched all night, going nine miles back down the river on the eastern side toward Trenton, New Jersey. The weather was horrible; there was a northeaster blowing. They marched through the snow, and since many of them had no shoes, they suffered frostbite and left bloody footprints in the snow. It was so cold that two young men froze to death on the march because they had no winter clothing. They struck at Trenton the next morning and defeated the British for the first time. This was a turning point of the war, and for our history as a nation. Washington's army struck again at Princeton a few days later—after marching through the night again, under extremely harsh conditions, they risked everything and won a second important engagement. As McCullough so eloquently stated, we honor the men who wrote and voted for the Declaration of Independence in Philadelphia. But that great document would have not been worth any more than the paper it was written on had it not been for those who were fighting and dying to secure our independence. Washington and those who fought with him gave selfless service and sacrificed for our shared Glorious Cause. In fact, George and Martha Washington lost their only son, who died of camp fever after joining his father at the battle of Yorktown. While the rest of the country was celebrating victory over the British and American independence, the Washingtons were mourning the loss of their son.

At the conclusion of the war, in one of the most important events in our entire history, Washington turned back his command to Congress. When George III heard Washington might take that action, he said that "if he does, he will be the greatest man in the world." After the war, Washington only reluctantly became our first president. It was not an office he aspired to, but he accepted it out a sense of duty and patriotism. He was dedicated to helping our young nation get established. He was a true patriot and humble servant of his God and fellow countrymen.

While I have a deep admiration and respect for George Washington, John Adams is my favorite Founding Father. In 1774, at only thirty-nine years of age, he was sent to represent Massachusetts in the Continental Congress. He was a brilliant man who could have easily chosen to dedicate his life to the pursuit of personal wealth. Instead he chose to dedicate his superior intellect and apparently endless energy to serving his country. He once wrote,

> There must be a positive Passion for the public good, the public Interest, Honor, Power, and Glory, established in the Minds of the People, or there can be no Republican Government, nor any real Liberty. And this public Passion must be Superior to all private Passions. Men must be ready, they must pride themselves, and be happy to sacrifice their private Pleasures, Passions, and Interests, nay their private Friendships and

dearest connections, when they Stand in Competition with the Rights of society.

This is how Adams lived his life—in unselfish service to our country. He and his wife Abigail endured great hardship and made tremendous sacrifices to support the development of our fledgling nation. It was largely due to Adams's recommendation that Washington was asked to command the Continental Army. Adams was one of our first ambassadors to Europe and spent a total of ten years there, most of them separated from his family, from 1778 to 1788. He was instrumental in negotiating a favorable peace treaty with Britain and, from the Netherlands, he secured our country's first loans. He authored the Massachusetts Constitution, the oldest functioning written constitution in continuous effect in the world, and played a key role in helping frame the U.S. Constitution. He was unable to attend the Constitutional Convention, since he was serving in Europe at the time. Adams became our first vice president and second president and his son John Quincy Adams became our sixth president. Adams was a man of unquestionable honesty, integrity, and devotion to his country. He was a true patriot in every sense of this word!

Honoring the Service and Sacrifices of Prior Generations through Our Actions

Most of us take our freedom for granted. As Abigail Adams feared, many of us have no comprehension of the hardships and sacrifices made by prior generations to ensure that the Glorious Cause of America was passed on to the next generation. Worse yet, not only do we take our freedom for granted, but too many of us have replaced virtue, honor, duty, and sacrifice with greed, unbridled passion, corruption, excessive leisure, and materialism. We have many political and business leaders in the public square who are like the Pharisees in the Old Testament. They wear their flag pins and boast of their love for America, but their actions tell a very different story. Many of them have avoided military service when called upon. Ironically, these same people are often the first to call for military action and are more than happy to send others into battle. They lie, cheat, steal, and will do anything for money and power. Like Judas Iscariot, they have no problem selling out America in exchange for campaign contributions or business opportunities that increase their personal wealth but damage our national economic well-being and security.

We can and must demand more of ourselves and our political and business leaders. We must individually and collectively recommit to virtue, honor, duty, sacrifice, and selfless service to honor the sacrifices of those who have gone before us and the young men and women who continue to lay down their lives to defend America. This is the kind of authentic patriotism exemplified by Washington and Adams, and it is the only way we can ensure that the Glorious Cause of America is passed on to future generations. We can improve our lives and the lives of our fellow countrymen by putting their values into action. Just think of the transformation we will see in our country when we begin holding ourselves along with our political and corporate leaders to higher standards, when we seek out opportunities to render selfless service. You can't claim to love America if you don't love Americans, and the ultimate expression of our national bond is selfless service. Together we can start a new age of Americanism!

> YOU CAN'T CLAIM TO LOVE AMERICA IF YOU DON'T LOVE AMERICANS, AND THE ULTIMATE EXPRESSION OF OUR NATIONAL BOND IS SELFLESS SERVICE.

CHAPTER ELEVEN

The Path Forward

Creating a New Age of Honorable Public Service and Accountability

Public Virtue cannot exist in a Nation without private, and public Virtue is the only Foundation of Republics. There must be a positive Passion for the public good, the public Interest, Honour, Power and Glory, established in the Minds of the People, or there can be no Republican Government, nor any real Liberty: and this public Passion must be Superiour to all private Passions.

—JOHN ADAMS, IN A LETTER TO
MERCY OTIS WARREN, 1776

Government is a trust, and the officers of the government are trustees. And both the trust and the trustees are created for the benefit of the people.

—HENRY CLAY

We are at a critical crossroads in American history and are facing historic challenges that threaten our democracy. These challenges can be met only by coming together as Americans to radically reform our corrupt political system and create a new age of honorable public service and accountability. To achieve that goal we need a political revolution that moves us beyond the corrupt two-party system. This is the first and most important task we must complete and upon which everything else depends. Until we free ourselves from the stranglehold of the two entrenched political parties, nothing will change—it will be business as usual in Washington. The two major political parties will continue to manipulate and dominate our political system, using their power to serve their own interests and the interests of their financial backers, to the detriment of our nation and the common good. We can and must put an end to this corrupt duopoly of power.

The first step is opening up and cleaning up our election process. An open and clean elections process, one that isn't controlled by any major political party, will make it possible, once again, for Americans to elect honorable men and women who refuse to put loyalty to a political party ahead of loyalty to their country. Opening up our elections process will also provide more opportunities to elect honest leaders who advise us, and aren't afraid to tell us what they think is right, even if it's unpopular. That's the type of true leadership and political courage exemplified by Washington, Adams, Lincoln, Theodore Roosevelt, Franklin Roosevelt, and other great American leaders. We are in dire need of true leaders of conscience, who place loyalty to their country above their party and are true to themselves and those they represent. An open elections process will also make it possible for more moderate and pragmatic political parties, like the Modern Whig Party, to participate in our political process. They have the potential to help us find and support honorable men and women who demonstrate, as Adams described it, a "positive Passion for the public good, the public interest, Honor, Power and Glory." We need leaders who recognize, as Clay did, that "Government is a trust, and the officers of the government are trustees. And both the trust and the trustees are created for the benefit of the people." Organizations like the Modern Whig Party can help us get closer to the ideals articulated by Adams and Clay.

Bringing about change of this scope is no easy task, especially since both major political parties have well-financed and established political machines that include a network of corporations, special interests, lobbyists, and major media outlets. All these groups benefit financially from their support of the corrupt two-party system and will doggedly resist change that threatens their power. Their resistance can only be overcome by "We the People" joining together in support of moderate, pragmatic third parties. We must all become active citizens who are directly involved in opening up and cleaning up our political process. We can no longer afford to sit on the sidelines and be spectators. Our active involvement will make it clear to those in government, at all levels, that their power is obtained from the people—not from corporate or other special interests. They need to be reminded that they exercise the power entrusted to them by the people only so long as, and to the extent that, they have our full backing. The power of the people of our nation must once again be at the center of our political system and government. Only then will we be realizing a true representative democracy as defined in the Constitution.

Independents and Third Parties Unite!

Political parties exist to secure responsible government and to execute the will of the people. From these great tasks both of the old parties have turned aside. Instead of instruments to promote the general welfare they have become the tools of corrupt interests, which use them impartially to serve their selfish purposes. Behind the ostensible government sits enthroned an invisible government owing no allegiance and acknowledging no responsibility to the people. To destroy this invisible government, to dissolve the unholy alliance between corrupt business and corrupt politics, is the first task of the statesmanship of the day.

—THEODORE ROOSEVELT, IN A SPEECH TITLED "THE PROGRESSIVE COVENANT WITH THE PEOPLE," 1912

In the past one hundred years, there have only been two significant third-party challenges to the corrupt two-party system: one from the Progressive Party, led by Theodore Roosevelt in 1912, and the other by Ross Perot, who ran for president as an Independent in 1992 and later organized the Reform Party. In both cases, the two major political parties used their considerable power and influence to attack and eliminate the threats posed by these third-party movements. Ballot access, which simply means getting your name listed as a candidate on a ballot, is their most powerful weapon. Until the late nineteenth century, there were generally no restrictions on ballot access in the U.S. In the 1880s a voters' reform movement led to officially designed secret ballots. This was both positive and negative. On the one hand, it improved the integrity of our voting system. On the other hand, it gave the government control over who could be on the ballot. Since the government in the 1880s was primarily controlled by the Democrats and Republicans, this allowed them to rig the election system by implementing restrictive ballot-access laws. Over the past 130 years, the Democrats and Republicans have constructed a maze of cumbersome regulations and procedures that make it extremely difficult for third parties and independent candidates to gain a spot on the general election ballot. The procedures vary by state, which makes them even more expensive and difficult to overcome. Meanwhile, Republican and Democratic candidates are automatically included on all general election ballots. Other weapons used by the two major parties to ensure their monopoly on political power continues unchallenged include:

- **Campaign Finance Reform Laws**—These laws are written to strongly favor the two major political parties, and they make it extremely difficult for third parties to receive any significant financing. This should be no surprise since the laws were written by and for members of the Republican and Democratic parties.

- **Media Coverage**—The major U.S. media sources are aligned closely with the two major political parties. This has been true historically and continues today. Televised presidential debates exclude third-party candidates. These debates have been rigged by the two major parties, as evidenced in 1996 when the Commission on Presidential Debates, an organization founded and funded by the Democratic and Republican Parties, changed its rules for the sole purpose of excluding Perot, who had done very well in the 1992 presidential debates. His exclusion dealt a decisive blow to the 1996 Perot campaign *(CNN)*.

- **Attacking the Legitimacy of Third Parties**—It is common for major-party candidates to argue that a third-party vote is wasted, or that third-party challengers are "fringe" candidates who stand outside the bounds of acceptable political discourse. The major parties have also employed a full array of dirty tricks against independent challengers, and they don't sit idly by while third-party candidates battle state election laws. They actively fight to prevent third parties from securing spots on the ballot.

The Democratic and Republican parties also have virtually unlimited resources at their disposal, which means that to have a realistic chance of breaking their monopoly on political power, Independents and third parties must unite! Those of us who do not belong to either of the two major parties must put aside any partisan differences and come together as patriotic Americans to form a nonpartisan coalition. This coalition could work together with other nonpartisan groups—such as No Labels and Occupy Wall Street—to clean up and open up our political system.

We can and must unite around a common goal: rescuing the country we love from the corrupt influence of corporations, Wall Street, and special interests. This will only be accomplished by electing independent candidates, not those bound by obligation to either major political party. Such a coalition would enable the pooling of resources and an expanded network to identify and support viable third-party candidates who could effectively compete and win against the Democrats and Republicans. If you are interested in joining this nonpartisan coalition of American patriots, please visit my website at Selling-US-Out.com.

Achieving Real and Lasting Campaign Finance Reform

The only way we will achieve real and lasting campaign finance reform is by taking the matter out of the control of the two major political parties, and passing an airtight constitutional amendment that eliminates the corrupting influence of money in our federal elections. Several such amendments have recently been proposed. You can view several of them at **http://unitedrepublic.org/amendments-guide**. I'm persuaded by this one:

Constitutional Amendment for the Public Financing of Federal Elections

Section 1. All elections for President and members of the United States House of Representatives and the United States Senate shall be publicly financed. No political contributions shall be permitted to any federal candidate, from any other source, including the candidate. No political expenditures shall be permitted in support of any federal candidate, or in opposition to any federal candidate, from any other source, including the candidate. Nothing in this section shall be construed to abridge the freedom of the press.

Section 2. The Congress shall, by statute, provide limitations on the amounts and timing of the expenditures of such public funds and provide criminal penalties for any violation of this section.

Section 3. The Congress shall have the power to enforce this article by appropriate legislation.

Section 4. This article shall be inoperative unless it is ratified as an amendment to the Constitution by conventions in the several States, as provided in the Constitution.

This amendment is proposed by Russell Simmons, of hip-hop fame. I know nothing about hip-hop, and had never heard of Russell Simmons before I happened across his proposed amendment. I like it because I agree that publicly financed campaigns are the only way to clean up our corrupt political system, and his proposal appears to leave no loopholes or wiggle room. All federal campaigns should be publicly financed—no exceptions— with limits placed on how much each candidate can spend. Also, debates should be televised using publicly funded media outlets such as C-SPAN or PBS, and they should include all candidates, not just those from the two major political parties. A publicly financed political system has the potential to create an intellectually rich political environment where those with the best ideas can compete for and win the opportunity to serve, regardless of party affiliations. This would benefit all Americans and put pressure on the two major political parties to either reform or go the way of the dinosaurs. This type of real political reform will return the power back to the people and breathe new life into the Glorious Cause of America.

We cannot trust the Democrats and Republicans to follow through on real campaign finance reform. They co-created, and are the shared benefactors of, our current corrupt political system. They're addicted to the billions of dollars they receive from corporations, special interests, wealthy individuals, and other sources. This is the fuel that runs their corrupt political machinery and ensures their continued hold on power. Do you think they have any serious intentions of changing this? They pay lip service to "reforming" the system, because they realize an overwhelming majority of Americans are fed up with their corruption. But that's nothing more than political theater designed to "appease" the masses. Behind the scenes, the power brokers in both major parties are devising ways to circumvent any real change that would disrupt their cash flow and threaten their lock on political power. We can and must prevent them from maintaining the same problematic system by electing moderate third-party and Independent candidates to congress in 2012 and beyond. If we put a substantial number of moderate third-party and Independent candidates in office, they can work together to ensure we get an airtight constitutional amendment that provides real and lasting campaign finance reform. Amending the constitution is no easy task. To get such an amendment passed will take the active involvement and commitment of each and every one of us. If you would like to know how you can help, please visit my website at Selling-US-Out.com.

Eradicating Professional Lobbyists and Influence Peddling

We should immediately pass laws banning all lobbying of federal government officials and their staffs. Our elected officials are in Washington to represent the interests of the citizens in their congressional districts (House) or states (Senate), not the interests of well-compensated professional lobbyists. Many Washington insiders justify the corrupt influence of lobbying in our political system by claiming that lobbyists provide lawmakers with valuable knowledge from "experts" that help formulate policies for the benefit of society. In some cases, this may have merit, but in most cases lobbying is nothing more than a legal way for corporations and special interests to bribe politicians to enact legislation that benefits the interests of whoever's paying the bills. The self-serving corrupting influence and harm done by professional lobbyists to the general welfare of the U.S. far outweighs any good they do. We all understand that lawmakers can't be experts in all areas, but in the age of modern communications and the Internet there are virtually unlimited ways that lawmakers and their staffs can access the information needed to formulate public policy. They can also consult with experts in their home districts or states, scholars, business leaders, professional and industry organizations, and many other resources that have no direct financial interest in providing assistance.

Until we ban all lobbying, we should immediately pass legislation barring all former elected officials and their staff members from becoming federal lobbyists. This will help put a stop to the corrupt influence peddling that is now rampant in Washington. To put the issue in perspective, consider that since the end of World War II, the number of people in greater Washington who are lobbyists or engaged in support of lobbying activities has grown from several thousand in the 1950s, to more than 150,000 in 2011 *(Farrell, Aslanian, and Barshay)*. Furthermore, the number of lawyers admitted to practice before the federal courts of Washington, D.C., jumped from less than 1,000 in 1950 to 80,000 in 2011. Since World War II, Washington has become a giant influence-peddling machine. As reported in *The New York Times* in 2011 *(Edsall)*, nearly one-half of all members of Congress become lobbyists. According to the Center for Responsive Politics, 372 former members are in the influence-peddling business, including at least 285 who are now registered as federal lobbyists. The remainder who are not formally registered as lobbyists are described by the center's website, OpenSecrets.org, as providing "strategic advice" to corporate clients or as performing work classified as public relations. When Washington politicians leave office, most of them no longer return home. They stay in Washington and become highly paid lobbyists, cashing in on their government service. A former member of the House or Senate, with even modest seniority, can expect to walk into a job worth up to one million or more a year. In December 2011, an inside-the-Beltway newsletter, *First Street*, published a report listing the thirty most influential and connected lobbyists in Washington *(First Street Research Group)*. Here are some highlights:

Top 10 Ex-Members of U.S. Congress

The 10 ex-members on this list were among the 135 former members of Congress who actively lobbied in the first three quarters of 2011. These 10 don't boast the most clients, but they have the highest-paying clients on average, reflecting the value that corporations and other organizations place on the relationships, reputations, and experiences of former members of Congress.

- **Representative Victor Fazio:** D CA-3 (1979–1999)—Akin Gump Strauss Hauer & Feld LLP

- **Senator John Breaux:** D LA-7 (1972–1987) & D-LA (1986–2005)—Breaux Lott Leadership Group & Patton Boggs LLP

- **Representative Robert Livingston:** R LA-1 (1977–1999)—The Livingston Group, LLC

- **Representative James McCrery, III:** R LA-4 (1988–1989) —Capitol Counsel, LLC

- **Senator Trent Lott:** R MS-5 (1973–1989) & R-MS (1989–2007) —Breaux Lott Leadership Group & Patton Boggs LLP

- **Senator Tim Hutchinson:** R AK-3 (1993–1997) & R-AK (1997–2003)—Dickstein Shapiro LLP

- **Representative Bill Paxon:** R NY-31 (1989–1993) & R NY-27 (1993–1999)—Akin Gump Strauss Hauer & Feld LLP

- **Representative Richard Gephardt:** D MO-3 (1977–2005)— Gephardt Group Government Affairs

- **Representative Vin Weber:** R MN-6 (1981–1983) & R MN-2 (1983–1993)—Clark & Weinstock

- **Representative Thomas Downey:** D NY-2 (1975–1993)— Downey McGrath Group, Inc.

Representative Victor Fazio—Akin Gump Strauss Hauer & Feld LLP

- Number of Clients: 51

- **Total Amount Clients Paid Firm: $10,340,000**

- Average Amount Each Client Paid Firm: $202,745

- Number of *Fortune 100* Clients: 5

- Notable Clients: Moody's, AT&T, Shell

Having spent two decades as a House member from California, several of them as a member of the Democratic leadership, Vic Fazio has established himself as one of Washington's best-connected lobbyists. His firm's client list is studded with *Fortune 100* giants such as Johnson & Johnson Inc., Anheuser-Busch, Archer Daniels Midland, and Honeywell International. Other colleagues include former representative Bill Paxon and Barney Skladany. With more than 50 clients, Fazio helped bring in more than $10.3 million through the third quarter of 2011. Fazio has close ties to House Minority Leader Nancy Pelosi.

Senator John Breaux—Breaux Lott Leadership Group & Patton Boggs LLP

- Number of Clients: 35
- **Total Amount Clients Paid Firm: $8,380,000**
- Average Amount Each Client Paid Firm: $239,429
- Number of *Fortune 100* Clients: 8
- Notable Clients: Tyson Foods, Raytheon, EADS North America

John Breaux was known for his fondness for negotiating when he served as a Democratic senator from Louisiana; **he once famously quipped that while his vote could not be bought, "it could be rented."** It was not surprising to most observers when Breaux decided to leave legislative office for the more lucrative deal-cutting world of K Street. Together with his friend, former Senate Majority Leader Trent Lott, he runs one of the most formidable lobbying operations in Washington, bringing in more than $8.3 million through the third quarter of 2011. The firm's roughly three-dozen clients include numerous *Fortune 100* firms, such as General Electric and Tyson Foods.

Representative Robert Livingston—The Livingston Group, LLC

- Number of Clients: 50
- **Total Amount Clients Paid Firm: $6,510,000**
- Average Amount Each Client Paid Firm: $130,200
- Number of *Fortune 100* Clients: 3
- Notable Clients: Oracle, Mayo Clinic, Accenture

As a former chairman of the House Appropriations Committee who almost became House speaker, the Louisiana Republican was well-versed in the art of doing favors for colleagues. He has traded in on that experience while becoming one of Washington's premier lobbyists, concentrating on foreign-policy work among other areas. His firm boasts of having played a lead role in approving a U.S. free-trade agreement with Morocco, as well as obtaining money for international assistance with several countries. The firm also has done considerable lobbying on behalf of Egypt. **Livingston's firm once represented Libyan leader Muammar Gaddafi's government** but terminated that relationship in 2009, two years before Gaddafi was toppled from power. Its current top clients include the *Fortune 100* companies Oracle and Verizon Wireless, and it brought in more than $6.5 million through the third quarter of 2011.

Representative James McCrery, III—Capitol Counsel, LLC

- Number of Clients: 45
- **Total Amount Clients Paid Firm: $6,290,000**
- Average Amount Each Client Paid Firm: $139,778
- Number of *Fortune 100* Clients: 3
- Notable Clients: Sanofi-Aventis, Wal-Mart, Fortune Brands

The former Louisiana Republican was known for his even demeanor and expertise on **tax, trade, and health care** matters during his stint on the House Ways and Means Committee, and he continues to delve into those subjects as a lobbyist for Capitol Counsel on behalf of Cardinal Health, Health Care Science Corp., and the American Health Care Association. His colleagues include Jim Gould, Shannon Finley, and Sara L. Franko. But McCrery—a close ally of House Speaker John Boehner—also has capitalized on his ties to the Gulf Coast energy industry by representing such clients as the Edison Electric Institute and American Petroleum Institute. His portfolio also includes such *Fortune 100* giants as General Electric and Wal-Mart. All of this activity helped him bring in nearly $6.3 million during the first three quarters of 2011. He was named in 2010 by the *Washington Post* as one of four "lobbyists to watch" with the Republican takeover of the House, and he also was recognized that year for playing a significant role in the inclusion of capital gains and dividends provisions that were signed into law as part of the tax cuts enacted under former president George W. Bush.

Senator Trent Lott—Breaux Lott Leadership Group & Patton Boggs LLP

- Number of Clients: 24
- **Total Amount Clients Paid Firm: $6,240,000**
- Average Amount Each Client Paid Firm: $260,000
- Number of *Fortune 100* Clients: 8
- Notable Clients: Citigroup, FedEx, Prudential

Trent Lott deploys many of the same skills as a lobbyist that he used as Senate Majority Leader and Majority Whip: a gregarious personality carried over from his days as a University of Mississippi yell leader, an acute attention to detail he developed as a legislative aide, and an astute pragmatism about just how far his former colleagues might go on a given vote. Lott left the Senate in December 2007 and opened his lobbying firm a month later with a former like-minded colleague—and fellow *First Street 30* member—Louisiana Democrat John Breaux. It has become one of Capitol Hill's powerhouse shops, pulling in nearly $8 million in just its first year; it also took in more than $8 million through the third quarter of 2011. It has represented a number of *Fortune 100* corporations—General Electric, Boeing, AT&T, and Goldman Sachs—that are willing to pay for top-flight access.

Senator Tim Hutchinson—Dickstein Shapiro LLP

- Number of Clients: 18
- **Total Amount Clients Paid Firm: $5,250,000**
- Average Amount Each Client Paid Firm: $291,667
- Number of *Fortune 100* Clients: 1
- Notable Clients: Peabody Energy, Fleishman-Hillard, LightSquared

The former conservative Republican Senator—known during his days as an Arkansas state legislator as "no tax Tim"—has taken the policy knowledge and connections earned during his service on the Armed Services,

Aging, Health, and Veterans' Affairs committees to bring in top dollars for Dickstein Shapiro, which he joined immediately upon leaving Congress in 2003. Working for clients on such issues as education, health, agriculture, and homeland security, he brought in $5.25 million in the first three quarters of 2011. His highest-paying client during that time was Lorillard Tobacco Co., which paid $2.2 million for Hutchinson and colleagues to monitor implementation of the Family Smoking Prevention and Tobacco Control Act and lobby on a measure that would impose a tax on "smokeless tobacco" products.

Representative Bill Paxon—Akin Gump Strauss Hauer & Feld LLP

- Number of Clients: 21
- **Total Amount Clients Paid Firm: $4,300,000**
- Average Amount Each Client Paid Firm: $204,762
- Number of *Fortune 100* Clients: 4
- Notable Clients: Boeing, Pfizer, NASDAQ

The former New York Republican representative, who served on the powerful Committee on Energy and Commerce during the 1990s and was once considered a rising star in the House GOP, has become a top lobbyist on behalf of Trimble Navigation Ltd., a Sunnyvale, California–based company that makes navigation gear like the GPS. Paxon—also the former chairman of the National Republican Congressional Committee—reported bringing in $4.3 million from 21 clients during the first three quarters of 2011, with Trimble as his top-paying customer. The company had paid $620,000 for Paxon and firm colleagues (including former California Democratic representative Vic Fazio) to help fight a plan by LightSquared to offer a high-speed national wireless network using airwaves previously reserved for satellites—a network Trimble contends will interfere with its GPS navigation technology. Paxon's second top-paying client is Dow Chemical Co., a *Fortune 100* company. Other key clients include Boeing Co., Pfizer, Archer Daniels Midland—all *Fortune 100* companies—and NASDAQ.

Representative Richard Gephardt—Gephardt Group Government Affairs

- Number of Clients: 18
- **Total Amount Clients Paid Firm: $3,650,000**
- Average Amount Each Client Paid Firm: $202,778
- Number of *Fortune 100* Clients: 4
- Notable Clients: Visa, Anheuser-Busch, Waste Management

The former Missouri congressman and House Democratic leader has always been known for a conciliatory approach to issues; his top aide, James M. Jaffe, once said: "He wants to make a deal on whatever issues people are interested in." That flexibility, along with a long list of connections, has helped him become one of the top-earning lobbyists among former members of Congress. Gephardt reported $3.6 million in billing in the first three quarters of 2011 for his firm. He launched his shop in 2007 with the help of several former staffers—including Michael Messmer, who once focused on such issues as defense and international affairs, and Tom O'Donnell, who had served as Rep. Gephardt's chief of staff for nearly a decade. Several of his other former staffers—including David Plouffe and Bill Burton—later went to work for Barack Obama's presidential campaign or in the Obama White House.

General Electric—ranked sixth among *Fortune 100* companies and his top-paying client—hired Gephardt primarily to help the company fight for continued federal support for a joint-strike fighter alternate engine program that GE was building with Rolls Royce. Also among his top clients in 2011 were Peabody Energy, a global coal company based in St. Louis, Missouri, that seeks long-term venture opportunities in Mongolia, and Rational Entertainment Enterprises, which operates an online poker site called PokerStars.com. Gephardt has lobbied on issues related to the financial services reform law of 2010 and debit fees for Visa, and was hired by LightSquared to help weather a high-profile political fight related to its new wireless network effort that is opposed by GPS makers. He represents several other *Fortune 100* companies, including Boeing Co., The Goldman Sachs Group Inc., and Google Inc.

Representative Vin Weber—Clark & Weinstock

- Number of Clients: 24
- **Total Amount Clients Paid Firm: $2,410,000**
- Average Amount Each Client Paid Firm: $100,417
- Number of *Fortune 100* Clients: 0
- Notable Clients: Sallie Mae, Hyundai, eBay

The former Republican congressman from Minnesota—nearly 20 years after leaving Capitol Hill—remains a prominent GOP strategist with strong party connections that have helped him become a top Washington lobbyist. Weber briefly served as top advisor to ex-Minnesota governor Tim Pawlenty's 2012 president campaign, then became special advisor for former Massachusetts governor Mitt Romney's White House bid, and is a long-time friend of another GOP contender: former House Speaker Newt Gingrich. And Weber's lending a hand to congressional races as a board member for a new super PAC, Congressional Leadership Fund, which will make independent expenditures on behalf of GOP candidates.

Weber brought in $2.4 million in the first three quarters of 2011 for Clark & Weinstock, where he is a managing partner. His leading client, American Institute of Certified Public Accountants, paid the firm $240,000 to monitor implementation of the 2010 financial services reform law and lobby on intellectual property issues. Student loan provider Sallie Mae, Inc. sought Weber's expertise to lobby on bankruptcy issues relating to the discharge of student loans. Other key clients include Hyundai and eBay. **Hyundai has sought to weigh in on issues ranging from driver safety to new fuel standards to labor-relations issues, and pushed for approval of the United States–Korea Free Trade Agreement.**

Representative Thomas Downey—Downey McGrath Group, Inc.

- Number of Clients: 23
- **Total Amount Clients Paid Firm: $1,820,000**
- Average Amount Each Client Paid Firm: $79,130
- Number of *Fortune 100* Clients: 2
- Notable Clients: Time Warner, Intercontinental Exchange, Credit Union National Association

Former New York Democratic representative Thomas J. Downey made a quick transition into a lobbyist after nearly two decades in the U.S. House, where he served on the Armed Services, Budget, and Ways and Means committees. He maintained close connections on the Hill and with various White House Democrats—he was a colleague of Al Gore, before Gore entered the Clinton White House. Downey served on Bill Clinton's presidential transition team, and **he helped Clinton rally congressional support for several trade deals, including NAFTA.** Those connections enabled him to quickly build a successful lobbying firm, now called Downey McGrath Group Inc.—where in the first three quarters of 2011, Downey reported bringing in $1.8 million from 23 clients. **His top client, UC Group Ltd.—based in Bromley in the United Kingdom—hired Downey to monitor measures related to Internet gambling regulations.** FedEx Corp., a *Fortune 100* company that is also a top-paying client, sought Downey's expertise on transportation issues, such as an FAA reauthorization measure that threatened to bring FedEx under the same labor laws as UPS.

The *First Street* report also provides information on former congressional staff members who are cashing in on their government service as well. This is a national disgrace and precisely the type of corruption that Washington, Adams, Roosevelt, and other great American leaders have warned us about. I am positive that they along with many former presidents and true statesmen would be appalled by this blatant corruption and abuse of public service and trust. Lobbying and other kinds of influence peddling are a cancer destroying our democracy, and the practice must be eradicated—not regulated! We must purge our nation's capital of criminals and traitors who love wealth more than their country and once again send true, incorruptible American patriots to represent us in Washington. This is the only way to bring about positive change that serves the common good.

Term Limits for Congress

To prevent every danger which might arise to American freedom from continuing too long in office, it is earnestly recommended that we set an obligation on the holder of that office to go out after a certain period.
—THOMAS JEFFERSON

We must amend the U.S. constitution to limit the number of terms members of congress can serve, just as we have done for the Presidency. Coupled with eradication of lobbying and influence peddling, term limits will help reduce the corruption in Washington by replacing career politicians with citizen legislatures, as was intended by the framers of our constitution. Several amendments to this effect have been proposed in recent years. They are unlikely to passed, however, without direct citizen involvement since neither major political party seriously supports the idea. Both major political parties have used this issue to gain popular support for their reelection campaigns, and I'm sure they'll trot it out again in 2012. It's just more political theater, though, since the corporate and special interests that support them are profiting from the current system. Limiting congressional terms would threaten their monopoly on power. This provides yet another reason why we must join together to elect moderate third-party and Independent candidates to congress. If you are interested in actively supporting a constitutional amendment imposing term limits, please visit my website at Selling-US-Out.com.

Replacing Free Trade with Reciprocal Trade

Reciprocity must be treated as the handmaiden of protection. Our first duty is to see that the protection granted by the tariff in every case where it is needed is maintained, and that reciprocity be sought for so far as it can safely be done without injury to our home industries. Just how far this is must be determined according to the individual case, remembering always that every application of our tariff policy to meet our shifting national needs must be conditioned upon the cardinal fact that the duties must never be reduced below the point that will cover the difference between the labor cost here and abroad. The well-being of the wage-worker is a prime consideration of our entire policy of economic legislation.

—THEODORE ROOSEVELT

Among the many things I learned writing this book is that looking back into our history will help us find the best path forward. Concerning our trade and economic policies, we should give serious consideration to the wise counsel provided by Roosevelt. The principles he articulates above and in his "The New Nationalism" speech are as relevant today as they were in his era. How could any rational, patriotic American not support:

1. Making the well-being of American workers (and families) the prime consideration when formulating all our economic and trade policies.

2. Ensuring that our trade and economic policies support—rather than injure—home industries (that employ American workers).

3. Having a U.S. trade policy that is reciprocal (not "free"), so long as this can be achieved without doing harm to American industries and workers.

4. Once again, using tariffs to offset the effects of currency manipulation and other trade distorting practices. We should ensure that no tariffs on any foreign import (including those

from foreign subsidiaries of U.S. corporations) are less than the difference between the foreign item's cost of production and the cost of production of a similar item produced in the U.S. The U.S. production cost should include wages and fringe benefits paid to American workers and environmental costs imposed on business by federal, state, and local governments. Production costs should also account for differences in currency valuation.

This is sensible American thinking—the same common sense and American pragmatism that built this great nation. In today's America, this kind of practical problem solving is rejected by the two major political parties because they are more concerned about appeasing their financial backers and retaining their political power than about doing what's best for America and American workers. They label any opposition to the so-called free-trade policies, which are destroying the American economy, as "protectionism." This is a deliberate distortion designed to suppress any rational discussion of U.S. trade and economic policy. From the research conducted, it seems clear that when our government reformed the tariff system and implemented the income tax along with a more liberal trading policy in 1913, they never intended this to degenerate into the offshoring and outsourcing we now inaccurately call free trade. I am confident that Roosevelt and his legislative colleagues from 1913, Republicans or Democrats, would not support the offshoring and outsourcing that destroy U.S. jobs and the overall U.S. economy. They would label those who do support such policies as traitors. I am even more confident that Washington, Adams, Jefferson, Hamilton, and the other Founding Fathers would have the same opinion.

It is time that we once again take control of our economic well-being and formulate a new trade policy that is part of a carefully considered national economic strategy. We need to bring together the best, most pragmatic, rational minds in our country to discuss and help formulate a national economic strategy and new trade policy that puts the American economy and Americans first again.

I have been involved in international business for most of the past twenty-five years. My business travels have taken me to Asia, Europe, South America, Mexico, Canada, and the Middle East. What I have learned and concluded from my experiences is that our approach to international trade is seriously flawed. Our government takes a "legalistic" approach instead of a pragmatic business approach to negotiating and managing our trade relationships. This seriously works to our disadvantage—especially in Asia. That conclusion is not a theory; I know it to be true from firsthand experience. To rebuild the U.S. economy, we must shift to a more pragmatic, business-based approach in structuring, negotiating, and managing our trade relationships. We must also decouple trade policy from foreign policy. Of course, we need to take foreign policy into consideration, but our trade policy should be designed to support a national economic strategy—not our foreign policy. This is how America functioned prior to World War II and it worked very well. We also need to stop giving away access to the U.S. market as a bribe or reward to foreign countries—especially when that access is detrimental to U.S. industry.

We must reclaim our national and economic sovereignty by withdrawing from the World Trade Organization (WTO). Our membership in the WTO is unconstitutional; it violates Article I, Section 8, Clause 3 of the U.S. Constitution, which states that Congress shall have the power "To regulate Commerce with foreign Nations . . . ." Under our constitution, Congress may not hand over these powers to the WTO or any other domestic or foreign organization. Following this same line of thought, we should immediately withdraw from the North American Free Trade Agreement (NAFTA), and all other so-called free-trade agreements. They are flawed agreements that do nothing but support the offshoring and outsourcing that enriches multinational corporations and first-world capitalists while destroying the U.S. economy. I see no need for the WTO, NAFTA, or any other type of trade agreement since our tariff system worked quite well for the first 150 years of our history. We should implement a tariff system to regulate trade again. However, if we decide that trade agreements are a necessary element of our new national economic strategy, then any such agreements should be structured and negotiated as reciprocal business agreements with clear and measurable outcomes. These agreements should be smart, balanced, and mutually beneficial. No violations should be tolerated. If either party fails to honor the agreement, it should be immediately terminated. We need to take a sober, tough business approach to structuring and enforcing any trade agreements we enter into, and stop playing cat-and-mouse games with those who claim to be our trading partners.

It is time for us to end the "free trade ride," to revive American pragmatism, and formulate sensible trade and economic policies that put America and Americans first. I wholeheartedly agree with Roosevelt's assertion that "[t]he well-being of the wage-worker is a prime consideration of our entire policy of economic legislation." We should keep this in mind when we formulate our new national economic strategy and trade policy. We need to ask ourselves: What kind of a society do we want to live in and pass on to our children? Do we want a hard-working and free society that creates industry and prosperity—rewarding current and future generations with the fruits of their labor? Or do we want an oppressive, dysfunctional society, where wealth is extremely concentrated, foreign and domestic labor is exploited, and masses of Americans are either unemployed or underemployed—not even able to make a living wage?

The choice is clear. Let's put aside partisan politics and start working together to create a new national economic strategy and reciprocal trade policy. If you want to know how you can help, please visit my website at Selling-US-Out.com.

Creating a National Economic Strategy

Not only the wealth, but the independence and security of a country,

appear to be materially connected with the prosperity of manufactures.

Every nation. . . ought to endeavor to posses within itself all the essentials

of a national supply. These comprise the means of subsistence, habitation,

clothing and defense.

—ALEXANDER HAMILTON

We need to create a national economic strategy that is directly linked to our trade policy. Contrary to today's political rhetoric, this is not socialism. A national economic strategy is as American as the Fourth of July! After we won our independence from Britain, our founders realized the only way to preserve our hard-won political independence was to achieve economic independence. As Alexander Hamilton knew, independence and national security "appear to be materially connected with the prosperity of manufactures." Based upon related principles, our founders developed a national economic strategy that later became known as the American System. This economic strategy built the American economy and laid the foundation for our rise to power in the twentieth century. It was a fairly simple, yet highly effective strategy, which consisted of: tariffs to protect and promote American industry, a national bank to foster commerce, and federal subsidies for roads, canals, bridges, and other "internal improvements" to develop profitable markets for agriculture.

If our young nation had not adopted this economic strategy and chose instead to engage in free trade with the British Empire, our economic future would have been the same as India's. Until the eighteenth century, India was one of the wealthiest nations in the world, generating over 27 percent of the world's wealth. All this changed after the British colonization and the forced adoption of their free-trade system. India quickly went from being one of the wealthiest nations to one of the poorest nations in the world. Our fate will be the same if we do not change course soon and develop a new national economic strategy.

The absence of a strong trade strategy is one of the primary reasons the U.S. has lost and continues to lose major industries to foreign competition. It is also why many U.S. corporations have adopted their own survival and growth strategies that often conflict with, and damage, U.S. economic and national interests. With no coherent national economic strategy, U.S. corporations have been left to figure out on their own how to compete with foreign corporations based in communist China, Japan, Germany, Taiwan, India, Singapore, and other places with well-thought-out, and well-executed, national economic strategies. American corporations understand they are competing against not just foreign corporations but also with governments and mixed government-private collaborations. Foreign governments often provide their corporations with subsidies, protection from competition, tax breaks, low-cost loans, and other forms of assistance as part of their national economic strategy. Our government responds by complaining their practices are "unfair" and a violation of "free-market" principles. Not wanting to anger the U.S. and thus risk losing access to its lucrative market, these foreign governments carefully and politely brush us off. While we continue to preach free trade and free markets, they quietly continue to execute their national economic strategies. As a result, they're winning and we're losing.

Our national economic strategy should be driven by American pragmatism, not political ideology. We must put aside partisan politics, and come together to objectively create a pragmatic national economic strategy that will rebuild America's economy and ensure our continued political and economic independence. We must humble ourselves and, once again, think like a developing nation—like the America of 1812! It is not enough just to invent new technologies and industries; we must also be able to launch and maintain these technologies and industries on our shores. We must also ensure that we bring back the industries vital to our national defense. Such industries must also be under U.S. ownership and control. The re-industrialization of America and the creation of high-wage American jobs must be at the core of this economic strategy along with:

1. Public-private partnerships to gather and analyze market intelligence for the purpose of monitoring trends and determining which industries the U.S. should target to support the objectives of our national economic strategy.

2. Public-private partnerships to promote the development of new technologies and industries—with special emphasis on using our national labs to help develop commercially viable, high-tech products to be manufactured in the U.S.

3. Significantly increased investments in basic research and development—with special emphasis on the development of new manufacturing technologies.

4. Investment in a national fiber-optic network that runs high-speed broadband to every home in America. This will fuel innovation, education, and inventive creativity.

5. The creation of consortiums enabling much closer cooperation between U.S. industry, public and private universities, and government research and development.

6. Public-private partnerships to support major capital investments that enable young U.S. companies to grow and keep their manufacturing operations within the U.S.

7. Stricter laws protecting intellectual property that ban U.S. companies from sharing leading-edge technologies with foreign subsidiaries and foreign corporations.

8. Stricter laws regarding incorporation that eliminate "neutral ground" for multinational corporations. Penalize companies that have the majority of their assets and business in the U.S. but are incorporated elsewhere. Demand national allegiance and accountability from U.S. financial institutions and corporations.

9. Restrictions on foreign ownership of U.S. corporations and a requirement that officers of U.S. corporations be U.S. citizens.

10. Sensible and balanced tax reform that includes higher tariffs on all foreign-produced products, including those produced by subsidiaries of U.S. corporations.

11. The elimination of "tax-free" trade by changing tax treaties and U.S. tax laws to ensure all foreign corporations pay U.S. taxes. The IRS must have sufficient resources to investigate and enforce our corporate tax laws.

12. The use of tariffs to offset the effects of currency manipulation and other trade distorting practices.

13. A decoupling of economic and trade policy from foreign policy.

14. A ban prohibiting state governments from directly soliciting foreign direct investments and using taxpayer money to subsidize foreign manufacturers. All international trade missions and foreign direct investments should be managed by the federal government. We are the *United States* not the *Divided States* of America. We should not allow foreign corporations or governments to divide and conquer us.

15. Restrictions on offshoring and outsourcing—including services such as telemarketing, engineering, medical diagnostics, etc.

16. Immigration reform and the elimination of the H-1B and L-1 visa programs.

17. Financial and banking system reforms—repeal Dodd-Frank and the Gramm-Leach-Blilely Act, and fully reinstate the Glass-Steagall Act.

18. Passage of local content laws—especially for items related to our national defense.

19. Requirements for strict, detailed country-of-origin labeling on all food and agricultural imports, and a limit on such imports only to those countries that fully comply with U.S. food-safety laws.

While our national economic strategy must take into account the realities of today's world, it should also look beyond our current moment toward our vision for the future. We have always been, and must continue to be, a nation that helps shape human history.

Some will read this and say that such a national economic strategy might invoke a trade war with communist China, Japan, or some other nation. Based upon my quarter-century of international business experience, I think this is highly unlikely since communist China, Japan, and other nations need access to the U.S. market to support their economies. However, even if I am wrong, what is the alternative? Should we continue on our current destructive path toward economic and political ruin? Allowing America to fail would be an act of cowardice that would simultaneously dishonor all who have gone before us and rob our children of their future. We have a responsibility to rebuild the American economy and the free society whose adaptability and stability we have taken for granted. If doing what is necessary to rebuild America's economy invokes a trade war with China, Japan, or others, then so be it. We'll fight to win! We must come together as Americans, with courage and conviction, remembering Patrick Henry's rallying cry: "Give me liberty, or give me death!" All of us must once again be willing to pledge our lives, fortunes, and sacred honor to reclaim America's economic and political independence. If we do this, with faith in God, nothing can stop us from rebuilding America!

To declare your support for creation of a national economic strategy, please visit my website at Selling-US-Out.com.

Unleashing the Power of Yankee Ingenuity

Some men see things as they are and ask why. Others dream things that never were and ask why not.
—George Bernard Shaw

Be courageous! Whatever setbacks America has encountered, it has always emerged as a stronger and more prosperous nation. . . . Be brave as your fathers before you. Have faith and go forward!
—Thomas Edison

For more than 200 years, America has been the invention engine of the world. Our inventions and discoveries have transformed the world and benefited all mankind. Take a moment to remind yourself of some you may have forgotten, and perhaps discover some for the first time *(Wikipedia)*.

1700s

Invention/ Discovery	Use	Invention/ Discovery	Use
swim fins or flippers	swimming, snorkeling, diving	bifocals	eyeglasses
octant	navigation	artificial diffraction grating	optical lenses
mail order catalogue	commerce	automatic flour mill	grain processing
lightning rod	lightning protection	cracker/dried biscuit	food
flexible urinary catheter	medical	cotton gin	textiles
armonica/glass harmonica	musical instrument	wheel cipher	message encryption
swivel chair	furniture	Rumford fireplace	fireplace heating
flat boat	inland waterways	cupcake	baked goods
submarine (turtle)	naval warfare	interchangeable parts	mass production

1800s

Invention/ Discovery	Use	Invention/ Discovery	Use
steam boat	transportation	spray gun	multiple
suspension bridge	transportation	sandblasting	multiple
armored warship	naval warfare	revolver	firearms
fire hydrant	fire protection	mixer	food processing
Burr truss	building construction	feather duster	cleaning
vapor-compression refrigeration	cold storage	railway air brake	transportation
amphibious vehicle	transportation	diner	restaurant

1800s

Invention/ Discovery	Use	Invention/ Discovery	Use
coffee percolator	brew coffee	earmuffs	clothing
lobster trap	lobster fishing	silo	agriculture
columbiad	canon-artillery	jeans	clothing
circular saw	construction	knuckle coupler (trains)	transportation
dental floss	hygiene	fire sprinkler	fire safety
milling machine	industrial tool	spork	cutlery
profile lathe	woodworking	ice cream soda	food
detachable collar	clothing	quadruplex telegraph	electronic communications
graham cracker	baked goods	jockstrap	safety
platform scale	weighing/ measurement	Forstner bit	woodworking
flanged t rail	transportation	qwerty	keyboard layout
multiple coil magnet	electric motors	biscuit cutter	food processing
electric doorbell	signaling	dental drill	healthcare
Morse code	electronic communications	mimeograph	printing
sewing machine	textiles	synthesizer	electronic instrument
combine harvester	agriculture	airbrush	multiple
steam shovel	construction	tattoo machine	multiple
wrench	multiple	phonograph	sound reproduction
solar compass	surveying	district heating	commercial and residential
relay	electrical switch	carbon microphone	sound conversion
gridiron	cooking	free jet water turbine	multiple
circuit breaker	electrical protection	bolometer	energy measurement

1800s

Invention/ Discovery	Use	Invention/ Discovery	Use
self-polishing cast steel plow	agriculture	photographic plate	photography
corn sheller	agriculture	carton	multiple
sleeping car	transportation	cash register	commerce
vulcanized rubber	tires and other uses	oil burner	heating and other uses
Babbitt metal	engine bearings and other uses	candlepin bowling	recreation
Howe truss	bridge construction	electric chair	capital punishment
anesthesia	medical	metal detector	multiple
grain elevator	agriculture	electric iron	clothing
ice cream maker	food processing	electric fan	multiple
multiple-effect evaporator	processing-multiple uses	salt water taffy	food
rotary printing press	printing	solar cell	converting light to electricity
Pratt truss	bridge construction	machine gun (fully automatic)	firearms
pressure sensitive tape	multiple	dissolvable pill	pharmaceuticals
Maynard tape primer	firearms	lap steel guitar	musical instrument
baseball	recreation	popcorn machine	food processing
transverse shuttle	sewing machines	photographic film	multiple
printing telegraph	electronic communications	skyscraper	building construction
gas mask	public safety	fuel dispenser (gas pump)	transportation
doughnut	baked goods	filing cabinet	multiple
pin tumbler lock	security	telephone	electronic communications
jackhammer	construction	telephone directory	multiple

1800s

Invention/ Discovery	Use	Invention/ Discovery	Use
safety pin	multiple	screen door	home construction
dishwasher	appliance	gramophone record	sound reproduction
feed dogs	sewing machines	slot machine	gambling
vibrating shuttle	sewing machines	softball	recreation
inverted microscope	multiple	comptometer	adding machine
rotary hook	sewing machines	ac motor	multiple
fire alarm box	fire protection	kinetoscope	motion pictures
elevator brake	transportation safety	trolley pole	transportation
burglar alarm	public safety	drinking straw	transfer liquid
potato chips	food	stepping switch	electrical connection
clothespin	multiple	revolving door	commercial construction
breast pump	healthcare	ballpoint pen	writing
calliope	musical instrument	telautograph (fax)	electronic communications
condensed milk	food	touch typing	communications
equatorial sextant	navigation	Flexible Flyer (sled)	recreation
toilet paper	hygiene	payphone	electronic communications
pink lemonade	food	stop sign	transportation
brown truss	bridge construction	tabulating machine	accounting
pepper shaker	food	shredded wheat	food
mason jar	food storage	Babcock test	food processing
pencil eraser	writing	smoke detector	fire safety
ironing board	clothing	Ferris wheel	amusement
twine knotter	agriculture	Dow process	material science

1800s

Invention/ Discovery	Use	Invention/ Discovery	Use
dustpan	cleaning	tesla coil	electronics-multiple uses
electric stove	appliance	rotary dial telephone	electronic communications
escalator	transportation	pastry fork	cutlery
vacuum cleaner	appliance	zipper	clothing
repeating rifle	firearms	Schrader valve	tires & other uses
jelly bean	food	bottle cap	beverage containers
twist drill	multiple	dimmer	lighting control
Kinematoscope	motion pictures	bicycle seat (padded)	bicycle
postcard	communication	tractor	agriculture
machine gun	firearms	laxative	pharmaceuticals
breakfast cereal	food	spectroheliograph	astronomy
ratchet wrench	multiple	pinking shears	clothing
quad roller skates	recreation	stadimeter	navigation
double-barreled cannon	artillery	mousetrap	pest control
spar torpedo	naval weapon	medical glove	health care
cowboy hat	clothing	cyclocomputer	bicycle
rotary printing press (web)	printing	clipless pedal	bicycle
urinal	public restrooms	volleyball	recreation
chuckwagon	food storage and preparation	cotton candy	food
motorcycle	transportation	muffler	engines and other uses
paper clip	multiple	tapered roller bearing	industrial-multiple
barbed wire	fencing/security	ice cream scoop	food
ticker tape	communication	charcoal briquette	food preparation
water-tube boiler	heating and other uses	billiards cue chalk	recreation

1800s

Invention/ Discovery	Use	Invention/ Discovery	Use
refrigerator car	transportation	candy corn	food
paper bag	multiple	remote control	electronics-multiple uses
tape measure	multiple	semi-automatic shotgun	firearms
vibrator	multiple	filing cabinet (vertical)	multiple
American football	recreation	installer bit	multiple
pipe wrench	multiple	Sousaphone	musical instrument
clothes hanger	multiple	wing warping	aviation
bee smoker	agriculture	flash-lamp	photography
can opener	appliance	duckpin bowling	recreation

1900-45

Invention/ Discovery	Use	Invention/ Discovery	Use
nickel-zinc battery	power source-multiple	masking tape	multiple
Merrill-Crowe process	gold processing	Reuben sandwich	food
carbide lamp	multiple	tilt-a-whirl	amusement ride
thumbtack	multiple	garage door opener	door control
key punch	data processing	power steering	transportation
mercury-vapor lamp	multiple	drive through	retail/banking
assembly line	manufacturing	liquid-fuel rocket	space vehicles/ missiles
safety razor (disposable)	personal hygiene	bread slicer	Food processing
windowed envelope	mail	jukebox	entertainment
radio direction finder	electronic navigation	garbage disposal	appliance

313

1900-45

Invention/ Discovery	Use	Invention/ Discovery	Use
hearing aid	healthcare	resonator guitar	musical instrument
postage meter	mail	Kool-Aid	beverage
teddy bear (named after Theodore Roosevelt)	stuffed toy	corn dog	food
periscope (collapsible)	visual observation	negative feedback amplifier	electronic communications
mercury arc valve	electric motors	recliner	furniture
air conditioning	indoor climate control	ice cube tray	ice cubes
tea bag	beverage	bubble gum	candy
offset printing press	printing	clip-on tie	clothing
airplane	air transportation	electric razor	personal hygiene
windshield wipers	multiple	iron lung	healthcare
wood's glass	communications	Freon	refrigerators/ac
wood's lamp	dermatology	tampon (applicator)	personal hygiene
baler (round)	agriculture	eyelash curler	personal hygiene
automatic transmission	transportation	sunglasses	eye care
ac power plugs and sockets	electrical connection	frozen food	food storage
banana split	food	cyclotron	scientific research
pantograph (diamond-shaped)	public transportation	car audio	radio
dragline excavator	mining and construction	polyvinylidene chloride (PVC)	multiple
batting helmet	safety	Cheesesteak sandwich	food
fly swatter	multiple	bathysphere	ocean exploration
liquid ring pump	multiple	chocolate chip cookie	food

1900-45

Invention/ Discovery	Use	Invention/ Discovery	Use
outboard motor	boating	sodium thiopental (sodium pentothal)	drug
ice pop	food	fluropolymers	multiple
typesetting	printing	thermistor	electrical-multiple uses
flushometer	plumbing	electric guitar	musical instrument
audion tube	electronic amplifier	strobe light	multiple
curtain rod	curtains	aerogel	multiple
electrostatic precipitator	air or gas filtering	bug zapper	insect control
paper towel	multiple	miniature snap-action switch	micro switch-multiple
candy apple	food	staple remover	
mixer (electric)	appliance	peristaltic pump	healthcare
skee ball	recreation	radio telescope	radio astronomy
paper shredder	document security	tape dispenser	dispensing adhesive tape
suppressor	firearms	landing vehicle tracked	WWII amphibious vehicle
gin rummy	game	Multiplane camera	animated motion pictures
headset	electronic communications	frequency modulation (FM)	radio/television
fifth wheel coupling	transportation	television	
erector set	educational toy	impact sprinkler	irrigation systems
binder clip	multiple	trampoline (modern)	gymnastics
automobile self-starter	transportation	acrostic (puzzle)	word puzzle
road surface marking	transportation	Richter magnitude scale	seismic measurement
autopilot	transportation	black light	uv lamp
electric blanket	health care	parking meter	transportation

1900-45

Invention/ Discovery	Use	Invention/ Discovery	Use
traffic light (electric)	transportation	surfboard fin	recreation
formica (plastic)	multiple	pH meter	pH measurement of liquid
regenerative circuit	electronic amplifier	gomco clamp	health care
traffic cone	transportation	reed switch	electronics-multiple
fortune cookie	food	Phillips-head screw	multiple
skeet shooting	recreation	stock car racing	automobile racing/ NASCAR
single-sideband modulation	electronic communications	programming languages	computers
hamburger bun	food	compact fluorescent lamp	lighting
Lincoln logs	educational toy	chair lift	transport system
supermarket	retail store	strain gauge	measure strain of an object
cloverleaf interchange	transportation	bass guitar	musical instrument
tow truck	transportation	O-ring	multiple
condenser microphone	electronic communications	photosensitive glass	multiple
light switch (toggle)	lighting control	digital computer	data processing
stream cipher	electronic communications	shopping cart	retail-multiple
superheterodyne receiver	radio/television	sunglasses (polarized)	eye care
French dip sandwich	food	klystron	electronics-multiple
torque wrench	multiple	cyclamate	artificial sweetener
crystal oscillator	electronics-multiple	beach ball	recreation

1900-45

Invention/ Discovery	Use	Invention/ Discovery	Use
grocery bag	multiple	fiberglass	multiple
hydraulic brake	transportation	xerography	photocopy
blender	appliance	nylon	multiple
silica gel	multiple	operant conditioning chamber	animal research
toaster (pop-up)	food preparation	soft serve ice cream	food
Eskimo pie	food	Teflon	multiple
jungle gym	recreation	yield sign	transportation
polygraph	lie detector	VU meter	audio measurement
flowchart	multiple	starting gate	horse/dog racing
adhesive bandage	health care	twist tie	multiple
headrest	transportation	automated teller machine (atm)	banking
garage door opener	transportation	vocoder	telephony
blowout preventer (ram)	oil/gas wells	fluxgate magnetometer	magnetic field measurement
convertible	transportation	deodorant	personal hygiene
water skiing	recreation	acrylic fiber	multiple
radial arm saw	multiple	electric guitar (solid body)	musical instrument
audiometer	health care	bazooka	military weapon
neutrodyne	electronic communications	magnetic proximity fuze	military ordnance detonator
bulldozer	construction	slinky	toy
cotton swab	multiple	microwave oven	food preparation
instant camera	photography	cruise control	transportation
locking pliers	multiple	block heater	engine warming
cheeseburger	food	plutonium	atomic bomb/ atomic energy

1900-45

Invention/ Discovery	Use	Invention/ Discovery	Use
propane	fuel	atomic reaction	atomic bomb/ atomic energy
heparin	health care-anticlotting	cyanoacrylate (super glue)	adhesive-multiple
earth inductor compass	navigation	streptomycin	antibiotic drug
Moviola	motion picture editing	americium (synthetic element)	smoke detectors, industrial guages-multiple
radio altimeter	aircraft navigation	curium (synthetic element)	scientific research
automatic volume control	electronic communications	promethium	scientific research, atomic battery, instrumentation

1946-60

Invention/ Discovery	Use	Invention/ Discovery	Use
cloud seeding	weather modification	wd-40	lubricant-multiple
warfarin	pesticide, anticlotting drug	apgar scale	health care
tetracycline	antibiotic drug	gilhoolie	appliance
space observatory	Hubble telescope	wheel clamp	public safety
blowout preventer (annular)	oil wells	porous silicon	multiple
Tupperware	food storage	antineutron, neutrino, antiproton	scientific research
Spoonplug	fishing lure	Wiffle ball	recreation
chipper teeth	chain saw	MASER	microwave amplifier-multiple
filament tape	packaging	carbonless copy paper	handwritten communications
diaper (waterproof)	health care	crossed-field amplifier	microwave amplifier-multiple

1946-60

Invention/ Discovery	Use	Invention/ Discovery	Use
transistor	electronics-multiple	zipper storage bag	food storage-multiple
defibrillator	health care	TV dinner	prepackaged frozen food
supersonic aircraft	aviation	acoustic suspension loudspeaker	multiple
acrylic paint	multiple	model rocketry	hobby
magnetic particle clutch	multiple	door (automatic sliding)	multiple
windsurfing	recreation	mogen clamp	health care
hair spray	personal hygiene	cardiopulmonary resuscitation	health care
cat litter	pet care	synthetic diamond	multiple
Halligan bar	public safety	radar gun	measure object speed
hand dryer	personal hygiene	sling lift	health care
rogallo wing	aviation	Crosby-Kugler capsule	health care
cable television	television	nuclear submarine	naval warfare
flying disc	recreation	hard disk drive	electronic data storage
video game	multiple	harmonic drive	multiple
radiocarbon dating	scientific research	vibrating sample magnetometer	measure magnetic properties
airsickness bag	motion sickness	lint roller	fiber removal
ice resurfacer	ice rinks	kart racing	auto racing
californium	nuclear energy, x-ray	industrial robot	multiple
berkelium	scientific research	operating system (batch processing)	computers
atomic clock	timekeeping	Fortran	computer programming
Holter monitor	health care	videotape	image and sound recording

1946-60

Invention/ Discovery	Use	Invention/ Discovery	Use
crash test dummy	transportation safety	particle storage ring	scientific research
compiler	computer programming	skid-steer loader	multiple
aerosol paint	spray painting	wireless microphone	multiple
artificial snowmaking	ski resorts	laser	multiple
credit card	banking/finance	confocal microscopy	optical imaging-multiple
leaf blower	gardening	sugar packet	multiple
hamming code	telecommunications	air-bubble packing	packaging
teleprompter	communications	borazon	multiple
sengstaken-blake-more tube	health care	gamma camera	imaging-multiple
stellarator	nuclear energy	cryotron	switch-supercon-ductivity
cooler	food storage	doppler fetal monitor	health care
wetsuit	recreation	cable tie	multiple
correction fluid	typing	lisp programming language	computer programming
well counter	measuring radioactivity	carbon fiber	multiple
airbag	vehicle safety	integrated circuit	electronics-multiple
bread clip	food storage	fusor	nuclear energy
barcode	data communication	weather satellite	meteorology
polio vaccine	health care	spandex	multiple
artificial heart	health care	child safety seat	transportation safety
heart-lung machine	health care	artificial turf	multiple

1946-60

Invention/ Discovery	Use	Invention/ Discovery	Use
einsteinium (synthetic element)	scientific research	magnetic stripe card	data storage-multiple
dna structure	scientific research	global navigation satellite system	gps navigation
voltmeter (digital)	electrical measurement	combined oral contraceptive pill	health care
mendelevium	scientific research	obsidian hydration dating	scientific research
marker pen	multiple	gas laser	multiple

1961-70

Invention/ Discovery	Use	Invention/ Discovery	Use
spreadsheet (electronic)	organize and analyze data	snowboarding	recreation
wearable computer	body-worn computers	adaptive equalizer (automatic)	electronics-multiple
frozen carbonated beverage	food-slurpee	Kevlar	fiber-multiple
biofeedback	health care	hypertext	data communications
communications satellite	telecommunica-tions	cordless telephone	telecommunica-tions
chimney starter	charcoal ignition	space pen	writing in space and other harsh environments
light-emitting diode (LED)	electronics-multiple	minicomputer	computer system-multiple
electret microphone	multiple	compact disc (cd)	digital data storage
jet injector	health care	chemical laser	multiple
laser diode	electronics-multiple	dynamic random access memory (dram)	data storage-multiple
glucose meter	health care	backpack (internal frame)	recreation

1961-70

Invention/ Discovery	Use	Invention/ Discovery	Use
kicktail	skateboards	calculator (hand-held)	mathematical calculations
computer mouse	computer user interface	racquetball	recreation
basic	computer programming	virtual reality	computer simulation
balloon catheter	health care	turtle excluder device	commercial fishing
geosynchronous satellite	multiple	zipper (ride)	amusement ride
buffalo wings	food	lunar module	moon landing
plasma display	flat panel electronic display	laser printer	computer printer
quark, up quark, down quark	scientific research	bioactive glass	health care
moog synthesizer	musical instrument	wide-body aircraft	aviation
aspartame	artificial sweetener	Taser	electroshock weapon
8-track cartridge	magnetic sound recording	charge coupled device	electronics- multiple
permanent press	fabric-multiple	mousepad	computer interface
carbon dioxide laser	multiple	chapman stick	musical instrument
liquid crystal display (dynamic scattering mode)	flat panel electronic display	markup language	computer text
squid	measure magnetic fields	wireless local area network	data communications
argon laser	multiple	surf leash (surfboard)	recreation

1971-80

Invention/ Discovery	Use	Invention/ Discovery	Use
personal computer	data processing	Post-it note	multiple

1971-80

Invention/ Discovery	Use	Invention/ Discovery	Use
fuzzball router	first internet data routing	scanning acoustic microscope	imaging analysis
Uno (card game)	game	quantum well laser	electronics-multiple
supercritical airfoil	transonic aviation	universal product code	electronic data tracking
microprocessor	computer central processor	optical character recognition and text-to-speech technology	multiple
floppy disk	data storage	digital camera	digital photography
ambulatory infusion pump	health care	ethernet	computer networking
string trimmer	weed/grass cutting	breakaway rim	basketball rim safety
Memristor	data storage	Gore-Tex	waterproof, breathable fabric-multiple
email	digital communications	hepatitis b virus vaccine	health care
C (programming language)	computer programming	human-powered aircraft	aviation
video game console	entertainment computer	chemical oxygen iodine laser	multiple
global positioning system	position, navigation, time	slide away bed	sofa bed
PET scanner	health care	popcorn bag	microwave popcorn
magnetic resonance imaging	health care	bulletin board system	data communications
personal watercraft (jet ski)	recreation	winglets	aviation fuel efficiency
e-paper	multiple such as e-books	polar fleece	synthetic "wool"-multiple

1971-80

Invention/ Discovery	Use	Invention/ Discovery	Use
recombinant dna	scientific research	winglets	aviation fuel efficiency
catalytic converter (three-way)	pollution control	voicemail	digital voice message storage
mobile phone	wireless communications	Heimlich maneuver	health care

1981-90

Invention/ discovery	Use	Invention/ discovery	Use
control-alt-delete	PC keyboard command	digital micromirror device	digital imaging
total internal reflection fluorescence microscope	scientific research	Perl	computer programming
space shuttle	reusable spacecraft	luggage (tilt-and-roll)	personal travel
paintball	recreation	fused deposition modeling	rapid prototyping and manufacturing
graphic user interface	computer interface	TCL (tool command language)	computer programming
internet	global computer network	ballistic electron emission microscopy	scientific research
blind signature	secure digital communication	electron beam ion trap	scientific research
laser turntable	phonograph	nicotine patch	health care
pneumococcal polysaccharide vaccine (Pneumovax)	prevention of streptococcus pneumoniae infections	firewall	network computer security
pointing stick	pc pointing device as used on the ibm "ThinkPad"	resin identification code	plastics type id
the flex-foot prosthesis	artificial limb	zip file format	data compression format

1981-90

Invention/ discovery	Use	Invention/ discovery	Use
polymerase chain reaction	scientific research	selective laser sintering	rapid prototyping and manufacturing
atomic force microscope	scientific research	electromagnetic lock	electronic locking system
stereolithography	rapid prototyping and manufacturing	sulfur lamp	highly efficient lighting system
tumor suppressor gene	cancer treatment		

1991-2000

Invention/ Discovery	Use	Invention/ Discovery	Use
ant robotics	simple and inexpensive robots with limited capabilities	JavaScript	computer programming
spinner (wheel)	auto hubcap	Adobe Flash	web-page animation
CMOS image sensor	electronic imaging-multiple	bait car	law enforcement
portable dialysis machine	health care	virtual reality therapy	health care
DNA computing	scientific research	embryonic stem cell lines	health care and scientific research
Segway PT	personal transport	HVLS fan (high-volume-low-speed)	air circulation
quantum cascade laser	multiple	Torino scale	measure impact hazard of near-earth objects
Bose–Einstein condensate	scientific research	phase-change incubator	water microorganism testing
Screenless hammer mill	grain processing	bowtie cotter pin	wire fastener-multiple
Xtracycle	load carrying bicycle	iBOT	mobile powered wheelchair

1991-2000

Invention/ Discovery	Use	Invention/ Discovery	Use
scroll wheel	computer mouse		

2001-present

Invention/ Discovery	Use	Invention/ Discovery	Use
SERF (magnetometer)	scientific research	nanowire battery	power source-multiple
self-cleaning windows (ppg)	residential and commercial	human genome and variation mapping	health care and scientific research
Doggles	sunglasses for dogs	electro needle biomedical sensor array (Sandia National Labs)	health care
nanoscale motor		bionic contact lens	digital contact lens
fermionic condensate	scientific research	trongs	eating utensils
Slingshot (water vapor distillation system)	portable water purification	flying windmills	wind energy from jet stream
Facebook	online social networking	Sixth Sense wearable gestural interface (MIT)	natural hand gesture computer interface
YouTube	online video forum	retinal implants	restores vision to patients with macular degeneration and blindness
solar roof shingles	solar energy	bed bug detective	electronic sensor to detect bed bugs
Twitter	online social networking		

As you can see from this expansive list, most of today's major industries—automotive, consumer electronics, information technology, aerospace, pharmaceutical, semiconductor, nuclear energy, oil and gas, and countless others—were created by American inventions and discoveries. Invention and discovery has played a vital role in building the U.S. economy. However, since the end of World War II, our country has given away the majority of its inventions and discoveries or had them stolen by foreign manufacturers—especially in Asia. This loss has been catastrophic to the U.S. economy and is further compounded by a slowdown in the rate of new inventions and discoveries within the U.S. since 1980, due to outsourcing and offshoring.

We must change course and once again unleash our Yankee ingenuity to rebuild the U.S. economy. Fortunately, we still have some of the best research universities in the world and a strong and extensive network of public and private institutions dedicated to scientific research. We must continue to invest heavily in these institutions as part of our national economic strategy. But we have to ensure that their inventions and discoveries are protected and used to rebuild American industry and our domestic economy, not outsourced or offshored by U.S. or foreign manufacturers. We must stop the foreign transfer and theft of U.S. inventions, technologies, and discoveries. At the same time, we should liberalize U.S. laws governing the protection of inventions, technologies, and discoveries to make it easier for U.S. companies, universities, and private and public research labs to collaborate and innovate. We should also continue to support international scientific collaboration but under a different set of rules that continue to promote human progress while protecting U.S. national and economic interests.

There are no limits or boundaries to what we can achieve as a nation by revitalizing and protecting the American invention and discovery engine as part of a carefully considered national economic strategy. Imagine the size and scope of the industries we can create together based on new technologies—cars and trucks that drive themselves, intelligent highway systems, flying cars and trucks, androids, teleporters, fully automated homes, decentralized personal power plants using cold fusion, bionic limbs and organs, space planes, space-based factories, space tourism, manned deep-space flight, and countless other possibilities. My nine-year-old son Blake always talks about inventing flying shoes someday. He spoke of his idea even before seeing the movie *Iron Man*. When we saw the movie together, he enthusiastically told me afterward, "Dad, those are the kind of shoes I've been talking about." Perhaps he will invent flying shoes someday—who knows? America can and must once again lead the way in making today's science fiction tomorrow's reality!

What is your vision of the future and how do you think we can revitalize America's invention and discovery engine? Please share your thoughts at Selling-US-Out.com.

Confronting Our National Debt

The greatness of America lies not in being more enlightened than any other nation, but rather in her ability to repair her faults.

—ALEXIS DE TOCQUEVILLE, FRENCH HISTORIAN AND
AUTHOR OF *Democracy in America*

Here's some good news: de Tocqueville is right. America is not destined by fate to fail as some misguided political ideologues falsely preach, and our adversaries hope. There is no historical pattern or predestined historical time clock that says our democracy will collapse after 200, 300, or even 500 years. As we have since 1776, we Americans have the freedom to choose what course we will take as individuals and as a nation. We can and must once again "repair our faults," so our democracy continues to endure for the benefit of future generations. There are many who cite the following spurious quote as proof that American democracy is predestined by history to fail.

A democracy cannot exist as a permanent form of government. It can only exist until the voters discover that they can vote themselves largesse from the public treasury.

From that moment on, the majority always votes for the candidate promising the most benefits from the public treasury, with the result that a democracy always collapses over loose fiscal policy, and is always followed by a dictatorship.

The average of the world's great civilizations has been 200 years. These nations have progressed through this sequence: from bondage to spiritual faith; from spiritual faith to great courage; from courage to liberty; from liberty to abundance; from abundance to selfishness; from selfishness to complacency; from complacency to apathy; from apathy to dependency; from dependency back again to bondage.

This is a fictitious quote falsely attributed to Sir Alex Fraser Tytler, a Scottish historian. While Tytler was real, this so-called quote is fraudulent political propaganda with no basis in historical fact. It has been circulating in various forms since the 1950s and was one of the first Internet myths in the 1980s *(Collins)*. In truth, we are the authors of our own history—not the passive victims of some predetermined historical outcome. We have the power, individually and collectively, to determine the future of America through the choices that we make. Even when events happen that are out of our control, we still have the freedom and power to decide how to respond, to determine what course of action to take as individuals and as a nation. This is the power and the greatness of American liberty!

With this in mind, it is time we honestly acknowledge and confront our skyrocketing national debt. Our national debt is the single greatest threat to our democracy and must immediately be brought under control. This is a complicated issue since this debt is a result of decreased tax revenues, increased spending, and the decline of U.S. manufacturing and the overall U.S. economy caused by outsourcing and offshoring. We must carefully address all the causes of our national debt simultaneously with a thoughtful and balanced approach. This is no easy or simple task. It is like trying do major repairs to a 747 airliner in flight without landing or crashing. We must use a well-orchestrated, surgical approach to avoid wrecking our economy while we rein in and begin to pay down our national debt. Our approach must be driven by American pragmatism, and not right-or left-wing ideology that has no basis in sound fiscal policy or economic reality. It must also include a sensible mix of spending cuts and increased revenues. This will require tough choices and sacrifices by all Americans. However, we can and must come together as a nation to confront our national debt to ensure our democracy endures for future generations. I believe that this will only happen by electing moderate third-party candidates since both major political parties have shown that they cannot be trusted to make the responsible decisions necessary to balance our federal budget and pay down our national debt. Please give your support to the Modern Whig Party or some other moderate third party of your choosing to make this happen. Our nation's future depends on it! For more information on how you can help, please visit my website at Selling-US-Out.com.

Raising Tariffs and Buying Back All Foreign Debt, Starting with China

Source: "Which Countries Hold The Most U.S. Government Debt?" Huffington Post

Almost 50 percent of our national debt is owned by foreign nations, with China being our number-one lender. As John Adams warned, "There are two ways to conquer and enslave a nation. One is by the sword. The other is by debt." His observation is as true today as it was in 1776, which is why we must make it a top national security priority to buy back all foreign debt, starting with China. Washington, Adams, Hamilton, and the other Founding Fathers must be looking down from the heavens on the foreign ownership of our national debt in disbelief and disgust! It is incomprehensible that we've allowed our country to become indebted to communist China and other such dictatorial nations that are hostile to American interests and that oppose our foundational ideals.

We must do whatever it takes to eliminate this foreign debt, including the use of higher tariffs on imports, as our nation did during its first 150 years. Currently only about 30 percent of all goods imported into the U.S. are subject to tariffs; the rest are on the "free list." Furthermore, the average tariff rates are at a historic low of 1.3 percent. We need to eliminate the free list and increase the average tariff rate from 1.3 percent to 12.6 percent, which is consistent with the rates that were in effect during the late 1930s and early 1940s, the recovery period from the Great Depression. It is also consistent with the average tariff rate in effect when we lowered tariffs and implemented the income tax to support a more liberal trade policy back in 1913. The rate increase will raise significant revenues that we can use to eliminate foreign debt while also creating a more level playing field with communist China, Japan, India, and other nations that have enjoyed open access to our market, while blocking access to their home markets. Higher import tariffs will also help us achieve balanced trade and set the conditions for bringing manufacturing back to our shores—helping us reindustrialize America and revitalize the U.S. economy.

We should also immediately enact laws limiting the foreign ownership of U.S. public debt. We must not allow other nations to control our national finances—especially those that are hostile to the democratic principles and freedoms that define who we are as a nation. Foreign ownership of U.S. debt threatens and undermines our independence and freedom. It places us in bondage to the nations and institutions that control our debt and gives them direct influence over our foreign and domestic affairs. The dictators in

Beijing clearly understand this as does Japan, the U.K., and OPEC nations. They are collectively influencing U.S. domestic and foreign affairs to their benefit, and our detriment, as the primary holders of our national debt. If you agree that we should raise import tariffs to:

1. eliminate foreign ownership of our national debt

2. achieve balanced trade

3. set the conditions for bringing manufacturing back to our shores—helping us reindustrialize America and revitalize the U.S. economy

Please sign the petition to Congress on my website, Selling-US-Out.com.

Balancing Our Federal Budget

Throughout most of U.S. history, we had balanced federal budgets. The only exception was in times of war or national emergency. However, once these crises passed, we quickly put our financial affairs in order again and rebalanced our budgets and paid our public debts. This all changed in the 1980s under the Reagan administration. We began running up large budget deficits as the government started spending more money than it was taking in. We began an irrational and irresponsible pattern of cutting taxes, increasing spending, and borrowing the difference. This pattern has continued throughout the 1990s and 2000s with the only exception being the period from 1998 through 2001, under the Clinton administration. During that period, the federal government actually had a budget surplus (revenues exceeded expenses). The worst period of debt accumulation occurred under President George W. Bush and this pattern has accelerated and continued under President Obama. Since 1981, we have borrowed $15.7 trillion! Of this, approximately $5.7 trillion was borrowed under Democratic administrations, and $10 trillion was borrowed under Republican administrations. The following charts show the 2010 Federal expenditures versus revenues.

FY2010 U.S. Federal Spending

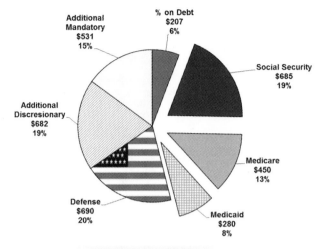

Total = $3.6 trillion

Source: usgovernmentrevenue.com

FY2010 U.S. Federal Revenues

| Tax Revenue ......$2.2 trillion |
| Borrowed ....$1.4 trillion |
| Total ....$3.6 trillion |

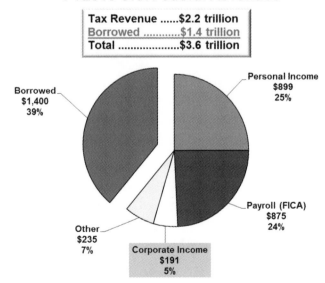

Source: usgovernmentrevenue.com

The federal government had to borrow $1.4 trillion in 2010 to make up the difference in expenditures versus revenues collected. This same pattern has been repeated for the past three decades and as a result, our national debt is skyrocketing. Neither major party has the political courage or will to do what is necessary to get the deficit under control. In fact, it seems that the Republicans are deliberately trying to bankrupt our federal government under a perverse neoconservative strategy known as "starve the beast." This concept was first introduced by Reagan and is now being driven to extremes by Grover Norquist, a powerful Washington lobbyist *(Wikipedia; Grover Norquist)*. "Starve the beast" *(Wikipedia)* is an overly simplistic, flawed, and dangerous strategy that seeks to cut taxes in order to deprive the government of revenue in a deliberate effort to create a fiscal budget crisis. The theory is that this will force the federal government to reduce spending. Instead, all this approach has done is run up an enormous public debt that is nearly 50 percent owned by foreign governments. This reckless and irresponsible partisan behavior is destroying America. It's another example of the harm that self-serving Washington politicians and lobbyists are doing to our country. We need to put an end to this type of irrational, ideologically driven behavior and come together as patriotic Americans to put thoughtful, fiscally responsible tax and spending policies in place that build—rather than destroy—America.

From the spending side, the two main drivers of our budget deficits and growing national debt are Social Security, Medicare, and Medicaid. From the revenue side, the gap is the decline in corporate and personal income tax, tariffs, and excise taxes. To balance our federal budget and begin paying down the principle on our national debt, we need to both reduce spending and increase revenues. Here are some possible solutions:

Proposals for Fixing Social Security

1. Gradually increase the retirement age and index this as life expectancy goes up.

2. Increase the FICA tax—raise the ceiling from $106,800 to $250,000 or remove the ceiling altogether (which means that you

would keep paying FICA tax even after your earnings exceed $106,800 in a year).

3. Reduce the automatic increase in benefits based on cost-of-living adjustments (COLA).

4. Reduce benefits for wealthy Americans.

Proposals for Fixing Medicare

1. Takes steps to reduce the rate of growth in health-care costs, such as:

   - Strongly promote prevention and wellness programs—encourage personal responsibility for overall health and well-being through proper eating and exercise.

   - Move away from a "fee-for-services" system of paying hospitals and doctors.

   - Implement more stringent cost controls.

   - Use technology to enable more efficient and better coordination of care throughout the health-care system.

   - Adopt electronic medical records.

   - Increase doctor and hospital accountability for patient outcomes.

   - Reform malpractice laws.

   - Reduce administrative procedures.

   - Reduce medical errors.

   - Use tools like WebMD to create more informed health-care consumers.

   - Promote personal responsibility and better decisions regarding end-of-life care—30 percent of Medicare costs are for patients who die within one year.

2. Reduce the rate of growth by eliminating automatic cost and benefit adjustments—replace with annual cost reviews and make adjustments as required.

3. Raise premiums for Medicare Parts B and D, and have a progressive scale based on income levels.

4. Gradually raise the eligibility age and index this as life expectancy goes up.

5. Reduce benefits for wealthy Americans.

6. Cap the total federal health-care spending for all programs—including Medicare.

7. Ensure health-care programs, such as Medicare Part D (prescription drug coverage) are fully funded—if we are unable or unwilling to fund such programs, they must be discontinued. No more unfunded mandates!

Proposals for Reducing Defense Spending

1. Reduce overall defense spending to prewar levels.

2. Eliminate inefficient and wasteful programs.

3. Reduce the number of nuclear weapons in our arsenal.

4. Reduce the number of troops in Europe and Asia.

5. Decrease the overall size of the ground forces.

Tax Simplification and Reform

1. Instead of adopting a new tax system, simplify the existing system.

   - Throw out the current U.S. tax code (72,536 pages) and revert back to an updated version of the 1939 U.S. tax code (504 pages).

   - The 1939 tax code was the original version and it was fair, simple, and worked well. It was focused on revenue collection—not social engineering.

- The earlier tax code is progressive and ensures individuals and corporations pay their fair share of taxes. (Best of all, there aren't any loopholes!)

- Ban any changes to the reinstated tax code without a public vote—this will eliminate tampering by Washington lobbyists, which is what created the additional 72,032 pages between 1939 and 2011.

2. Increase excise taxes from 3 percent to 12 percent of total revenue collected, which is in line with historical averages.

3. Increase the average tariff rate on imported goods from 1.3 percent to 12.6 percent, which is consistent with the tariff rates that were in effect during the late 1930s and early 1940s.

4. Streamline and strengthen the IRS. Give them the support and resources needed to enforce U.S. tax laws domestically and internationally. Consolidate all federal revenue collections and enforcement under this agency, including excise taxes and tariffs.

Restructuring Our Federal Government

1. Restructure our federal government using an objective and rational approach, not one driven by irrational ideology. This restructuring should be based on function and effectiveness, not size. Ideological arguments about the size of government are pointless. We need to focus on function, effectiveness, and cost.

2. Regarding function, get back to the basics as defined by our constitution. Carefully and objectively evaluate the functions taken on by the federal government that are not defined constitutionally. Are these government functions required? If so, why are they being performed at the federal level? Would they be more effectively performed at the state or local level?

3. Eliminate or transfer any functions that do not belong at the federal level. (One good example is education—I propose that this department be eliminated so that education will be managed at the state and local levels.)

4. Consolidate redundant functions within the federal government.

5. Change many of the senior positions within the federal government from political appointees to career civil service. This will increase competency and professionalism while reducing cronyism and corruption.

6. Use technology to further improve the efficiency and effectiveness of the federal government.

7. As part of the restructuring process, make an honest assessment of the costs associated with the redefined functions of the federal government and ensure we have the revenues necessary to support the changes while paying down the principle on our national debt.

8. One of the core functions of the federal government, as defined in the Constitution, is the U.S. Postal Service. I believe it is vital that we preserve and support the postal service.

9. Congress must reassert itself and play a more active role in managing our government affairs, as defined in the Constitution, and not delegate its authority to the executive branch or external organizations, such as the WTO.

These and other possible solutions need to be discussed and debated in a rational, nonpartisan manner to determine what is truly best for America. More than ever before in our history, we need people in government who are true patriots and consensus-builders in the tradition of Henry Clay. We need people who put loyalty to their country above loyalty to a political party. Nothing will change unless and until we once again start electing such people to Congress and other public offices. This is why I strongly encourage you to become actively engaged in the political process and give your support to the Modern Whig Party or another moderate third party of your choice. The reason I stress *moderate* is because we desperately need well-educated and rational American patriots in Washington, not more politicians who are ignorant of American history and blinded by irrational, extreme ideology. Electing educated, thoughtful, reasonable people is the only way that we will achieve real and lasting change in America—the type of change that puts our country back on a strong fiscal and economic path by making the tough choices necessary to balance our federal budget and begin paying down our national debt. To learn how you can help, please visit my website at Selling-US-Out.com.

Closing Thoughts . . .

I promised my 9 year old son Blake that he could write the last words in this book. These words appeared at the end of the movie *Dr. Seuss' The Lorax* which we enjoyed as a family.

"Unless someone like you cares a whole awful lot, nothing is going to get better. Its <u>not</u>." - Dr.Seuss☺

Blake Martin, 9 years old

Addendum

The New Nationalism

A speech delivered by Theodore Roosevelt
Osawatomie, Kansas
August 31, 1910

We come here to-day to commemorate one of the epoch-making events of the long struggle for the rights of man—the long struggle for the uplift of humanity. Our country—this great Republic—means nothing unless it means the triumph of a real democracy, the triumph of popular government, and, in the long run, of an economic system under which each man shall be guaranteed the opportunity to show the best that there is in him. That is why the history of America is now the central feature of the history of the world; for the world has set its face hopefully toward our democracy; and, O my fellow citizens, each one of you carries on your shoulders not only the burden of doing well for the sake of your own country, but the burden of doing well and of seeing that this nation does well for the sake of mankind.

There have been two great crises in our country's history: first, when it was formed, and then, again, when it was perpetuated; and, in the second of these great crises—in the time of stress and strain which culminated in the Civil War, on the outcome of which depended the justification of what had been done earlier, you men of the Grand Army, you men who fought through the Civil War, not only did you justify your generation, not only did you render life worth living for our generation, but you justified the wisdom of Washington and Washington's colleagues. If this Republic had been founded by them only to be split asunder into fragments when the strain came, then the judgment of the world would have been that Washington's work was not worth doing. It was you who crowned Washington's work, as you carried to achievement the high purpose of Abraham Lincoln.

Now, with this second period of our history the name of John Brown will be forever associated; and Kansas was the theater upon which the first act of the second of our great national life dramas was played. It was the result of the struggle in Kansas which determined that our country should be in deed as well as in name devoted to both union and freedom; that the great experiment of democratic government on a national scale should succeed and not fail. In name we had the Declaration of Independence in 1776; but we gave the lie by our acts to the words of the Declaration of Independence until 1865; and words count for nothing except in so far as they represent acts. This is true everywhere; but, O my friends, it should be truest of all in political life. A broken promise is bad enough in private life. It is worse in the field of politics. No man is worth his salt in public life who makes on the stump a pledge which he does not keep after election; and, if he makes such a pledge and does not keep it, hunt him out of public life. I care for the great deeds of the past chiefly as spurs to drive us onward in the present. I speak of the men of the past partly that they may be honored by our praise of them, but more that they may serve as examples for the future.

It was a heroic struggle; and, as is inevitable with all such struggles, it had also a dark and terrible side. Very much was done of good, and much also of evil; and, as was inevitable in such a period of revolution, often the same man did both good and evil. For our great good fortune as a nation, we, the people of the United States as a whole, can now afford to forget the evil, or, at least, to remember it without bitterness, and to fix our eyes with pride only on the good that was accomplished. Even in ordinary times there are very few of us who do not see the problems of life as through a glass, darkly; and when the glass is clouded by the murk of furious popular passion, the vision of the best and the bravest is dimmed. Looking back, we are all of us now able to do justice to the valor and the disinterestedness and the love of the right, as to each it was given to see the right, shown both by the men of the North and the men of the South in that contest which was finally decided by the attitude of the West. We can admire the heroic valor, the sincerity, the self-devotion shown alike by the men who wore the blue and the men who wore the gray; and our sadness that such men should have had to fight one another is tempered by the glad knowledge that ever hereafter their descendants shall be found fighting side by side, struggling in peace as well as in war for the uplift of their common country, all alike resolute to raise to the highest pitch of honor and usefulness the nation to which they all belong. As for the veterans of the Grand Army of the Republic, they deserve honor and recognition such as is paid to no other citizens of the Republic; for to them the republic owes its all; for to them it owes its very existence. It is because of what you and your comrades did in the dark years that we of to-day walk, each of us, head erect, and proud that we belong, not to one of a dozen little squabbling contemptible commonwealths, but to the mightiest nation upon which the sun shines.

I do not speak of this struggle of the past merely from the historic standpoint. Our interest is primarily in the application to-day of the lessons taught by the contest of half a century ago. It is of little use for us to pay lip-loyalty to the mighty men of the past unless we sincerely endeavor to apply to the problems of the present precisely the qualities which in other crises enable the men of that day to meet those crises. It is half melancholy and half amusing to see the way in which well-meaning people gather to do honor to the man who, in company with John Brown, and under the lead of Abraham Lincoln, faced and solved the great problems of the nineteenth century, while, at the same time, these same good people nervously shrink from, or frantically denounce, those who are trying to meet the problems of the twentieth century in the spirit which was accountable for the successful solution of the problems of Lincoln's time.

Of that generation of men to whom we owe so much, the man to whom we owe most is, of course, Lincoln. Part of our debt to him is because he forecast our present struggle and saw the way out. He said:

"I hold that while man exists it is his duty to improve not only his own condition, but to assist in ameliorating mankind."

And again:

"Labor is prior to, and independent of, capital. Capital is only the fruit of labor, and could never have existed if labor had not first existed. Labor is the superior of capital, and deserves much the higher consideration."

If that remark was original with me, I should be even more strongly denounced as a Communist agitator than I shall be anyhow. It is Lincoln's. I am only quoting it; and that is one side; that is the side the capitalist should hear. Now, let the working man hear his side. "Capital has its rights, which are as worthy of protection as any other rights. . . . Nor should this lead to a war upon the owners of property. Property is the fruit of labor; . . . property is desirable; is a positive good in the world."

And then comes a thoroughly Lincolnlike sentence:

"Let not him who is houseless pull down the house of another, but let him work diligently and build one for himself, thus by example assuring that his own shall be safe from violence when built."

It seems to me that, in these words, Lincoln took substantially the attitude that we ought to take; he showed the proper sense of proportion in his relative estimates of capital and labor, of human rights and property rights. Above all, in this speech, as in many others, he taught a lesson in wise kindliness and charity; an indispensable lesson to us of today. But this wise kindliness and charity never weakened his arm or numbed his heart. We cannot afford weakly to blind ourselves to the actual conflict which faces us to-day. The issue is joined, and we must fight or fail.

In every wise struggle for human betterment one of the main objects, and often the only object, has been to achieve in large measure equality of opportunity. In the struggle for this great end, nations rise from barbarism to civilization, and through it people press forward from one stage of enlightenment to the next. One of the chief factors in progress is the destruction of special privilege. The essence of any struggle for healthy liberty has always been, and must always be, to take from some one man or class of men the right to enjoy power, or wealth, or position, or immunity, which has not been earned by service to his or their fellows. That is what you fought for in the Civil War, and that is what we strive for now.

At many stages in the advance of humanity, this conflict between the men who possess more than they have earned and the men who have earned more than they possess is the central condition of progress. In our day it appears as the struggle of freemen to gain and hold the right of self-government as against the special interests, who twist the methods of free government into machinery for defeating the popular will. At every stage, and under all circumstances, the essence of the struggle is to equalize opportunity, destroy privilege, and give to the life and citizenship of every individual the highest possible value both to himself and to the commonwealth. That is nothing new. All I ask in civil life is what you fought for in the Civil War. I ask that civil life be carried on according to the spirit in which the army was carried on. You never get perfect justice, but the effort in handling the army was to bring to the front the men who could do the job. Nobody grudged promotion to Grant, or Sherman, or Thomas, or Sheridan, because they earned it. The only complaint was when a man got promotion which he did not earn.

Practical equality of opportunity for all citizens, when we achieve it, will have two great results. First, every man will have a fair chance to make of himself all that in him lies; to reach the highest point to which his capacities, unassisted by special privilege of his own and unhampered by the special privilege of others, can carry him, and to get for himself and his family substantially what he has earned. Second, equality of opportunity means that the commonwealth will get from every citizen the highest service of which he is capable. No man who carries the burden of the special privileges of another can give to the commonwealth that service to which it is fairly entitled.

I stand for the square deal. But when I say that I am for the square deal, I mean not merely that I stand for fair play under the present rules of the games, but that I stand for having those rules changed so as to work for a more substantial equality of opportunity and of reward for equally good service. One word of warning, which, I think, is hardly necessary in Kansas.

When I say I want a square deal for the poor man, I do not mean that I want a square deal for the man who remains poor because he has not got the energy to work for himself. If a man who has had a chance will not make good, then he has got to quit. And you men of the Grand Army, you want justice for the brave man who fought, and punishment for the coward who shirked his work. Is not that so?

Now, this means that our government, National and State, must be freed from the sinister influence or control of special interests. Exactly as the special interests of cotton and slavery threatened our political integrity before the Civil War, so now the great special business interests too often control and corrupt the men and methods of government for their own profit. We must drive the special interests out of politics. That is one of our tasks to-day. Every special interest is entitled to justice—full, fair, and complete—and, now, mind you, if there were any attempt by mob-violence to plunder and work harm to the special interest, whatever it may be, and I most dislike and the wealthy man, whomsoever he may be, for whom I have the greatest contempt, I would fight for him, and you would if you were worth your salt. He should have justice. For every special interest is entitled to justice, but not one is entitled to a vote in Congress, to a voice on the bench, or to representation in any public office. The Constitution guarantees protections to property, and we must make that promise good. But it does not give the right of suffrage to any corporation. The true friend of property, the true conservative, is he who insists that property shall be the servant and not the master of the commonwealth; who insists that the creature of man's making shall be the servant and not the master of the man who made it. The citizens of the United States must effectively control the mighty commercial forces which they have themselves called into being.

There can be no effective control of corporations while their political activity remains. To put an end to it will be neither a short nor an easy task, but it can be done.

We must have complete and effective publicity of corporate affairs, so that people may know beyond peradventure whether the corporations obey the law and whether their management entitles them to the confidence of the public. It is necessary that laws should be passed to prohibit the use of corporate funds directly or indirectly for political purposes; it is still more necessary that such laws should be thoroughly enforced. Corporate expenditures for political purposes, and especially such expenditures by public-service corporations, have supplied one of the principal sources of corruption in our political affairs.

It has become entirely clear that we must have government supervision of the capitalization, not only of public-service corporations, including, particularly, railways, but of all corporations doing an interstate business. I do not wish to see the nation forced into the ownership of the railways if it can possibly be avoided, and the only alternative is thoroughgoing and effective regulation, which shall be based on a full knowledge of all the facts, including a physical valuation of property. This physical valuation is not needed, or, at least, is very rarely needed, for fixing rates; but it is needed as the basis of honest capitalization.

We have come to recognize that franchises should never be granted except for a limited time, and never without proper provision for compensation to the public. It is my personal belief that the same kind and degree of control and supervision which should be exercised over public-service corporations should be extended also to combinations which control necessaries of life, such as meat, oil, and coal, or which deal in them on an important scale. I have not doubt that the ordinary man who has control of them is much like ourselves. I have no doubt he would like to do well, but I want to have enough supervision to help him realize that desire to do well.

I believe that the officers, and, especially, the directors, of corporations should be held personally responsible when any corporation breaks the law.

Combinations in industry are the result of an imperative economic law which cannot be repealed by political legislation. The effort at prohibiting all combination has substantially failed. The way out lies, not in attempting to prevent such combinations, but in completely controlling them in the interest of the public welfare. For that purpose the Federal Bureau of Corporations is an agency of first importance. Its powers, and, therefore, its efficiency, as well as that of the Interstate Commerce Commission, should be largely increased. We have a right to expect from the Bureau of Corporations and from the Interstate Commerce Commission a very high grade of public service. We should be as sure of the proper conduct of the interstate railways and the proper management of interstate business as we are now sure of the conduct and management of the national banks, and we should have as effective supervision in one case as in the other. The Hepburn Act, and the amendment to the act in the shape in which it finally passed Congress at the last session, represent a long step in advance, and we must go yet further.

There is a wide-spread belief among our people that under the methods of making tariffs, which have hitherto obtained, the special interests are too influential. Probably this is true of both the big special interests and the little special interests. These methods have put a premium on selfishness, and, naturally, the selfish big interests have gotten more than their smaller, though equally selfish brothers. The duty of Congress is to provide a method by which the interest of the whole people shall be all that receives consideration. To this end there must be an expert tariff commission, wholly removed from the possibility of political pressure or of improper business influence. Such a commission can find the real difference between cost of production, which is mainly the difference of labor cost here and abroad. As fast as its recommendations are made, I believe in revising one schedule at a time. A general revision of the tariff almost inevitably leads to logrolling and the subordination of the general public interest to local and special interests.

The absence of effective State, and, especially, national, restraint upon unfair money-getting has tended to create a small class of enormously wealthy and economically powerful men, whose chief object is to hold and increase their power. The prime need is to change the conditions which enable these men to accumulate power which is not for the general welfare that they should hold or exercise. We grudge no man a fortune which represents his own power and sagacity, when exercised with entire regard to the welfare of his fellows. Again, comrades over there, take the lesson from your own experience. Not only did you not grudge, but you gloried in the promotion of the great generals who gained their promotion by leading the army to victory. So it is with us. We grudge no man a fortune in civil life if it is honorably obtained and well used. It is not even enough that it should have gained without doing damage to the community. We should permit it to be gained only so long as the gaining represents benefit to the community. This, I know, implies a policy of a far more active governmental interference with social and economic conditions in this country than we have yet had, but I think we have got to face the fact that such an increase in governmental control is now necessary.

No man should receive a dollar unless that dollar has been fairly earned. Every dollar received should represent a dollar's worth of service rendered—not gambling in stocks, but service rendered. The really big fortune, the swollen fortune, by the mere fact of its size acquires qualities which differentiate it in kind as well as in degree from what is possessed by men of relatively small means. Therefore, I believe in a graduated income tax on big fortunes, and in another tax which is far more easily collected and far more effective—a graduated inheritance tax on big fortunes, properly safeguarded against evasion and increasing rapidly in amount with the size of the estate.

The people of the United States suffer from periodical financial panics to a degree substantially unknown among the other nations which approach us in financial strength. There is no reason why we should suffer what they escape. It is of profound importance that our financial system should be promptly investigated, and so thoroughly and effectively revised as to make it certain that hereafter our currency will no longer fail at critical times to meet our needs.

It is hardly necessary for me to repeat that I believe in an efficient army and a navy large enough to secure for us abroad that respect which is the surest guaranty of peace. A word of special warning to my fellow citizens who are as progressive as I hope I am. I want them to keep up their interest in our internal affairs; and I want them also continually to remember Uncle Sam's interest abroad. Justice and fair dealing among nations rest upon principles identical with those which control justice and fair dealing among the individuals of which nations are composed, with the vital exception that each nation must do its own part in international police work. If you get into trouble here, you can call for the police; but if Uncle Sam gets into trouble, he has got to be his own policeman, and I want to see him strong enough to encourage the peaceful aspirations of other peoples in connection with us. I believe in national friendships and heartiest good-will to all nations; but national friendships, like those between men, must be founded on respect as well as on liking, on forbearance as well as upon trust. I should be heartily ashamed of any American who did not try to make the American Government act as Justly toward the other nations in international relations as he himself would act toward any individual in private relations. I should be heartily ashamed to see us wrong a weaker power, and I should hang my head forever if we tamely suffered wrong from a stronger power.

Of conservation I shall speak more at length elsewhere. Conservation means development as much as it does protection. I recognize the right and duty of this generation to develop and use the natural resources of our land; but I do not recognize the right to waste them, or to rob, by wasteful use, the generations that come after us. I ask nothing of the nation except that it so behave as each farmer here behaves with reference to his own children. That farmer is a poor creature who skins the land and leaves it worthless to his children. The farmer is a good farmer who, having enabled the land to support himself and to provide for the education of his children leaves it to them a little better than he found it himself. I believe the same thing of a nation.

Moreover, I believe that the natural resources must be used for the benefit of all our people, and not monopolized for the benefit of the few, and here again is another case in which I am accused of taking a revolutionary attitude. People forget now that one hundred years ago there were public men of good character who advocated the nation selling its public lands in great quantities, so that the nation could get the most money out of it, and giving it to the men who could cultivate it for their own uses. We took the proper democratic ground that the land should be granted in small sections to the men who were actually to till it and live on it. Now, with the water-power with the forests, with the mines, we are brought face to face with the fact that there are many people who will go with us in conserving the resources only if they are to be allowed to exploit them for their benefit. That is one of the fundamental reasons why the special interest should be driven out of politics. Of all the questions which can come before this nation, short of the actual preservation of its existence in a great war, there is none which compares in importance with the great central task of leaving this land even a better land for our descendants than it is for us, and training them into a better race to inhabit the land and pass it on. Conservation is a great moral issue for it involves the patriotic duty of insuring the safety and continuance of the nation. Let me add that the health and vitality of our people are at least as well worth conserving as their forests, waters, lands, and minerals, and in this great work the national government must bear a most important part.

I have spoken elsewhere also of the great task which lies before the farmers of the country to get for themselves and their wives and children not only the benefits of better farming, but also those of better business methods and better conditions of life on the farm. The burden of this great task will fall, as it should, mainly upon the great organizations of the farmers themselves. I am glad it will, for I believe they are all able to handle it. In particular, there are strong reasons why the Departments of Agriculture of the various States, and the United States Department of Agriculture, and the agricultural colleges and experiment stations should extend their work to cover all phases of farm life, instead of limiting themselves. as they have far too often limited themselves in the past, solely to the question of the production of crops. And now a special word to the farmer. I want to see him make the farm as fine a farm as it can be made; and let him remember to see that the improvement goes on indoors as well as out; let him remember that the farmer's wife should have her share of thought and attention just as much as the farmer himself.

Nothing is more true than that excess of every kind is followed by reaction; a fact which should be pondered by reformer and reactionary alike. We are face to face with new conceptions of the relations of property to human welfare, chiefly because certain advocates of the rights of property as against the rights of men have been pushing their claims too far. The man who wrongly holds that every human right is secondary to his profit must now give way to the advocate of human welfare, who rightly maintains that every man holds his property subject to the general right of the community to regulate its use to whatever degree the public welfare may require it.

But I think we may go still further. The right to regulate the use of wealth in the public interest is universally admitted. Let us admit also the right to regulate the terms and conditions of labor, which is the chief element of wealth, directly in the interest of the common good. The fundamental thing to do for every man is to give him a chance to reach a place in which he will make the greatest possible contribution to the public welfare. Understand what I say there. Give him a chance, not push him up if he will not be pushed. Help any man who stumbles; if he lies down, it is a poor job to try to carry him; but if he is a worthy man, try your best to see that he gets a chance to show the worth that is in him. No man can be a good citizen unless he has a wage more than sufficient to cover the bare cost of living, and hours of labor short enough so that after his day's work is done he will have time and energy to bear his share in the management of the community, to help in carrying the general load. We keep countless men from being good citizens by the conditions of life with which we surround them. We need comprehensive workmen's compensation acts, both State and national laws to regulate child labor and work for women, and, especially, we need in our common schools not merely education in book learning, but also practical training for daily life and work. We need to enforce better sanitary conditions for our workers and to extend the use of safety appliances for our workers in industry and commerce, both within and between the States. Also, friends, in the interest of the working man himself we need to set our faces like flint against mob-violence just as against corporate greed; against violence and injustice and lawlessness by wage-workers just as much as against lawless cunning and greed and selfish arrogance of employers. If I could ask but one thing of my fellow countrymen, my request would be that, whenever they go in for reform, they remember the two sides, and that they always exact justice from one side as much as from the other. I have small use for the public servant who can always see and denounce the corruption of the capitalist, but who cannot persuade himself, especially before elections, to say a word about lawless mob-violence. And I have equally small use for the man, be he a judge on the bench, or editor of a great paper, or wealthy and influential private citizen, who can see clearly enough and denounce the lawlessness of mob-violence, but whose eyes are closed so that he is blind when the question is one of corruption in business on a gigantic scale. Also remember what I said about excess in reformer and reactionary alike. If the reactionary man, who thinks of nothing but the rights of property, could have his way, he would bring about a revolution; and one of my chief fears in connection with progress comes because I do not want to see our people, for lack of proper leadership, compelled to follow men whose intentions are excellent, but whose eyes are a little too wild to make it really safe to trust them. Here in Kansas there is one paper which habitually denounces me as the tool of Wall Street, and at the same time frantically repudiates the statement that I am a Socialist on the ground that is an unwarranted slander of the Socialists.

National efficiency has many factors. It is a necessary result of the principle of conservation widely applied. In the end it will determine our failure or success as a nation. National efficiency has to do, not only with natural resources and with men, but is equally concerned with institutions. The State must be made efficient for the work which concerns only the people of the State; and the nation for that which concerns all the people. There must remain no neutral ground to serve as a refuge for lawbreakers, and especially for lawbreakers of great wealth, who can hire the vulpine legal cunning which will teach them how to avoid both jurisdictions. It is a misfortune when the national legislature fails to do its duty in providing a national remedy, so that the only national activity is the purely negative activity of the judiciary in forbidding the State to exercise power in the premises.

I do not ask for overcentralization; but I do ask that we work in a spirit of broad and far-reaching nationalism when we work for what concerns our people as a whole. We are all Americans. Our common interests are as broad as the continent. I speak to you here in Kansas exactly as I would speak in New York or Georgia, for the most vital problems are those which affect us all alike. The national government belongs to the whole American people, and where the whole American people are interested, that interest can be guarded effectively only by the national government. The betterment which we seek must be accomplished, I believe, mainly through the national government.

The American people are right in demanding that New Nationalism, without which we cannot hope to deal with new problems. The New Nationalism puts the national need before sectional or personal advantage. It is impatient of the utter confusion that results from local legislatures attempting to treat national issues as local issues. It is still more impatient of the impotence which springs from overdivision of governmental powers, the impotence which makes it possible for local selfishness or for legal cunning, hired by wealthy special interests, to bring national activities to a deadlock. This New Nationalism regards the executive power as the steward of the public welfare. It demands of the judiciary that it shall be interested primarily in human welfare rather than in property, just as it demands that the representative body shall represent all the people rather than any one class or section of the people.

I believe in shaping the ends of government to protect property as well as human welfare. Normally, and in the long run, the ends are the same; but whenever the alternative must be faced, I am for men and not for property, as you were in the Civil War. I am far from underestimating the importance of dividends; but I rank dividends below human character. Again, I do not have any sympathy with the reformer who says he does not care for dividends. Of course, economic welfare is necessary, for a man must pull his own weight and be able to support his family. I know well that the reformers must not bring upon the people economic ruin, or the reforms themselves will go down in the ruin. But we must be ready to face temporary disaster, whether or not brought on by those who will war against us to the knife. Those who oppose all reform will do well to remember that ruin in its worst form is inevitable if our national life brings us nothing better than swollen fortunes for the few and the triumph in both politics and business of a sordid and selfish materialism.

If our political institutions were perfect, they would absolutely prevent the political domination of money in any part of our affairs. We need to make our political representatives more quickly and sensitively responsive to the people whose servants they are. More direct action by the people in their own affairs under proper safeguards is vitally necessary. The direct primary is a step in this direction, if it is associated with a corrupt-practices act effective to prevent the advantage of the man willing recklessly and unscrupulously to spend money over his more honest competitor. It is particularly important that all moneys received or expended for campaign purposes should be publicly accounted for, not only after election, but before election as well. Political action must be made simpler, easier, and freer from confusion for every citizen. I believe that the prompt removal of unfaithful or incompetent public servants should be made easy and sure in whatever way experience shall show to be most expedient in any given class of cases.

One of the fundamental necessities in a representative government such as ours is to make certain that the men to whom the people delegate their power shall serve the people by whom they are elected, and not the special interests. I believe that every national officer, elected or appointed, should be forbidden to perform any service or receive any compensation, directly or indirectly, from interstate corporations; and a similar provision could not fail to be useful within the States.

The object of government is the welfare of the people. The material progress and prosperity of a nation are desirable chiefly so far as they lead to the moral and material welfare of all good citizens. Just in proportion as the average man and woman are honest, capable of sound judgment and high ideals, active in public affairs—but, first of all, sound in their home life, and the father and mother of healthy children whom they bring up well—just so far, and no farther, we may count our civilization a success. We must have—I believe we have already—a genuine and permanent moral awakening, without which no wisdom of legislation or administration really means anything; and, on the other hand, we must try to secure the social and economic legislation without which any improvement due to purely moral agitation is necessarily evanescent. Let me again illustrate by a reference to the Grand Army. You could not have won simply as a disorderly and disorganized mob. You needed generals; you needed careful administration of the most advanced type; and a good commissary—the cracker line. You well remember that success was necessary in many different lines in order to bring about general success. You had to have the administration at Washington good, just as you had to have the administration in the field; and you had to have the work of the generals good. You could not have triumphed without that administration and leadership; but it would all have been worthless if the average soldier had not had the right stuff in him. He had to have the right stuff in him, or you could not get it out of him. In the last analysis, therefore, vitally necessary though it was to have the right kind of organization and the right kind of generalship, it was even more vitally necessary that the average soldier should have the fighting edge, the right character. So it is in our civil life. No matter how honest and decent we are in our private lives, if we do not have the right kind of law and the right kind of administration of the law, we cannot go forward as a nation. That is imperative; but it must be an addition to, and not a substitution for, the qualities that make us good citizens. In the last analysis, the most important elements in any man's career must be the sum of those qualities which, in the aggregate, we speak of as character. If he has not got it, then no law that the wit of man can devise, no administration of the law by the boldest and strongest executive, will avail to help him. We must have the right kind of character—character that makes a man, first of all, a good man in the home, a good father, a good husband—that makes a man a good neighbor. You must have that, and, then, in addition, you must have the kind of law and the kind of administration of the law which will give to those qualities in the private citizen the best possible chance for development. The prime problem of our nation is to get the right type of good citizenship, and, to get it, we must have progress, and our public men must be genuinely progressive.

Bibliography

AFL-CIO. "Executive Pay Watch." 2010. AFL-CIO.org. 2011. <http://www.aflcio.org/Corporate-Watch/CEO-Pay-and-the-99>.

Alexander, Rachel. "Rick Perry's NAFTA Superhighway Problem." 12 August 2011. TownHall.com. 2012. <http://townhall.com/columnists/rachelalexander/2011/08/12/rick_perrys_nafta_superhighway_problem/page/full/>.

Alonso-Zaldivar, Ricardo. "FDA says Chinese fish tainted." 29 June 2007. *Los Angeles Times*. 2009. <http://articles.latimes.com/2007/jun/29/business/fi-fish29>.

Amadeo, Kimberly. "The Auto Industry Bailout." 2011. About.com. 2011. <http://useconomy.about.com/od/criticalissues/a/auto_bailout.htm>.

American Automotive Policy Council. *How Japan has Maintained The Most Protected and Closed Auto Market In the Industrialized World*. Washington, D.C: American Automotive Policy Council, 2009.

—. *STATISTICAL OVERVIEW OF THE JAPAN AUTOMOTIVE INDUSTRY/ MARKET & U.S. TRADE RELATIONSHIP*. Industry. Washington, D.C.: American Automotive Policy Council, 2010.

—. *STATISTICAL OVERVIEW OF THE KOREA AUTOMOTIVE INDUSTRY/ MARKET & U.S. TRADE RELATIONSHIP*. Industry. Washington, D.C.: American Automotive Policy Council, 2010.

Associated Press. "China Rejects FDA Warning on Possibly Toxic Toothpaste." 3 June 2007. FOXNews.com. 2009. <http://www.foxnews.com/story/0,2933,277442,00.html>.

Automotive Trade Policy Council. *The Economic Impact of Japanese Currency Manipulation*. Industry. Washington, D.C.: Automotive Trade Policy Council, 2006.

Avlon, John P. "What Independent Voters Want—They tend to be fiscally conservative and strong on security." 20 October 2008. *The Wall Street Journal*.

2012. <http://online.wsj.com/article/
SB122445963016248615.html>.

Barlett, Donald L. and James B. Steele.
"Tax time: Are corporations paying
their share?" 16 April 2011. *What Went
Wrong: The Betrayal of the American
Dream*. American University School
of Communication. 2011. <http://
americawhatwentwrong.org/story/
taxes-and-corporations/>.

BBC News. "India allows copy of cancer
drug." 13 March 2012. BBC News.
2012. <http://www.bbc.co.uk/news/
world-asia-india-17348766>.

—. *US warns against Chinese build-up.*
23 May 2006. 2010. <http://news.bbc.
co.uk/2/hi/asia-pacific/5010632.stm>.

Bogdanich, Walt and Jake Hooker.
"From China to Panama, a Trail of
Poisoned Medicine." 6 May 2007.
The New York Times. 2009. <http://
www.nytimes.com/2007/05/06/world/
americas/06poison.html?pagewanted=all>.

Bradford, Harry. "10 Job Slashers That
Benefited From a Tax Holiday: IPS."
8 October 2011. *Huffington Post*.
2011. <http://www.huffingtonpost.
com/2011/10/08/top-ten-job-cutters-to-
benefit-overseas-tax-holiday_n_998787.
html#s394509&title=1_Citigroup>.

Bradsher, Keith. "China recalls infant
formula." 12 September 2008. *The New
York Times*. 2009. <http://www.nytimes.
com/2008/09/12/world/asia/12iht-
13milk.16094054.html>.

Business Maps of India. "American
Companies in India." 2012. Business
Maps of India.com. 2012. <http://busi-
ness.mapsofindia.com/india-company/
america.html>.

Cantrell, Ann. "Growth in India Leads to
Acquisitions in the U.S." 26 March 2011.
GlobalAtlanta.com. 2012. <http://www.
globalatlanta.com/article/24661/>.

Carroll, Joe. "BP's Solar Retreat Signals
Exodus of U.S. Renewable-Energy Jobs."
29 March 2010. Bloomberg. 2011. <http://
www.bloomberg.com/apps/news?pid=news
archive&sid=aGVOmSgSj_hk>.

Carty, Sharon Silke. "Tata Motors to buy
Jaguar, Land Rover for $2.3B." 26 March
2008. *USA Today*. 2012. <http://www.
usatoday.com/money/autos/2008-03-25-
ford-sells-jaguar-land-rover-tata_N.htm>.

CBC News. "From collapse to convictions: a timeline." 23 October 2006. CBC.
ca. 2010. <http://www.cbc.ca/news/
background/enron/>.

Center for Responsive Politics. "Hillary
Clinton—CAREER PROFILE (SINCE
1989)." 2009. OpenSecrets.org. 2011.
<http://www.opensecrets.org/politicians/
summary.php?cid=n00000019&cycle=C
areer>.

Central Intelligence Agency. *The 2008
World Fact Book*. Washington, D.C.: U.S.
Central Intelligence Agency, 2008.

Chang, James C. P. *U.S. POLICY
TOWARD TAIWAN*. Research.
Cambridge: WEATHERHEAD
CENTER FOR INTERNATIONAL
AFFAIRS, HARVARD UNIVERSITY,
2001.

CIOL. "India sold pirated s/w worth
$2.7 bn in 2010." 12 May 2011. CIOL.
com. 2012. <http://www.ciol.com/news/
news/news-reports/india-sold-pirated-sw-
worth-27-bn-in-2010/149898/0/>.

Clark, Victor S. *History of Manufactures in the United States 1607–1860*. Washington, D.C.: Carnegie Institution of Washington, 1916.

Cline, William R. *The United States as a Debtor Nation*. Washington, D.C.: Institute for International Economics, 2005.

CNN. "Perot sues to stop presidential debates." 23 September 1996. CNN. 2012. <http://articles.cnn.com/1996-09-23/us/9609_23_perot_1_vice-presidential-candidates-presidential-debates-federal-court?_s=PM:US>.

Collins, Loren. "The Truth About Tytler." 25 January 2009. Lorencollins.net. 2012. <http://www.lorencollins.net/tytler.html>.

COMMITTEE ON GOVERN-MENTAL AFFAIRS. *INVESTIGATION OF ILLEGAL OR IMPROPER ACTIVITIES IN CONNECTION WITH 1996 FEDERAL ELECTION CAMPAIGNS*. Special Investigation. Washington, D.C.: U.S. Government, 1998. <http://www.fas.org/irp/congress/1998_rpt/sgo-sir/index.html>.

Cooney, Stephen and Brent Yacobucci. *U.S. Automotive Industry: Policy Overview and Recent History*. U.S. Government. Washington, D.C.: Congressional Research Service-The Library of Congress, 2005.

Cornell University ILR School. *Wal-Mart Imports From China, Exports Ohio Jobs*. Industry. New York: Cornell University ILR School-AFL-CIO Wal-Mart Campaign, 2005.

Costa, Daniel. *ABUSES IN THE L-VISA PROGRAM—Undermining the U.S. Labor Market*. Research. Washington, D.C.: Economic Policy Institute, 2010.

<http://www.epi.org/publication/abuses_in_the_l-visa_program_undermining_the_us_labor_market/>

Council Report. *Sustaining the Nation's Innovation Ecosystem: Maintaining the Strength of Our Science & Engineering Capabilities*. U.S. Government. Washington, D.C.: PRESIDENT'S COUNCIL OF ADVISORS ON SCIENCE AND TECHNOLOGY, 2004. <http://www.whitehouse.gov/sites/default/files/microsites/ostp/pcast-04-sciengcapabilities.pdf>.

Creswell, Julie and Nomi Prins. "The Emperor Of Greed With the help of his bankers, Gary Winnick treated Global Crossing as his personal cash cow—until the company went bankrupt." 24 June 2002. *Fortune*. 2010. <http://money.cnn.com/magazines/fortune/fortune_archive/2002/06/24/325183/index.htm>.

Cuomo, Andrew M. *NO RHYME OR REASON: The Heads I Win, Tails You Lose' Bank Bonus Culture*. Government. Albany: New York State Attorney General, 2009.

Curry, Timothy and Lynn Shibut. *The Cost of the Savings and Loan Crisis: Truth and Consequences*. U.S. Government. Washington, D.C.: Federal Deposit Insurance Corporation, 2000. <http://www.fdic.gov/bank/analytical/banking/2000dec/brv13n2_2.pdf>.

DaimlerChrysler Corporation, Ford Motor Company, and General Motors Corporation. *America's Auto Industry: Economic Contributions & Competitive Challenges*. Industry. Detroit: DaimlerChrysler Corporation, Ford Motor Company, and General Motors Corporation, 2006.

Deficits Do Matter.org. DeficitNews. com. April 2012. <http://www. deficitnews.com/?gclid=CJeytO_QzZoCFQOIFQodln3y2w>.

DeVol, Ross C., et al. "Manufacturing 2.0—A More Prosperous California." June 2009. MilkenInstitute.org. 2011. <http://www.milkeninstitute.org/pdf/CAManu-facturing.pdf>.

Dower, John. *Japan in War and Peace, 9–32.* New York: New Press, 1995.

Eckert, Paul and Stella Dawson. "US' China dreams may now be a chimera." 2011 11 December. MSNBC.com. 2012. <http://www.msnbc.msn.com/id/45614308/ns/business-world_business/t/us-china-dreams-may-now-be-chimera/>.

Editorials: *The Washington Post.* "Editorials: Tibet and the Olympics ." 19 March 2008. *The Washington Post.* 2009. <http://www.washingtonpost.com/wp-dyn/content/article/2008/03/18/AR2008031802706.html>.

Edsall, Thomas B. "The Trouble With That Revolving Door." 18 December 2011. *The New York Times.* <http://campaign-stops.blogs.nytimes.com/2011/12/18/the-trouble-with-that-revolving-door/>.

encyclopedia.jrank.org. "Consumer Electronics—History, The Modern Marketplace, Trends, Miniaturization, Digitization, Convergence." n.d. encyclo-pedia.jrank.org. 2011. <<a href="http://encyclopedia.jrank.org/articles/pages/6483/Consumer-Electronics.html">Consumer>.

Ensinger, Dustin. "America's Losing WTO Track Record." 1 May 2011. *Economy In Crisis.* 2011. <http://economyincrisis.org/content/americas-losing-wto-track-record>.

—. "Japan's Cash-For-Clunkers Program Excludes U.S. Cars." 23 December 2009. *Economy in Crisis.* 2011. <http://economyincrisis.org/content/japans-cash-clunkers-program-excludes-us-cars>.

Falkenberg, Kai. "How Business Crooks Cut Their Jail Time." 18 December 2008. *Fortune.* 2010. <http://www.forbes.com/forbes/2009/0112/064.html>.

Fang, Lee. "Exclusive: Foreign-Funded 'U.S.' Chamber Of Commerce Running Partisan Attack Ads." 5 October 2010. ThinkProgress.org. 2011. <http://think-progress.org/politics/2010/10/05/121701/foreign-chamber-commerce/>.

Farrell, Chris, Sasha Aslanian and Jill Barshay. "Imperial Washington—A Culture of Conceit?" November 2006. Americanradioworks.publicradio.org. 2012. <http://americanradioworks.publi-cradio.org/features/congress/a2.html>.

Faux, Jeff and Andrea Orr. "Trade policy and the American worker." 3 May 2010. *Economic Policy Institute.* 2011. <http://www.epi.org/publication/trade_policy_and_the_american_worker/>.

Feldman, Claudia. "Ken and Linda Lay's condo for sale for $12.8 million." 22 September 2009. *Houston Chronicle.* 2010. <http://www.chron.com/business/energy/article/Ken-and-Linda-Lay-s-condo-for-sale-for-12-8-1734593.php#photo-1290676>.

Figliola, Patricia Moloney, Casey L. Addis and Thomas Lum. *U.S. Initiatives to Promote Global Internet Freedom: Issues, Policy, and Technology.* U.S. Govern-ment. Washington, D.C.: Congressional

Research Service, 2011. <http://www.fas. org/sgp/crs/row/R41120.pdf>.

Fingleton, Eamonn. *In the Jaws of the Dragon: America's Fate in the Coming Era of Chinese Hegemony*. New York: Thomas Dunne Books, 2008.

First Street Research Group. *The First Street 30-Top Federal Lobbyists Named to 2011 List*. Research. Washington, D.C.: CQ Press, 2011.

Fitzgerald, Alison. "The Power Brokers." 2011. *Businessweek*. 2011. <http://images. businessweek.com/slideshows/20110119/ the-power-brokers/>.

Fletcher, Ian. "America Aping Britain's Historic Decline Through Free Trade." 23 September 2010. *Huffington Post*. 2011. <http://www.huffingtonpost.com/ ian-fletcher/america-aping-britains- hi_b_735967.html>.

—. *Economy in Crisis-Japan, the Forgotten Protectionist Threat*. 29 July 2011. 2012. <http://economyincrisis.org/content/ japan-forgotten-protectionist-threat>.

Food Safety News. "WTO Strikes Down Country-of-Origin Labeling." 19 November 2011. *Food Safety News*. 2012. <http://www. foodsafetynews.com/2011/11/ wto-strikes-down-cool-except-for-meat/>.

Forbes. "America's Highest Paid Chief Executives." 25 March 2011. *Forbes*. 2012. <http://www.forbes.com/lists/2011/12/ ceo-compensation-11_rank.html>.

Froomkin, Dan. "How Foreign Money Can Find Its Way Into Political Campaigns." 18 July 2011. *Huffington Post*. 2011. <http://www. huffingtonpost.com/2011/07/18/

foreign-money-campaign-finance- lobbying_n_897189.html?page=2>.

Gao, Bai. *Japan's Economic Dilemma: The Institutional Origins of Prosperity and Stagnation*. New York & Cambridge: Cambridge University Press, 2001.

Gillmore, Jesse. *Disastrous Financial Panics—1837 to 1908*. San Diego: Press of Frye & Smith, 1908.

Giridharadas, Anand. "Outsourcers corner market for U.S. skilled worker visas." 12 April 2007. *The New York Times*. 2012. <http://www. nytimes.com/2007/04/12/business/ worldbusiness/12iht-visa.4.5257621. html?_r=1&pagewanted=all>.

Gordon, Andrew. *A Modern History of Japan: From Tokugawa Times to the Present*. New York & Oxford: Oxford University Press, 2003.

Green World Investor. "Wind Energy Companies Categorized by Country and Wind Power Industry Major Trends." 25 November 2010. GreenWorld- Investor.com. 2011. <http://www. greenworldinvestor.com/2010/11/25/ wind-energy-companies-categorized-by- country-and-wind-power-industry-major- trends/>.

Grove, Andy. "Andy Grove: How America Can Create Jobs." 1 July 2010. *BusinessWeek*. <http://www.business- week.com/magazine/content/10_28/ b4186048358596.htm>.

Haberkorn, Jennifer and Jerry Seper. "EXCLUSIVE: AIG chiefs pressed to donate to Dodd." 30 March 2009. *The Washington Times*. 2011. <http://www. washingtontimes.com/news/2009/mar/30/ aig-chiefs-pressed-to-donate-to-dodd/>.

Hanna, Jason. "Chinese-made drywall ruining homes, owners say." 18 March 2009. CNN. 2009. <http://articles.cnn.com/2009-03-18/us/chinese.drywall_1_chinese-made-drywall-home-owners-appliances?_s=PM:US>.

Harrington, Craig. "Disastrous Effects of Free Trade." 24 January 2010. *Economy in Crisis*. 2011. <http://economyincrisis.org/content/disastrous-effects-free-trade>.

Harris, Gardiner. "U.S. Identifies Tainted Heparin in 11 Countries." 22 April 2008. *The New York Times*. 2009. <http://www.nytimes.com/2008/04/22/health/policy/22fda.html?pagewanted=all>.

Hart, Jeffrey A. "The Consumer-Electronics Industry in the United States: Its Decline and Future Revival." *BUSINESS IN THE CONTEMPORARY WORLD*, Summer 1991: 46–54.

Heeks, Richard. *Indian IT Sector Statistics*. Research. Manchester: Centre for Development Informatics, University of Manchester, UK, 2009.

Herbert, Bob. "Enron and the Gramms." 17 January 2002. *The New York Times*. 2011. <http://www.nytimes.com/2002/01/17/opinion/enron-and-the-gramms.html>.

High Beam Business. "Household Audio and Video Equipment: SIC 3651." 2011. *High Beam Business*. 2011. <http://business.highbeam.com/industry-reports/equipment/household-audio-video-equipment>.

Hille, Kathrin. "China hits at US over Taiwan arms deal." 22 September 2011. *Financial Times*. 2011. <http://www.ft.com/cms/s/0/2ae01e5c-e4f4-11e0-9aa8-00144feabdc0.html#axzz1uDEwl84x>.

Hira, Ron. *THE H-1B AND L-1 VISA PROGRAMS Out of Control*. Research. Washington, D.C.: Economic Policy Institute, 2010.

—. *The Offshoring of Innovation: U.S. innovation system morphs as investments in R&D increasingly go to low-cost countries*. Research. Washington, D.C.: Economic Policy Institute, 2008.

Huffington Post. "Corporate Profits At All-Time High As Recovery Stumbles." 25 March 2011. *Huffington Post*. 2011. <http://www.huffingtonpost.com/2011/03/25/corporate-profits-2011-all-time-high_n_840538.html>.

Hui, Kenneth Y. "National Security Review of Foreign Mergers and Acquisitions of Domestic Companies in China and the United States." Research. 2009.

Human Rights Watch. "How Multinational Internet Companies assist Government Censorship in China." 2006. hrw.org. 2011. <http://www.hrw.org/reports/2006/china0806/5.htm>.

IHS Global Insight. *Indian Companies Garner 33% of ANDA Approvals in 2011*. Englewood: IHS Global Insight, 2012. <http://www.ihs.com/products/global-insight/industry-economic-report.aspx?id=1065932080>.

IMaCS VIRTUS Global Partners. *US-BOUND ACQUISITIONS BY INDIAN COMPANIES*. Industry. New York: IMaCS VIRTUS Global Partners, 2010. 2012.

International Iron and Steel Institute. *World Steel in Figures*. Industry. Belgium: International Iron and Steel Institute, 2006.

Irwin, Douglas A. "Trade Policies and the Semiconductor Industry." Anne O. Krueger, ed. *The Political Economy of American Trade Policy*. Chicago: University of Chicago Press, 1996. 11-72. <http://www.nber.org/chapters/c8703.pdf>.

Japan Automobile Manufacturers Association, Inc. *THE MOTOR INDUSTRY OF JAPAN 2010*. Tokyo: Japan Automobile Manufacturers Association, Inc., 2010.

Jilani, Zaid. "The Other Occupation: How Wall Street Occupies Washington." 12 October 2011. ThinkProgress. org. 2011. <http://thinkprogress. org/special/2011/10/12/341801/ the-other-occupation-how-wall-street-occupies-washington/>.

Jr., Alfred D. Chandler. "Gaps in the Historical Record: Development of the Electronics Industry." 20 October 2003. *Harvard Business School Working Knowledge*. 2011. <http://hbswk.hbs.edu/ item/3738.html>.

Kan, Shirley. *China's Military and Security Developments*. U.S. Government. Washington, D.C.: Congressional Research Service, 2011.

Kindy, Kimberly, Peter Whoriskey and Madonna Lebling. "Toyota heads to Capitol Hill with team of lobbyists, history of political giving." 22 February 2010. *The Washington Post*. 2011. <http://www.washingtonpost.com/ wp-dyn/content/article/2010/02/21/ AR2010022104295.html>.

Kocieniewski, David. "G.E.'s Strategies Let It Avoid Taxes Altogether." 24 March 2011. *The New York Times*. 2011. <http:// www.nytimes.com/2011/03/25/business/ economy/25tax.html?pagewanted=all>.

Kwong, Robin. "Microsoft strikes search deal with Baidu." 4 July 2011. *Financial Times*. 2011. <http://www.ft.com/intl/ cms/s/2/318695a6-a642-11e0-8eef-00144feabdc0.html#axzz1uRMeaJ5w>.

Lappin, Joan. "American Superconductor Destroyed For A Tiny Bribe." 21 September 2011. *Forbes*. 2011. <http://www.forbes.com/sites/ joanlappin/2011/09/21/american-super-conductor-destroyed-for-a-tiny-bribe/>.

Lee, Hyun Young. *The Japan-U.S. and Korea-U.S. Semiconductor Trade Dispute*. Research. Tokyo: Center for Far Eastern Studies, Toyama University, 2004.

Lemon, Sumner. "Cisco starts China offensive with R&D." 27 September 2004. ComputerWeekly. com. 2011. <http://www.comput-erweekly.com/news/2240057885/ Cisco-starts-China-offensive-with-RD>.

Lerer, Lisa. "McCain guru linked to subprime crisis." 28 March 2008. *Politico*. 2011. <http://www.politico.com/news/ stories/0308/9246.html>.

Leung, Rebecca. "Out of India." 11 February 2009. CBS News. 2012. <http://www.cbsnews.com/ stories/2003/12/23/60minutes/ main590004.shtml>.

Levine, Linda. *Offshoring (or Offshore Outsourcing) and Job Loss Among U.S. Workers*. U.S. Government. Washington, D.C.: Congressional Research Service, 2011.

Levy, Steven. "Inside Google's China misfortune." 15 April 2011. *Fortune*. 2011. <http://tech.fortune.cnn.com/2011/04/15/ googles-ordeal-in-china/>.

Lewis, Charles, Alejandro Benes and Meredith O'Brien. *The Buying of the President.* New York: Avon Books, 1996.

Lewis, Charles, et al. *THE TRADING GAME: Inside Lobbying for the North American Free Trade Agreement.* Research. Washington, D.C.: THE CENTER FOR PUBLIC INTEGRITY, 1993. <http://www.publicintegrity.org/assets/pdf/THETRADINGGAME.pdf>.

Liptak, Adam. "Justices, 5-4, Reject Corporate Spending Limit." 21 January 2010. *The New York Times.* 2011. <http://www.nytimes.com/2010/01/22/us/politics/22scotus.html?_r=1>.

Lother, Wiliam. "US congressman call for overhaul of Taiwan policy." 21 May 2009. *Taipei Times.* 2012. <http://www.taipeitimes.com/News/front/archives/2009/05/21/2003444152>.

Lozano, Juan A. "Ex-Enron Financial Chief Andrew Fastow Moved To Halfway House." 18 May 2011. *Huffington Post.* <http://www.huffingtonpost.com/2011/05/18/enron-prison-andrew-fastow-halfway-house_n_863457.html>.

Lucchetti, Aaron and Stephen Grocer. "On Street, Pay Vaults to Record Altitude." 2 February 2011. *The Wall Street Journal.* 2011. <http://online.wsj.com/article/SB10001424052748704124504576118421859347048.html>.

MacLeod, Calum. "China admits tainted food link." 29 April 2007. *USA Today.* 2009. <http://www.usatoday.com/money/industries/2007-04-26-pet-food-china_N.htm>.

Martin, Andrew. "Chinese Tires Are Ordered Recalled." 26 June 2007. *The New York Times.* 2009. <http://www.nytimes.com/2007/06/26/business/worldbusiness/26tire.html>.

McCormack, Richard. "The Plight of American Manufacturing." 21 December 2009. *The American Prospect.* 2011. <http://prospect.org/article/plight-american-manufacturing>.

McCullough, David. *1776.* New York: Simon & Schuster, Inc., 2005.

—. *John Adams.* New York: Simon & Schuster, 2001.

—. *Mornings on Horseback.* New York: Simon & Schuster, 1982.

—. "The Glorious Cause of America." 2006. *BYU Magazine.* 2009. <http://magazine.byu.edu/?act=view&a=1746>.

McIntire, Mike. "Clintons Made $109 Million in Last 8 Years." 5 April 2008. *The New York Times.* 2011. <http://www.nytimes.com/2008/04/05/us/politics/05clintons.html?_r=2&scp=1&sq=clinton+tax+return&st=nyt&oref=slogin>.

McIntyre, Robert S., et al. *Corporate Taxpayers & Corporate Tax Dodgers 2008–10.* Research. Washington, D.C.: Citizens for Tax Justice & the Institute on Taxation and Economic Policy, 2011. <http://www.ctj.org/corporatetaxdodgers/CorporateTaxDodgersReport.pdf>.

McMahon, Robert and Isabella Bennett. *U.S. Internet Providers and the 'Great Firewall of China'.* Research. Washington, D.C.: Council on Foriegn Relations, 2011. <http://www.cfr.org/china/us-internet-providers-great-firewall-china/p9856#p4>.

Moses, Asher. "Fighting China's Golden Shield: Cisco sued over jailing and torture of dissidents." 16 August 2011. *The Sydney Morning Herald*. 2011. <http://www.smh.com.au/technology/technology-news/fighting-chinas-golden-shield-cisco-sued-over-jailing-and-torture-of—dissidents-20110816-1ivkv.html>.

NASSCOM. "Resource Center—Indian IT-BPO Industry." 2012. *NASSCOM*. April 2012. <http://www.nasscom.in/indian-itbpo-industry>.

NDTV. "India to play big part in outsourcing despite talks of protectionism: Chandrasekaran." 26 January 2012. Profit. NDTV.com. 2012. <http://profit.ndtv.com/News/Article/india-to-play-big-part-in-outsourcing-despite-talks-of-protectionism-chandrasekaran-296598>.

Nevers, Kevin. "ISG sold in huge global steel deal." 25 October 2004. *Chesterton Tribune*. April 2012. <http://chestertontribune.com/Business/isg_sold_in_huge_global_steel_de.htm>.

New York State Department of Labor and Empire State Development. *THE OFFSHORE OUTSOURCING OF INFORMATION TECHNOLOGY JOBS IN NEW YORK STATE*. New York State Government. Albany: State of New York, 2010. <http://www.labor.ny.gov/stats/PDFs/Offshore_Outsourcing_ITJobs_NYS.pdf>.

Office of the Secretary of Defense. *Military Power of the People's Republic of China*. U.S. Government. Washington, D.C.: United States Department of Defense, 2009.

Palazzolo, Joe. "Where The Bribes Are." 16 November 2011. *The Wall Street Journal*. 2011. <http://blogs.wsj.com/corruption-currents/2011/11/16/where-the-bribes-are-2/?mod=google_news_blog>.

Patsuris, Penelope. "The Corporate Scandal Sheet." 26 August 2002. *Forbes*. 2010. <http://www.forbes.com/2002/07/25/accountingtracker.html>.

PBS. "The Long Demise of Glass-Steagall." 8 May 2003. PBS.org. 2011. <http://www.pbs.org/wgbh/pages/frontline/shows/wallstreet/weill/demise.html>.

Pearson, Natalie Obiko. "Essar Confirms Trinity Coal Acquisition, Seeking Other Deals ." 6 March 2010. Bloomberg. 2012.

Pennington, Adrian. "Global Consumer Electronics Market Rebounds to $873 Billion; Tablet and Connected TV Sales Expected to Skyrocket." 5 January 2011. *Streaming Media Europe*. 2011. <http://www.streamingmediaglobal.com/Articles/News/Featured-News/Global-Consumer-Electronics-Market-Rebounds-to-$873-Billion%3B-Tablet-and-Connected-TV-Sales-Expected-to-Skyrocket-73074.aspx>.

Pile, Kenneth. *The Making of Modern Japan, 2nd ed.* Lexington, MA: D.C. Heath, 1996.

Preston, Julia and Vikas Bajaj. "Indian Company Under Scrutiny Over U.S. Visas." 21 June 2011. *The New York Times*. 2012. <http://www.nytimes.com/2011/06/22/us/22infosys.html?_r=2&pagewanted=all>.

Public Campaign. *For Hire: Lobbyist of the 99%?—How Corporations Pay More for Lobbyists Than in Taxes*. Research. Washington, D.C.: Public Campaign, 2011. <http://publicampaign.org/sites/default/

files/ReportTaxDodgerLobbyingDec6.
pdf>.

Ram, Sudhakar. "India's Next
Outsourcing Wave: To modernize after
its crisis, the U.S. financial industry needs
help from India's IT outsourcers more
than ever, says Sudhakar Ram." 9 March
2010. *BusinessWeek*. 2012. <http://www.
businessweek.com/globalbiz/content/
mar2010/gb2010039_433787.htm>.

Ray, Tapan. "INDIAN PHARMA-
CEUTICAL MARKET IN A NEW
PARADIGM." 21 September 2010. api.
ning.com. 2012. <http://api.ning.com/files/
dgy7m4URvFXHkHyu7WxMFTe4e6G-
gbVMosALotn447jqJrGHLl6EGUDT-
Wl99nyeqbGC53yQ812ETqUZydMfX—
XeFCzzSEv60/DHLDubaiTR13.9.2010.
pdf>.

Reeves, Eric. "Understanding Genocide
in Darfur: The View from Khartoum."
26 January 2007. *Sudan Tribune*.
2009. <http://www.sudantribune.
com/Understanding-Genocide-in-
Darfur,19956>.

Reference for Business. "SIC 3651
HOUSEHOLD AUDIO AND
VIDEO EQUIPMENT." n.d.
*Reference for Business: Encyclopedia of
Business, 2nd ed.* 2011. <http://www.
referenceforbusiness.com/industries/
Electronic-Equipment-Components/
Household-Audio-Video-Equipment.
html>.

—. "SIC 3674 SEMICONDUCTORS
AND RELATED DEVICES." n.d.
*Reference for Business: Encyclopedia of
Business, 2nd ed.* 2011. <http://www.
referenceforbusiness.com/industries/
Electronic-Equipment-Components/
Semiconductors-Related-Devices.html>.

Reuters. "India launches WTO case
against US steel duties." 13 April 2012.
IBNLive.IN.com. 2012. <http://ibnlive.
in.com/news/india-launches-wto-case-
against-us-steel-duties/248219-7.html>.

Roberts, Paul Craig. 24 February 2009.
July 2011. <http://www.counterpunch.
org/2009/02/24/how-the-economy-was-
lost/>.

—. "American Job Loss Is Permanent."
28 October 2010. *Foriegn Policy Journal*.
2012. <http://www.foreignpolicyjournal.
com/2010/10/28/american-job-loss-is-
permanent>.

Romero, Simon and Alexei Barrionuevo.
"Deals Help China Expand Sway in
Latin America." 15 April 2009. *The New
York Times*. 2009. <http://www.nytimes.
com/2009/04/16/world/16chinaloan.
html?_r=2&ref=global-home>.

Savitz, Eric. "CES: Global Consumer
Electronics Retail Sales Seen Up
10% In 2011." 4 January 2011. *Forbes*.
2011. <http://www.forbes.com/sites/
ericsavitz/2011/01/04/ces-global-
consumer-electronics-retail-sales-seen-
up-10-in-2011/>.

Schwenninger, Sherle R. and Samuel
Sherraden. "The American Middle
Class." Research. 2011.

Scott, Robert E. *GROWING U.S.
TRADE DEFICIT WITH CHINA COST
2.8 MILLION JOBS BETWEEN 2001
AND 2010*. Research. Washington,
D.C.: Economic Policy Institute, 2011.
<http://www.epi.org/publication/
growing-trade-deficit-china-cost-2-8-
million/>

—. *Heading South U.S.-Mexico trade
and job displacement after NAFTA.*

Research. Washington, D.C.: Economic Policy Institute, 2011. <http://www.epi.org/publication/heading_south_u-s-mexico_trade_and_job_displacement_after_nafta1/>

Seiger, Theresa. "Record number of voters identify as Independent." 9 January 2012. WMCTV.com. 2012. <http://www.wmctv.com/story/16479766/record-number-of-voters-identify-as-independent>.

Shorrock, Tim. "The Japanese "miracle" was built on technology broken unions, and U.S. aid." May 1983. *Multinational Monitor.* 2011. <http://www.multinationalmonitor.org/hyper/issues/1983/06/index.html>.

SiliconIndia. "Top 10 global acquisitions by Indian companies." 23 June 2011. *SiliconIndia News.* 2012. <http://www.siliconindia.com/shownews/Top_10_global_acquisitions_by_Indian_companies-nid-85123-cid-3.html/1>.

Slocum, Tyson. *Blind Faith: How Deregulation and Enron's Influence Over Government Looted Billions from Americans.* Research. Washington, D.C.: Public Citizen's, 2001. <http://www.citizen.org/documents/Blind_Faith.PDF>.

Stempel, Jonathan. "Enron settles with ex-CEO's wife Linda Lay." 20 June 2011. Reuters. 2011. <http://www.reuters.com/article/2011/06/20/us-enron-lay-idUSTRE75J3GC20110620>.

Story, Louise. "Lead Paint Prompts Mattel to Recall 967,000 Toys ." 2 August 2007. *The New York Times.* 2009. <http://www.nytimes.com/2007/08/02/business/02toy.html>.

Strachan, Maxwell. "Corporate Tax Revenues Nearing Historic Lows as a Percentage of GDP, Report Says." 2 March 2011. *Huffington Post.* 2011. <http://www.huffingtonpost.com/2011/03/02/corporate-tax-revenues-ne_n_830361.html>.

Stumo, Michael. "Bernie Sanders on Immelt." 24 January 2011. TradeReform.org. 2011. <http://www.tradereform.org/2011/01/bernie-sanders-on-immelt/>.

Tabuchi, Hiroko. "Steel Giants Nippon and Sumitomo Talk of Merger." 3 February 2011. *Deal Book New York Times.* 2011. <http://dealbook.nytimes.com/2011/02/03/nippon-steel-and-sumitomo-metal-to-merge/>.

Tang, Rachel. *China's Steel Industry and Its Impact on the United States: Issues for Congress.* U.S. Government. Washington, D.C.: Congressional Research Service, 2010.

The China Post. "Chinese military chief vows faster missile build-up." 3 February 2009. *The China Post.* 2009. <http://www.chinapost.com.tw/china/national-news/2009/02/03/194383/Chinese-military.htm>.

The U.S.-China Business Council. "Reports, Analysis, & Statistics." 2011. uschina.org. 2011. <https://www.uschina.org/statistics/tradetable.html>.

The Washington Post. "Who Runs Gov—Christopher J. Dodd." 2011. The Washington Post. 2011. <http://www.washingtonpost.com/politics/christopher-j-dodd/gIQAmFfM9O_topic.html>.

The Washington Times. *China speeds pace of military buildup.* 3 March 2008. 2010. <http://www.washingtontimes.com/news/2008/mar/03/china-speeds-pace-of-military-buildup/>.

Thompson, Loren. "Intelligence Community Fears U.S. Manufacturing Decline." 14 February 2011. *Forbes.* <http://www.forbes.com/sites/beltway/2011/02/14/intelligence-community-fears-u-s-manufacturing-decline/>.

Time Magazine. "25 People to Blame for the Financial Crisis." 2008. *Time Specials.* 2010. <http://www.time.com/time/specials/packages/completelist/0,29569,1877351,00.html>.

Time Magazine. "Japan: The New No. 3 in Steel." 17 July 1964. *Time.* 2011. <http://www.time.com/time/magazine/article/0,9171,875998,00.html>.

Tocqueville, Alexis de. *Democracy in America.* Project Gutenburg, 1899.

Trade Lawyers Advisory Group. *CHINA'S COMPLIANCE WITH WTO COMMITMENTS AND OBLIGATIONS: 2005–2007 UPDATE.* Washington, D.C.: U.S. Small Business Administration, 2007.

Trigaux, Robert. "Corporate scandal: Same story, different company." 17 February 2002. *St. Petersburg Times.* 2010. <http://www.sptimes.com/2002/02/17/Columns/Corporate_scandal__Sa.shtml>.

TV History. *Television History— The First 75 Years.* 2011. July 2011. <http://www.tvhistory.tv/1960-2000-TVManufacturers.htm>.

Tyco. *2010 Annual Report.* Corporate. Zurich: Tyco International Ltd., 2011.

U.S. Census Bureau. *Trade in Goods with India.* U.S. Government. Washington, D.C.: U.S. Census Bureau, 2012. <http://www.census.gov/foreign-trade/balance/c5330.html#2011>.

U.S. Department of Commerce. *On the Road: U.S. Automotive Parts Industry Annual Assessment.* U.S. Government. Washington, D.C.: Office of Transportation and Machinery—U.S. Department of Commerce, 2011.

U.S. GAO. *Comparison of the Reported Tax Liabilities of Foreign- and U.S.-Controlled Corporations.* U.S. Government. Washington, D.C.: Government Accountability Office, 2008. <http://www.gao.gov/new.items/d08957.pdf>.

—. *Large U.S. Corporations and Federal Contractors with Subsidiaries in Jurisdictions Listed as Tax Havens or Financial Privacy Jurisdictions.* Congressional Research. Washington, D.C.: Government Accountability Office, 2008. <http://www.gao.gov/new.items/d09157.pdf>.

U.S. Geological Survey. "Historical statistics for mineral and material commodities in the United States: U.S. Geological Survey Data Series 140: IRON AND STEEL STATISTICS." 7 December 2010. pubs.usgs.gov. 2011. <http://pubs.usgs.gov/ds/2005/140/>.

U.S. SEC. *Spotlight on Enron.* U.S. Government. Washington, D.C.: SEC, 2010. <http://www.sec.gov/spotlight/enron.htm>.

United States Census Bureau. *Foreign Trade*. 2011. 2011. <http://www.census.gov/foreign-trade/balance/>.

Valdes-Dapena, Peter. "Toyota: Saved $100 million dodging recall." 22 February 2010. CNN Money. 2011. <http://money.cnn.com/2010/02/21/autos/toyota_document/>.

—. *U.S. lost $14B on auto bailout... Excellent!* 22 July 2011. 2012. <http://money.cnn.com/2011/07/21/autos/chrysler_bailout_costs_gains/index.htm>.

Wadhwa, Vivek, et al. *Seeing through Preconceptions: A Deeper Look at China and India*. 2005. 2012. <http://www.issues.org/23.3/wadhwa.html>.

West, Thomas G. and Douglas A. Jeffrey. "The Rise & Decline of Constitutional Government in America." West, Thomas G. and Douglas A. Jeffrey. *The Rise & Decline of Constitutional Government in America*. Claremont, CA: The Claremont Institute, 2006. 4–9.

Wikipedia. "1996 United States campaign finance controversy." 2011. Wikipedia. 2011. <http://en.wikipedia.org/wiki/1996_United_States_campaign_finance_controversy>.

—. "2007–2012 global financial crisis." 2011. Wikipedia. 2011. <http://en.wikipedia.org/wiki/2007%E2%80%932012_global_financial_crisis >.

—. "ArcelorMittal." 2012. Wikipedia. 2012. <http://en.wikipedia.org/wiki/ArcelorMittal>.

—. "Automotive industry in Japan." 2011. Wikipedia. 2011. <http://en.wikipedia.org/wiki/Automotive_industry_in_Japan>.

—. "Baidu." 2011. Wikipedia. 2011. <http://en.wikipedia.org/wiki/Baidu>.

—. "Banking in the United States." 2011. Wikipedia. 2011. <http://en.wikipedia.org/wiki/Banking_in_the_United_States>.

—. "Business process outsourcing in India." 2012. Wikipedia. 2012.

—. "Causes of the United States housing bubble." 2011. Wikipedia. 2011. <http://en.wikipedia.org/wiki/Causes_of_the_United_States_housing_bubble#cite_note-9>.

—. "Dodd–Frank Wall Street Reform and Consumer Protection Act." 2011. Wikipedia. 2011. <http://en.wikipedia.org/wiki/Dodd%E2%80%93Frank_Wall_Street_Reform_and_Consumer_Protection_Act>.

—. *Economic history of India*. 2012. Wikipedia. 2012. <http://en.wikipedia.org/wiki/Economic_history_of_India#GDP_estimate>.

—. *Economy of the United States*. 2012. Wikipedia. June 2011. <http://en.wikipedia.org/wiki/Economy_of_the_United_States>.

—. "Enron scandal." 2010. Wikipedia. 2010. <http://en.wikipedia.org/wiki/Enron_scandal>.

—. "Glass–Steagall Act." 2011. Wikipedia. 2011. <http://en.wikipedia.org/wiki/Glass%E2%80%93Steagall_Act>.

—. "Gramm–Leach–Bliley Act." 2011. Wikipedia. 2011. <http://en.wikipedia. org/wiki/Gramm%E2%80%93Leach%E 2%80%93Bliley_Act>.

—. "H-1B visa." 2012. Wikipedia. 2012. <http://en.wikipedia.org/wiki/H-1B_ visa#H-1B_demographics>.

—. *History of Taiwan.* 2012. Wikipedia. 2012. <http://en.wikipedia.org/wiki/ History_of_Taiwan>.

—. *History of the United States public debt.* 2012. Wikipedia. June 2011. <http://en.wikipedia.org/wiki/History_ of_the_U.S._public_debt>.

—. "List of corporate scandals." 2010. Wikipedia. 2010. <http://en.wikipedia. org/wiki/List_of_corporate_scandals>.

—. "List of federal political scandals in the United States." 2011. Wikipedia. 2011. <http://en.wikipedia.org/wiki/ List_of_federal_political_scandals_in_ the_United_States>.

—. "List of photovoltaics companies." n.d. Wikipedia. <http://en.wikipedia. org/wiki/List_of_photovoltaics_ companies#2011_Global_Top_Ten_ Solar_Cell_Manufacturer>.

—. "List of recessions in the United States." 2012. Wikipedia. June 2011. <http://en.wikipedia.org/wiki/List_of_ recessions_in_the_United_States>.

—. "List of steel producers." 2012. Wikipedia. <http://en.wikipedia.org/ wiki/List_of_steel_producers>.

—. "List of United States Representatives expelled, censured, or reprimanded." 2011. Wikipedia. 2011. <http://en.wikipedia.org/wiki/ List_of_United_States_Representatives_ expelled,_censured,_or_reprimanded>.

—. "List of United States senators expelled or censured." 2011. Wikipedia. 2011. <http://en.wikipedia.org/wiki/ List_of_United_States_senators_ expelled_or_censured>.

—. "Manufacturing in Japan." 2011. Wikipedia. 2011. <http://en.wikipedia. org/wiki/Manufacturing_in_Japan>.

—. "North American Free Trade Agreement." n.d. Wikipedia. <http:// en.wikipedia.org/wiki/North_ American_Free_Trade_Agreement>.

—. "Starve the beast." 2012. Wikipedia. 2012. <http://en.wikipedia.org/wiki/ Starve_the_beast>.

—. "Tariffs in United States history." 2011. Wikipedia. <http://en.wikipedia. org/wiki/Tariffs_in_United_States_ history>.

—. "Timeline of United States inventions." 2012. Wikipedia. 2012.

—. "United States federal budget." 2012. Wikipedia. June 2011. <http:// en.wikipedia.org/wiki/United_States_ federal_budget>.

—. "United States public debt." 2012. Wikipedia. June 2011. <http:// en.wikipedia.org/wiki/United_States_ public_debt#Estimated_ownership>.

—. "World Trade Organization." 2011. Wikipedia. 2011. <http://en.wikipedia. org/wiki/World_Trade_Organization>.

Wikipedia; Grover Norquist. "Grover Norquist." 2012. Wikipedia. 2012.

<http://en.wikipedia.org/wiki/Grover_
Norquist>.

Xiaokun, Li. "Clinton urges China
to buy US Treasuries." 23 February
2009. *China Daily.* 2009. <http://www.
chinadaily.com.cn/china/2009-02/23/
content_7501011.htm>.

Yardley, Jim and Andrew Martin.
"More candy from China, tainted, is in
U.S." 2 October 2008. *The New York
Times.* 2009. <http://www.nytimes.
com/2008/10/02/world/asia/02iht-
02milk.16631017.html>.

Zepeda, Eduardo, Timothy A. Wise
and Kevin P. Gallagher. *Rethinking
Trade Policy for Development:
Lessons From Mexico Under
NAFTA.* Research. Pittsburgh:
CARNEGIE ENDOWMENT FOR
INTERNATIONAL PEACE, 2009.

About the Author

J. R. Martin was born in Pittsburgh, Pennsylvania and completed his Master's Degree with Central Michigan University while serving in the U.S. Navy as a Cryptologist. He has since held key leadership positions in the semiconductor, computer, and medical device industries, receiving numerous awards for leadership and excellence. Visiting or living in 45 of the 50 states has deepened his appreciation and love of America. His extensive international experience includes development of business in Asia, Europe, The Middle East, and South America.